SMASHING
WordPress

Publisher's Acknowledgments

Some of the people who helped bring this book to market include the following:

Editorial and Production

VP Consumer and Technology Publishing Director: Michelle Leete
Associate Director – Book Content Management: Martin Tribe
Associate Publisher: Chris Webb
Assistant Editor: Colleen Goldring
Publishing Assistant: Ellie Scott
Project Editor: Juliet Booker
Content Editor: Juliet Booker
Development Editor: Brian Herrmann
Technical Editor: Tyler Hayes
Copy Editor: Gareth Haman

Marketing

Senior Marketing Manager: Louise Breinholt
Marketing Executive: Kate Batchelor

Composition Services

Compositor: Thomson Digital
Proof Reader: Sarah Price
Indexer: Jack Lewis – j&j indexing

SMASHING
WordPress
BEYOND THE BLOG

Thord Daniel Hedengren

A John Wiley and Sons, Ltd, Publication

There are a lot of people involved in writing a book. Friends, family, lovers, pets, and not to mention patient editors—all have had some sort of influence since they have put up with me over this somewhat hectic period. I could dedicate this book to any one of them, or to lost family members that have meant a lot to what I am today.

I won't, though.

This book is dedicated to the wonderful WordPress community. Without them, no WordPress, and without WordPress, no book from yours truly. In fact, if it weren't for WordPress in particular, and open source in general, I probably would be doing something entirely different today.

You've got to love WordPress. I do.

Thord Daniel Hedengren

About the Author

Thord Daniel Hedengren is a web designer and developer, as well as a freelance writer and a WordPress expert. He has created numerous WordPress themes, developed plugins, and put WordPress to good use powering both blogs and big editorial sites. In the blogosphere, you probably know Thord as TDH, and as the former editor of great blogging resources such as the Blog Herald and Devlounge, as well as the creator of the Notes Blog theme for WordPress.

Contents

Contents

Contents

Introduction

Writing a book about WordPress isn't the easiest endeavor one could tackle. When my editor and I first started discussing this project, the idea was to create something that not only acts as an introduction to web developers and professionals who want to utilize the power of the WordPress platform, but also to spark the minds to create things beyond the obvious.

Or beyond the blog, as it were, which is also the subtitle of the book.

The whole point is really to prove that WordPress is so much more than a blog-publishing platform. You can build just about anything on it, and you should as well if you like fast deployments and great flexibility. It is not always the perfect choice, but it should definitely be considered at all times. The ease with which you can both build and use this platform is a selling point, just as is the living community that can back you up when you run into problems, and the fact that this is open source at its finest.

To convey this message, *Smashing WordPress: Beyond the Blog* is divided into five parts.

Part 1: The WordPress Essentials

The first part tackles the WordPress essentials, from install to what actually makes the system tick. It does, indeed, give you everything you need to get started with WordPress, albeit at a slightly quicker pace than traditional beginner books. However, coverage doesn't stop there because there are a lot of things you should be aware of when getting started with WordPress, such as security measures, moving the install, and so on. The idea is to not only help beginners get started, but also enlighten current users to the problems and options available.

Part 2: Designing and Developing WordPress Themes

WordPress themes are what the user sees; this is the skin of your site, the one that controls how the content is presented. In effect, when working with a site running on WordPress you'll be spending a lot of time altering the theme files to get it to do what you want. This second part not only introduces themes technically, but also gives you the required knowledge to start building your own.

Part 3: Developing WordPres Plugins

The third part is all about developing WordPress plugins. The fact that you can extend WordPress with plugins means that there really is no limit to what you can do with the platform. If you can make it work in PHP, you can run it in WordPress, more or less. This also means that this part of the book is highly conceptual, dealing with the basic communication between your plugin (which in fact is your PHP code) and WordPress itself.

Part 4: Beyond the Blog

A claim that a lot of non-blogs could be running WordPress needs to be backed up, and that is what the fourth part is all about. Here you're looking at how WordPress can be used as a CMS to power more traditional websites, and you build a couple of sites from the ground up to prove that the platform can indeed do other things than just run bloggish websites. Finally, you're looking at plugins that can help you take WordPress one step further. Sometimes you just don't need to develop things from scratch, someone else might have done it for you and released it for free.

This fourth part is all about making you think differently about WordPress. The goal is to do away with all your thoughts about WordPress as a blogging platform. This is a publishing platform, nothing else.

Part 5: WordPress Toolbox

The fifth and final part of *Smashing WordPress: Beyond the Blog* is a selection of nifty little tricks and techniques that you can use to further enhance your site. A lot of the things you might need in your WordPress projects have been done already, and this part is meant to give you a little peek into that.

Start Thinking, Get Publishing!

Smashing WordPress: Beyond the Blog was written with the web developer in mind, but anyone who has fiddled a little bit with XHTML, CSS, PHP, or WordPress, can benefit from this book. It is truly a breeze to get started with WordPress, and WordPress is all you'll need to roll out your project to begin with. After that you'll have to get your hands dirty, with modifying or building themes as well as creating the necessary plugins to build the site you've envisioned.

In other words, start thinking and get publishing with WordPress, whether you're building the next Engadget or Huffington Post, or something entirely different.

THE WORDPRESS ESSENTIALS

1

ANATOMY OF A WORDPRESS INSTALL

Installing WordPress is neither difficult nor time consuming, and the available instructions on `wordpress.org` are more than adequate to guide you through the basic install. That being said, there are some things that you should know and take into account if you want to set up the perfect WordPress site. Therefore, this chapter is all about giving you the solid platform you need for further development. WordPress in itself is a powerful publishing tool, and you can supercharge it with themes and plugins. Running a site on top of WordPress is all about that, so it is important to get the basics right so you can build on top of it. WordPress is the bricks and mortar of the site, but themes and plugins are what make it tick for real.

Also, before moving on, remember that "WordPress" in this book means the stand-alone version of Word-Press available for free from `wordpress.org`. Don't get this mixed up with the multiuser version, called WordPress MU, which is touched upon briefly later, nor with AutoMattic hosted version on `wordpress.com`. This book is all about the main version available from `wordpress.org`, and more specifically with version 2.8 in mind.

The Basic Install

As you probably know, installing WordPress is a breeze. There is a reason the "five-minute install" PR talk isn't getting blasted to pieces by the otherwise so talkative blogosphere. In fact, the only reason that the install should take that long is because uploading the files sometimes takes time due to slow Internet connections or sluggish Web hosts. Most likely you'll have gone through a fair amount of WordPress installs yourself, so I'll be brief on this matter.

First, you need to make sure that your system meets the minimum requirements. The most recent ones can be found here: `wordpress.org/about/requirements/`. If your host supports PHP 4.3 or higher, and runs MySQL 4.0 or higher, then you're good. However, you should make sure your host has mod_rewrite installed since that will be needed for prettier links.

Figure 1-1: The Install interface

To install, you'll need the following:

- To download the most recent version of WordPress (from `wordpress.org/download/`).
- A MySQL database with a user that has write privileges (ask your host if you don't know how to set this up).
- Your favorite FTP program.

To install, unzip your WordPress download and upload the contents of the wordpress folder to your destination of choice on your server. Then, open wp-config-sample.php and find the database parts where you fill out the database name, and the username and password with write privileges. This is what wp-config-sample.php looks like:

```
define('DB_NAME', 'putyourdbnamehere');    // The name of the  database
define('DB_USER', 'usernamehere');     // Your MySQL username
define('DB_PASSWORD', 'yourpasswordhere'); // ...and password
define('DB_HOST', 'localhost');    // 99% chance you won't need to change this value
```

Next, still in wp-config-sample.php, find the part about Secret Keys. This part will start with a commented information text titled "Authentication Unique Keys" followed by four lines (as of writing) where you'll enter the Secret Keys. This is a security function to help make your install more secure and less prone to hacking. You'll only need to add these keys once, and while they can be entered manually and be whatever you like, there is an online generator courtesy of wordpress.org that gives you random strings with each load. Just copy the link (`api.wordpress.org/secret-key/1.1/`) to the generator from your wp-config-sample. php file and open it in your favorite Web browser. You'll get a page containing code looking something like this:

```
define('AUTH_KEY',         'PSmO59sFXB*XDwQ!<uj)h=vv#Kle')dBEOM:OoBzj'V(qd0.nP2|BT~T$a(;6-&!');
define('SECURE_AUTH_KEY', 'o>p3K{TD.tJoM74.Oy5?B@=dF_lcmlB6jm6D|gXnlJ#Z4K,M>E;[ +,22O?Lnarb');
define('LOGGED_IN_KEY',   'c}gR{389F*IG@/V+hg1 45J*H+9i_^HaF;$q(S[5Er[:DVOUjmS@(20E~t0-C*II');
define('NONCE_KEY',        'gz2D:n52|5wRvh)es:8OO|O ufZL@C|G.-w/H-E*}K:ygp4wI*.QHO-mUV_PR|6M');
```

Copy the contents from the generator page and replace the code shown below in wp-config-sample. php with them:

```
define('AUTH_KEY', ');
define('SECURE_AUTH_KEY', ');
define('LOGGED_IN_KEY', ');
define('NONCE_KEY', ');
```

By replacing the code above with the one from the generated page, you've made your install a little bit more secure from those nasty hackers.

The last thing you may want to change in wp-config-sample.php is the language. WordPress is in English (US English to be exact) by default, and if you're Swedish you would naturally want the default language to be Swedish, if you're German you would want German, and so on. To change the language, you'll need a language file (these are .mo files; most of them can be found here: codex.wordpress.org/WordPress_in_Your_Language) that you then upload to wp-content/language/. You also need to alter this little snippet in wp-config-sample.php to let WordPress know what language you want it to be in:

```
define ('WPLANG', '');
```

What you need to do is add the language code: this is the same as the language file, without the file extension. So if you really did want your install in Swedish, you'd download the sv_SE.mo, upload it to wp-content/languages/, and then pass the language to the WPLANG function, like this:

```
define ('WPLANG', 'sv_SE');
```

This won't necessarily make the themes or plugins you use display in your language of choice, but WordPress and its core functionality will, as will any code that supports it. We'll get to localization of themes and plugins in Chapter 6.

And that's it! Rename wp-config-sample.php to wp-config.php, and point your Web browser to your install location. This will show a link that initiates the install procedure, where you'll fill in the blog title, the admin user's e-mail address, and choose whether or not the blog should be open to search engines for indexing (most likely this will be the case, but if you want to fiddle with it first, then disable it; you can enable it in the settings later). After this, you'll get an admin username and a random password (save that!) and hopefully a success message along with a link to the blog.

Not very complicated, right?

Using an External Database Server

One of the most common issues when it comes to a failed WordPress install is that the MySQL database is located on a separate server. If you're getting database connection errors, and you're quite sure that both the username and password for the database user are correct, along with the full write capabilities, then this is most likely the case.

To fix this, just find this code snippet in wp-config.php (or wp-config-sample.php if you haven't renamed it yet) and change localhost to your database server:

```
define('DB_HOST', 'localhost');
```

What the MySQL server may be called depends on your host. It may be mysql67.thesuperhost.com, or something entirely different. Just swap localhost with this, and try and run the install script again.

Naturally, if you can't find your database server address you should contact your Web host and ask them for details.

Other Database Settings

You may want to consider some more database options before installing WordPress. (Probably not though, but still, they warrant mention.)

First of all, there's the database character set and collation. This is basically telling WordPress what character language the database is in, and it should just about always be UTF-8. This is also the default setting in wp-config-sample.php, hence you won't need to fiddle with it unless you have a special need to do so. If you do, however, this is what you're looking for:

```
define('DB_CHARSET', 'utf8');
```

That's the character set, with UTF-8 (obviously spelled out as utf8 in code) by default.

The collation, which is basically the sort order of the character set that WordPress will apply to the MySQL database in the install phase, can be changed in this line:

```
define('DB_COLLATE', );
```

It is empty here, which means it will pass the character set in DB_CHARSET as the collation. By default, that is UTF-8, but if you need this to be something specific you can add it like this:

```
define('DB_COLLATE', 'character_set_of_choice');
```

A Few Words on Installers

Some Web hosts offer installers that will get your WordPress install up and running with just a click from within the Web host admin interface. The most popular one is probably Fantastico. At first, this sounds like a really good idea, since you won't have to fiddle with config files or anything; it'll just slap the blog up there and you can get started.

However, take a moment to do some research before going down this route. The most important aspect to consider is what version of WordPress the installer is actually setting up. Old versions shouldn't be allowed because they are outdated and, at worst, a security hazard. After all, with every WordPress release a lot of security holes are jammed shut, so it is not all about releasing funky new features for your favorite blogging platform.

Installers like Fantastico are great and can save time. However, if they don't install the latest version of WordPress you really shouldn't bother with them at all. If they do, then Google it just to make sure other users haven't reported anything weird going on, and if the coast is clear and you really don't want to do the five-minute manual install, then by all means go for it.

After having installed WordPress using an installer you should use the built-in upgrade feature, or perform upgrades manually using FTP should your host not support automatic upgrades. Make sure the installer doesn't do something strange with the install that stops you from doing this: you don't want to be tied to the installer script for updates.

Moving the WordPress Install to a Different Directory

If you're like me, your dislike of clutter goes as far as your Web hosting environment. In other words, the mere thought of all those WordPress files and folders in the root of your domain makes you nauseous. This may not be such an issue for others, although it will be easier to manage your various Web endeavors if you put the WordPress install in its own folder. Say you want to add other Web software installs; you may have a hard time finding the files you need if they're all mixed in together (although it helps that everything WordPress at this level is named wp-something). It just gets messy if you want to do anything other than just use WordPress.

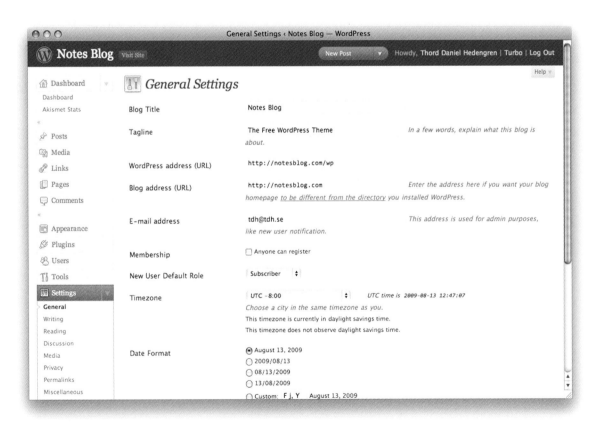

Figure 1-2: General Settings, found under General in the Settings part of the Admin Interface

Installing to a subfolder is the same as installing to the root of a domain, so I won't go into that. The purpose of this is to have the WordPress install in a subfolder, but have the blog displaying as if it were in the root folder, and keep the root folder on the server clean. You can either install Word-Press to the subfolder directly, or to the root and then move the files to a subfolder. How you decide to tackle it is up to you; they are both easy to do.

You should really set up permalinks before doing this, since you'll want them to work regardless. The permalink options are found under Settings → Permalinks.

The first thing you should do is create the folder in which you want to put the WordPress install. Then, go to the General Settings page (see Figure 1-2) and change the WordPress address URL field to where you want to move your install to, and the Blog address URL field to where you want your site to be. Then click the update button and move all the WordPress files to their new directory except for the index.php and .htaccess files, which should be where you want your site to be. When they are there, open index.php and change this to match where you moved your WordPress install to:

```
require('./wp-blog-header.php');
```

That's a relative link with PHP trying to include wp-blog-header.php, which is where the WordPress magic starts. Just change the link to point to the file, which should be in your WordPress directory (whatever you've chosen to call it), and you'll be fine.

After this, login and update your permalinks structure again to get everything to point to their new destinations.

I think a quick example is in order. Say you have WordPress installed in the root folder (domain.com), and want it to be in a subfolder called wpsystem instead while keeping the actual site in root. That means that when people visit domain.com they'll see your WordPress site, but when you log in and manage it you'll do that within the wpsystem folder (or `domain.com/wpsystem/wp-admin/`, to be precise).

Now, this means that you'll need to change the WordPress address URL to `domain.com/wpsystem`, because that's where you want the WordPress install to be, and the blog address URL to `domain.com`, because that's where you want the site to be. Save these settings (don't worry if anything is acting funky just now), and move all the WordPress files to the domain.com/wpsystem folder except index.php and .htaccess, which you put in the root of domain.com since that's where the site is supposed to be. Then, open index.php and locate this code snippet:

```
require('./wp-blog-header.php');
```

And replace it with this code snippet:

```
require('./wpsystem/wp-blog-header.php');
```

9

As you can see, the code now points to the wpsystem folder instead, and to the wp-blog-header.php file.

Log in to the WordPress admin interface (which is now on `domain.com/wpsystem/wp-admin/`) and update the permalinks, and there you have it.

Hacking the Database

Most of the time you needn't worry about the database; WordPress will do that for you. There are database changes between versions sometimes, but program updates will take care of everything, and other than keeping a backup of your content the database can be left to live its own life.

That being said, if things go wrong you may need to do some edits in the database to fix them. Common issues are password resets, weird URLs as a result of a failed move, domain name changes, and not forgetting the dreaded widget issue.

Before moving on, you should remember that making alterations in the database is serious stuff. There are no undos here; what is deleted is deleted for good. Even if you know what you're doing you should always make a fresh backup before altering anything at all. Should you not know your way around a MySQL database and PhpMyAdmin, then don't mess with it until you do. You will break things.

Where Everything Is

Finding your way in the WordPress database is pretty easy. It consists of 10 tables, which in turn are full of content. Just browsing the database should answer most of your questions, and any edits can be made right then and there if you know what you're after. Naturally, there is a full database description in the documentation (`codex.wordpress.org/Database_Description`) and you should consult that whenever you need to find something.

The 10 main tables are:

- wp_comments: contains all comments
- wp_links: contains added links and links data
- wp_options: the blog options
- wp_postmeta: metadata for the posts
- wp_posts: the actual posts
- wp_terms: categories and tags
- wp_term_relationships: associates categories and tags with posts
- wp_term_taxonomy: descriptions for categories and tags
- wp_usermeta: user metadata
- wp_users: the actual users

All these tables are important, of course, but if you need to fix or change something directly in the database, chances are that it is in wp_options (for blog settings, like URLs and such), wp_posts (for mass editing of your blog posts), or wp_users (for password resets and such).

Fixing Issues by Hacking the Database

One of the more common issues with WordPress upgrades is the widgets going crazy, sometimes outputting only a blank page on your blog. While this seems to be a lot less common these days, the upgrade instructions still state that you should disable all plugins and revert to the default theme. If you do, most likely you'll never get that blank page.

However, should you get a blank page, it is probably a widget issue. A possible solution is to clean out the widgets in the database; they are hiding in the wp_options table. Exactly what you need to do and what the various widgets are called depends on what plugins you have, so tread carefully. Most likely the data is named in a way that seems logical compared to the plugins you use, and with that in mind you should be able to find what you're looking for. It may sound a bit hazardous, but it is worth giving it a go should you encounter a blank screen on your blog after an upgrade.

Another issue you may want to resolve in the database is changing or resetting a password for a user. You can't actually retrieve the password from the database because it is encrypted and all you'll see is gibberish, but you can change it to something else. Just remember that the passwords needs the MD5 treatment, which can be done through PhpMyAdmin or just about any MySQL managing tool you may use. Basically, what you do is type the new password in plain text, and choose MD5 for that particular field. You'll end up with a new line of gibberish, which actually says what you typed in the first place. Again, if this sounds scary to you, don't do it without exploring other solutions first!

Finally, you may want to mass edit your posts. Maybe you've got a new domain and want to change the source for all images you've used over the years, from olddomain.com/wp-content/image.jpg to newdomain.com/wp-content/image.jpg, for example. There are plugins that will help you with this, so most of us should probably check them out first. If you're comfortable with the database, though, you can run a SQL query to search for all these elements and replace them with the new ones. It could be some thing like this:

```
UPDATE wp_posts SET post_content = REPLACE (
post_content,
'olddomain.com/wp-content/',
'newdomain.com/wp-content/');
```

That would search the wp_posts table for any mention of olddomain.com/wp-content/ and replace it with newdomain.com/wp-content/. That in turn would fix all the image links in the example above. Nifty little SQL queries for batch editing can come in handy, but remember: there are no undos here and what's done is done, so make sure you've got backups before even considering doing these things.

Backing Up

Anyone who has lost data in a hard drive crash or similar knows the importance of backing up, and it goes without saying that this applies to your online content as well. Backing up WordPress is actually a two-step process, since your blog consists of both a database (with all the content) and static files (image uploads and other attachments). Then you have your theme, your plugins, and so on, that you may or may not have altered but still don't want to lose because doing so would mean that you would have to collate them all over again. In fact, as of the inclusion of automatic updates within the admin interface in WordPress (a great feature in itself), backing up these things has become even more important.

The only thing you can lose without it causing too much trouble is the core WordPress files. These you can always download again, although you may want to keep a copy of wp-config.php somewhere safe.

For your database backup needs, several options are available. The most obvious one would be to use a Web interface like PhpMyAdmin and just download a compressed archive containing the data, and that is all well and good. However, you need to remember to do it on a regular basis, and that may be a problem. Also, PhpMyAdmin and similar database management interfaces aren't exactly the most user-friendly solutions out there, and most of us would rather not mess around with the database more than we truly have to.

Enter the wonderful world of WordPress plugins, and especially one called wp-db-backup. This plugin, which is featured in Chapter 11 in full, will let you set up various rules for database backups, and have your plugins stored on a server, e-mailed to you, or otherwise backed up, at regular intervals.

That's the database content; now for the static files. This is very simple: just keep backing up the wp-content folder. This folder contains all your uploads (images, videos, and other files that are attachments to your blog posts) along with your themes and plugins. In fact, it is the only part in the WordPress install that you should have been fiddling with, not counting the wp-config.php file, the .htaccess file, and possibly the index.php file in the root folder. Backing up wp-content will save all your static files, themes, plugins, and so on, as long as you haven't set up any custom settings that store data outside it.

So how can you backup wp-content? Unfortunately, the simplest backup method relies on you remembering to do so, which of course is downloading it using an FTP program. Some Web hosts have nifty little built-in scripts that can send backups to external storage places, such as Amazon S3 or any FTP server, really. This is a cheap way to make sure your static data is safe, so you should really look into it and not just rely on remembering to make an FTP download yourself. In fact, these built-in solutions often manage databases as well, so you can set up a backup of that as well. Better safe than sorry, after all.

The last stand, and final resort should the worst happen to your install, is the Web host's own backup solution. There is no way anyone can convince me to trust that my Web host, no matter how good they may be, will solve any matter concerning data loss. Some are truly doing what they claim, which may be hourly backups, RAID disks, and other fancy stuff, but even the most well thought out solution can malfunction or backfire. Most hosts have some automatic backup solution in place, but what happens if the whole datacenter is out for some reason, or there's a power outage? You may not think that this could happen today, but if Google can go offline, so can your Web host.

In other words, make sure you have your very own backup solution in place. I hope you'll never have to use it, but if you do, you'll be happy you thought it through from the start.

WordPress and Switching Hosts

There are several ways of moving to a new server. My preferred one is using the Export/Import functionality found under Tools in WordPress admin (see Figure 1-3). However, before moving, make sure your WordPress install is up to date. Then, go to Tools and choose to export the content. You'll get a file containing the data.

Next, install WordPress on your new server. Any decent Web host will have alternate URLs to access your content on the server online, without actually having to have your domain pointing to

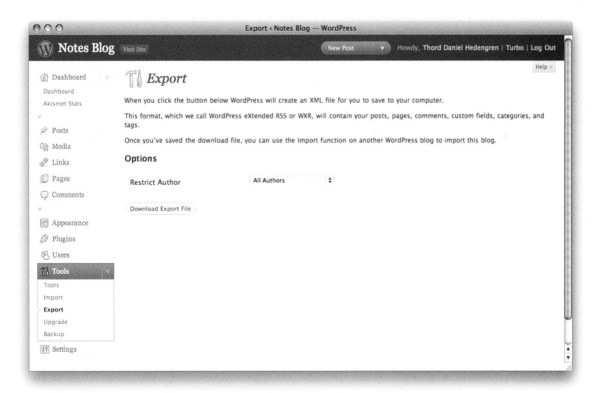

Figure 1-3: Exporting data

it. When you've got a running WordPress install, delete the automatic pages and posts since these won't be overwritten. You want the install to be clean.

Now, download the wp-content folder from your old server, and upload it to your new one. Now you've got all your images, plugins, themes, and so forth in place. There is a built-in option in the post importer that will try to download the images from your posts to your new server, but it fails more often than not, so it is better to manage the static files in wp-content manually using your favorite FTP program.

Finally, you're ready to import the exported file from your old server. Just go to Tools and go through the import wizard (see Figure 1-4), taking care that your exported file from the old server is up to date. Import it, let the script chew through the content, and then you're all done! Verify that everything is working properly, give yourself a pat on the back, and then redirect your domain to your new server. You may have to edit your new blog's settings, since it may have taken URLs from the Web host's internal system, so change them to correspond with your blog's domain name. While waiting for the domain to be pointed to your new server the blog will break of course, but then again your old one is still working. You may want to close comments on it, though, since those will be "lost" when the visitor is suddenly pointed to the new server with your new WordPress install, which is based on the content of your old one at the point when you exported the file.

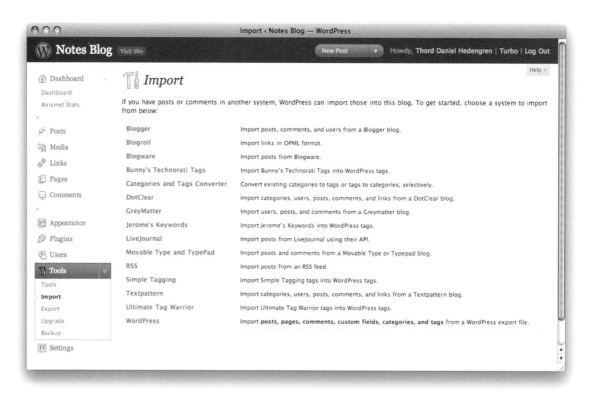

Figure 1-4: WordPress can import from a number of systems, but you want WordPress this time since that's what you exported from

When Export/Import Won't Work

Unfortunately, there are times when the Export/Import way won't work—usually because there is just too much content for PHP to parse in the import. This is only an issue if you have a big blog, and possibly due to your host's server settings as well.

If this is the case, you'll have to do things a little bit differently. Ideally, you can recreate your environment identically on your new server, with the same database name, and the same username and password to manage it. If you can do this, moving will be a breeze. All you have to do is get a dump from the MySQL database using your favorite MySQL admin tool, and then import it into the new one. This probably means using PhpMyAdmin and the backup instructions from the WordPress Codex (found at `codex.wordpress.org/Backing_Up_Your_Database`). Here's how you do it:

1. Log in to PhpMyAdmin and select the database you want to back up.
2. Click the Export tab in the top menu.
3. On the left-hand side, make sure all the necessary tables are marked (the Select All link will help). This would be all of them, unless you have other stuff in the same database as well.
4. On the right-hand side, you want to tick the Structure box checkbox, then the Add DROP TABLE box and Add AUTO_INCREMENT as well as Enclose table and field names with backquotes. Also tick the Data checkbox, but leave the choices within unchecked.
5. Down below, tick Save as file and pick the kind of file you want to download, probably a zipped one.
6. Click the Go button. This will download the database, which you will import on your new server.
7. Importing a dump in PhpMyAdmin is even easier. Make sure you have created a database with the same name, username, and password as you had on your previous server. This means you won't have to alter the wp-config.php file.

Import the dump to the new database by logging in with your favorite MySQL manager. If this is PhpMyAdmin, just select the database and choose the Import tab (sits next to the Export tab) at the top. Use the importer to find your downloaded dump, and import it.

Then download your full WordPress install from your old server, and upload it in an identical manner to your new one. Again, give it a spin using your Web host's temporary addresses and make sure that everything seems to be working. Point the domain to the new server, and when it resolves everything should be running smoothly.

However, you may not be able to recreate the environment in exactly the same way. If this is the case, just alter wp-config.php accordingly; most likely it is the database name, username and password, as well as possibly the need for an external database server, that you'll have to edit.

Moving WordPress from one server to another may seem scary at first, but it isn't as bad as it once was. Sure, if you've got a big blog and aren't comfortable doing stuff in database admin interfaces like PhpMyAdmin, then this may be a bit much. Get help, or give it a go yourself. Just make sure that you have all the backups you could possibly need, and don't mess things up on your old (current) server, but rather on the new one. After all, you can always just create a new database and WordPress install there and give it another go.

How to Make a WordPress Install More Secure

There are a few simple things you can do to make your WordPress install more secure, and a few that are pretty much hardcore. The first and foremost one, however, is to keep WordPress up to date. Each new version removes a bunch of security holes, bugs, and other possible exploits that can make your install vulnerable, and not updating regularly means you won't get these fixes.

This brings us to the first tip. Check your theme's header.php file to see if the following code is there (it almost always is):

```php
<?php remove_action('wp_head', 'wp_generator'); ?>
```

Then remove it! What it does is output what version of WordPress you're using, and while that may be a nice thing for bots and spiders looking for statistics, it's not worth the additional risk it brings. After all, if a certain version is known to have an open security hole, and people are looking for installs of that version to exploit, why make it easier on them and tell them outright?

You should also make sure that your wp-config.php file has the Secret Keys. Those make the install more secure. If you have an old version of WordPress and haven't bothered with the wp-config.php file in a while, you should at the very least add the four Secret Key lines to your file. You can get them from here: `api.wordpress.org/secret-key/1.1/`. You'll remember the Secret Keys from the installation instructions earlier in this chapter: just add them in the same way as you do when doing a brand-new install.

Users and Passwords

The first thing I do after having installed WordPress is to create a new user with admin privileges, log in with that user, and delete the default "admin" one. Why? Because everyone knows that if there is a user named admin, then that account has full admin capabilities. So if you wanted to hack your way into a WordPress install, you'd start by looking for the admin user to try to brute force a login. Once you're in via this method, you can do anything you want. So it's worth getting rid of the admin user, after you have logged in for the first time and created a proper account, because it has fulfilled its purpose.

That being said, deleting the admin user won't guarantee that hackers won't find another user to build their attempts on. If you have user archives on your blog, those will give you away. One solution would be to not display these, nor any links to an author page (other than ones you've created outside of WordPress's own functionality), but what do you do if you feel you need them?

The solution is to keep account credentials sparse. There is no need to have an administrator account for writing or editing posts and pages; an editor's credentials are more than enough. Granted, should an account with editor status be hacked then it will be bad for your site because the editor can do a lot of things, but at least it is not an administrator account and that will keep the worst things at bay. And besides, you keep backups, right?

Besides questioning the types of accounts you and your fellow users have, passwords are another obvious security risk. You've probably been told to use a strong password, to make it long and to use letters, numbers, special characters, and so on. Do that: the more complicated the password is, the harder will it be to crack.

Server-side Stuff

The MySQL user for your WordPress database, which incidentally shouldn't be shared with any other system, doesn't actually need all write privileges. In fact, you don't need to be able to lock tables, index, create temporary tables, references, or create routines. In other words, you can limit the capabilities somewhat to make the system more secure.

Another thing some people will tell you to do is add extra logins using Apache's .htaccess. I don't do that myself because these login forms are annoying. Besides, there are plugins that can do the job better (see Chapter 11 for more information).

One thing you may want to do is make sure that there is an empty index.php or index.html file in every folder that doesn't have an index file. This is usually the case by default in WordPress, but it doesn't hurt to check. What this does is make it impossible to browse the folders directly, something that some Web hosts support.

Another server-side issue is forcing SSL encryption when logging in to the WordPress admin. This means that the traffic sent when you're doing your thing in the admin interface will be a lot harder to sniff out for potential bad guys. It's pretty easy to force SSL; just add this code snippet to your wp-config.php file, above the "That's all, stop editing! Happy blogging" comment:

```
define('FORCE_SSL_ADMIN', true);
```

SSL won't work without support from your host. Some Web hosts give you all you need to start this service from within their admin interface, but others will have to activate it for you, and may even charge you for it.

Summary

It doesn't matter if this is your first foray into the wonderful world of WordPress, or if you're an experienced user and developer. The important thing is that you have the basic installation figured out, have made it secure, and understand the publishing beast that is WordPress. From here on you'll start building sites and creating plugins to achieve your goals.

Next up is diving into what makes WordPress tick. That means you'll get to play with the loop, start looking at themes and plugins, and hopefully also activate that idea machine in the back of the head that comes up with all those cool adaptations. The brilliance of WordPress is that it is so flexible and that you can build so many things with it, and the mere fact that it is so means that just thinking about the possibilities will undoubtedly inspire you.

If you have a WordPress install to play with (preferably something that isn't too public, since you may break something), get your sandbox set up and get ready to dive into the WordPress syntax.

2

THE WORDPRESS SYNTAX

Now that you've got your WordPress install set up, it's time to do something with it. Naturally, you can just download a theme and the plugins you want, start tinkering, and learn by doing/hacking. That's a proven method for sure, employed all the time. It is, in fact, how I got started with WordPress way back.

However, since you ponied up for this book you may as well get a head start. This chapter is all about what makes WordPress tick. It doesn't go into depth on every file in the system, but rather serves an introduction to how WordPress works so that you gain the knowledge needed to start developing sites running on WordPress.

From here on, it will help if you know a little bit of PHP, as well as (X)HTML and CSS. If these are alien concepts to you, be sure to read up on them at least a bit. You don't need to know either one by heart, but some sort of understanding is definitely needed.

WordPress and PHP

WordPress is written in PHP, a popular scripting language used online. You probably know this, and if you're even the least bit knowledgeable in PHP you'll quickly find your way around Word-Press and the various functions it offers on the plugin and theme development end of things. That being said, you don't need any prior PHP experience to do funky stuff with WordPress. Granted, you won't be able to create WordPress plugins without knowing PHP, but you can certainly make things happen with the built-in template tags used in themes, and that will get you a long way, if not all the way there.

The WordPress Codex, which is to say the manual in wiki form found on `codex.wordpress.org` (see Figure 2-1), will be very helpful when you start working with the code. You should make yourself familiar with it, since whenever you branch out from the examples in the coming chapters, or when you want to know more about a concept, the Codex will be where you'll find the information needed to keep moving. While the Codex contains basic information and tutorials, you'll often find yourself returning to a few reference listings, such as the template tags (`codex.wordpress.org/Template_Tags/`), which are explained shortly, and the function reference (`codex.wordpress.org/Function_Reference`) for your more advanced needs.

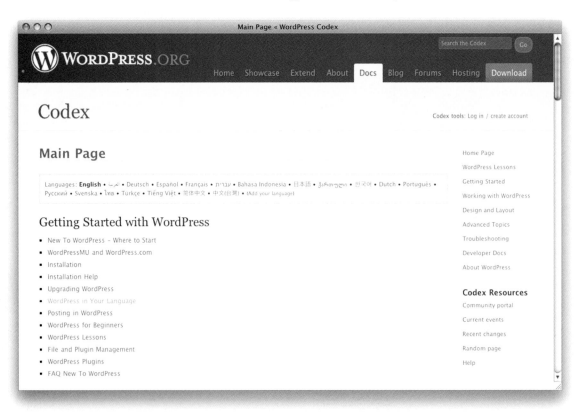

Figure 2-1: You'd better get used to browsing the WordPress Codex

Does this sound like Greek to you? Don't worry, even if you've never written a *Hello World!* PHP script you'll be able to build just about anything content-driven with WordPress before you're done with this book.

Themes and Templates

Before moving on, you need to know about themes and template files, since that will be what we'll be looking at next. To put it simply, a theme is a skin for your blog. It holds the design that your content, which WordPress outputs from the database, will be displayed in.

However, that is a simplification that undermines the possibilities of theme development. Sure, you can use a really basic theme that more or less just outputs the default presentation that WordPress falls back on, but you can also completely alter the way your site's content is displayed, making it look and behave in any way but as a blog if you want to.

A theme consists of a stylesheet file called style.css. This file holds your basic style, the theme name, and data. Along with it are a bunch of PHP files, some absolutely necessary and some just good practice to make life easier on you or make interesting stuff happen. These PHP files are called template files. You'll find index.php, which will be the main file for listings and search results, and is the fallback file for situations where there is no other template file available. Other common ones include sidebar.php, which holds the sidebar content, comments.php for comment functionality, and header.php/footer.php that are for your site's header and footer, respectively. You may also have a single.php for single post view, and a page.php for static WordPress pages, and maybe a dedicated template file for search results (search.php), along with your category listings in category.php, and so on. Add any number of page templates that you can apply to WordPress pages, and you get a tiny little glimpse of how versatile WordPress is.

With your template files, and the WordPress functions as well as plugins and traditional PHP code, you can make your site behave in just about any way imaginable. Don't want the commenting capability enabled? Just remove the code! Maybe you want a specific product page to look completely different? Then create a page template and style it any way you like. It goes on and on, and later in the book you'll see how to build sites that are nothing like the common blog at all.

Just to make things a little more complicated, you can have even more functionality in your themes. The file functions.php can provide plugin-like features to your theme, and we haven't even gotten started on widgets yet, areas where you can drop elements from within the admin interface.

The best way to learn about themes is to use them. Install a theme on a test blog, play around, and then take a look at the files it consists of. Don't bother with images and forget about the stylesheet as well (it is just a design), but do take a look at index.php and both header.php and footer.php to understand the way they are built up. It's not very complicated in essence: first you load header.php, then whatever main template file is used (like index.php, single.php, or something else), possibly a sidebar.php file, and then footer.php.

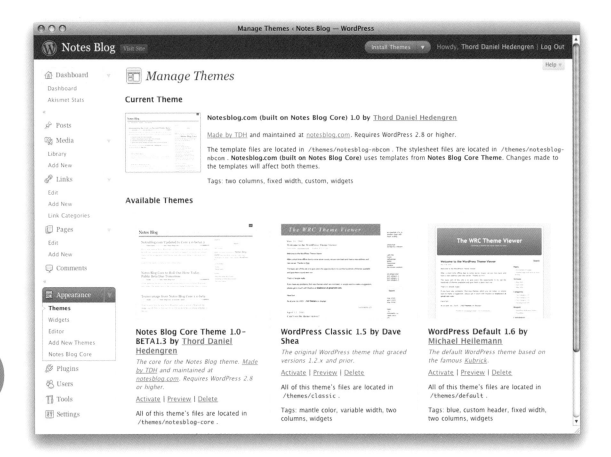

Figure 2-2: The WordPress admin interface makes theme management easy

We'll play with themes later and go through it all, but for now all you need to know is that it's in the theme's template files that the magic happens. There you'll find the code that outputs the content you've posted using WordPress, and while various themes may look and behave differently, they are just displaying the same thing in different ways thanks to the template files.

About the WordPress Core

Any good CMS will keep its core files apart so that you don't ruin the code that makes the system work, and WordPress is no exception. Here, we're talking about the WordPress core, which is basically everything that isn't in the wp-content folder, where you'll drop themes as well as plugins and uploaded files. All these things work on top of WordPress, so there's no risk of actually ruining the actual system files (unless you've installed malicious code, but that's a completely different matter) when you develop a site.

In fact, the whole idea is that the only time you're editing or even doing anything outside of the wp-content folder is when you're installing the system, and possibly when moving the install files to a different folder. Naturally, there is some cool stuff that requires .htaccess editing, and I'm sure you'll come across plugins that want you to do things outside of wp-content, and that's fine of course, although you should be a bit cautious.

The whole point, however, is that the WordPress core is untouchable. Don't mess with it unless you really need to, and if you do, you should rethink and rethink again because the chances are there's a better solution. Hacking the core is bad, and that's why the wp-content-based theme structure is so good.

Using the Template Tags

Although WordPress is written in PHP, it is in fact a framework in itself. You can use PHP to do stuff with your WordPress theme or plugin, but most of the functionality is managed with template tags. If you open a theme file (just about any file with the extension .php, like index.php or single.php) you'll find a lot of PHP-like functions, such as this one, for example:

```
<?php bloginfo('name'); ?>
```

That is a template tag, and it outputs the blog's name. The PHP part, which consists of `<?php` at first, and `; ?>` at the end, tells WordPress to process whatever's inside it, and in this case it is the template tag `bloginfo()`. Inside the parenthesis you'll find the parameter, passed inside the quotation marks. In other words, `'name'` is the parameter above.

You'll be using `bloginfo()` a lot in your themes, for example for finding the theme's directory. Let's output an image called smashing.gif in a theme file, just to drive the point home:

```
<img src="<?php bloginfo('template_directory'); ?>/smashing.gif" />
```

You'll recognize the img HTML tag of course. The `bloginfo()` template tag has another parameter here, `template_directory`. This outputs the path to the theme's folder, called template directory instead of theme directory just to make things a little more complicated. And then you just add the smashing.gif file name to complete the path, and you've got a potentially working image path in your theme. Of course, you would need the image in the theme folder as well.

So template tags are basically PHP functions that can handle parameters to do different things. Some have default values, others don't, and some have more settings for you to play with than others. Most of them will work anywhere in your WordPress theme files, but some need to be within the loop. The loop is basically the code that outputs the content, like posts or pages. (Loops are examined in the next chapter.)

You'll find a complete listing of template tags in the Codex: codex.wordpress.org/Template_Tags/. Consult it whenever you need to do something out of the ordinary within your themes, or when you want to alter things in an existing theme. Each template tag is described, along with usage and sample code to help you understand it. This is the beauty of WordPress: you can actually copy and paste your way to a different result without knowing any PHP at all.

23

The Include Tags

There are a couple of template tags that you'll find in just about any theme template file. The include tags are basically PHP include functions to output the content of the necessary files within your theme. In other words, it is just a way to make it a bit easier to grab that header, footer, and sidebar.

```php
<?php get_header(); ?>
<?php get_footer(); ?>
<?php get_sidebar(); ?>
```

You'll find them in your theme's index.php, for instance, and they automatically include header.php, footer.php, and sidebar.php, respectively, where the tags are placed. The first two won't take any parameters, but get_sidebar() actually supports alternate sidebars by adding a string to the tag, like this:

```php
<?php get_sidebar('left'); ?>
```

This would include sidebar-left.php rather than the default sidebar.php, so you'd need to create that file of course.

Should you want to include other files such as an alternate header, for example, you can use this nifty little PHP snippet:

```php
<?php include (TEMPLATEPATH . '/altheader.php'); ?>
```

That is a traditional PHP include with TEMPLATEPATH that shows PHP where to look for the file, which is your theme folder. This is what the other include template tags do as well: they look in the theme folder for their respective files. This example includes altheader.php wherever the PHP code snippet is put. You can just as easily include something else this way, so it is very handy.

Finally, there's an include tag for the comments, which any good theme has in comments.php. Should there be no comments.php, WordPress will include the one in the default theme. Just put the comments_template() tag where you want comment functionality, and remove it where you don't think you need it.

```php
<?php comments_template(); ?>
```

Note that you can't pass parameters to comments_template().

The include tags are what you use to output the various template files within your theme. They differ from the template tags in that respect, since what you're doing is including other files rather than adding a specific type of functionality or element. Or, to put it frankly, the include tags include the template files that contain the template tags.

Passing Multiple Parameters to a Template Tag

Outputting content with template tags is easy enough. Some won't take parameters at all, and others will just take one, like `bloginfo()` used in the previous example. Others, however, will take several parameters.

Two really useful template tags, for the blogger at least, are `edit_post_link()` and `edit_comment_link()`. They basically do the same thing, which is to add an edit link to posts and comments so that, when logged in as a user with the necessary credentials, you can fix errors quickly by clicking the edit link: this will take you to the admin interface where you can alter your blunder or censor that particularly nasty (but most likely valid) comment.

What you do with these tags—using `edit_post_link()` as an example (but they are basically the same)—is put them in your theme's file along with the posts/comments. Both tags need to be within the loop, which is discussed in the next chapter, but for now all you need to know that `edit_post_link()` goes with the code that outputs the posts.

First, this is how it looks when passing its default parameters:

```php
<?php edit_post_link(); ?>
```

If you put that in your theme, you'll get a link that says "Edit This" wherever you put the code, and that's it. Now, say you want this link to show up on its own row, say "Admin" before the actual link, and say "Edit this post" rather than the "Edit This" default. Simple—just put this in instead:

```php
<?php edit_post_link('Edit this post', '<p>Admin: ', '</p>'); ?>
```

As you can see, `edit_post_link()` supports three parameters. The first one is the link text, `'Edit this post'` in this case, and the second is what goes before the link. Remember, you wanted a separate paragraph for the edit link, and we wanted it to say "Admin" in front, so here's `'<p>Admin: '`. (Note the blank space after the text to make some room in front of the link.) Finally, the third parameter is what goes after the link, which is just `'</p>'` because you need to close the <p> tag.

In other words, `edit_post_link()` can handle three parameters, and they are passed, in this sense, to speak a little PHP:

```php
<?php edit_post_link( $link, $before, $after ); ?>
```

Remember, parameters are usually passed within quotation marks, and separated with commas and a space to make them more readable.

Not all that complicated, right? All you need to know is which parameters there are to pass, and in what order they need to be. The order is important: imagine if you threw it around? You may get the wrong text linked and would definitely break your design, or at least the validation of the site.

Now to try something a bit more complicated:

```php
<?php wp_tag_cloud(); ?>
```

This template tag will output a tag cloud displaying at most 45 tags, with the smallest one at the font size of 8 pt (points), and the largest at 22 pt. They are displayed in a flat listing and sorted by name, in ascending order. You know this because these are the default values, and there are a lot of them as you can see. In fact, `wp_tag_cloud()` can pass 12 parameters; the following table takes a look at them.

smallest	Smallest tag size; 8 is default
largest	Largest tag size; 22 is default
unit	What font size unit is used; pt is default
number	How many tags to display at most; 45 is default
format	How to display the tags; flat separated with white space is default
orderby	How to order the tags; name is default
order	How to sort the tags; ascending is default
exclude	What tags to exclude; none is default
include	What tags to include; all is default
link	View is default
taxonomy	The basis for the tag cloud; post is default
echo	Whether to show the tag cloud or not; true is default

Some of these may be new to you even if you're an experienced WordPress user, especially echo and taxonomy. Both were introduced in WordPress 2.8.

Now, if you compare these values to the description of the default output of `wp_tag_cloud()`, you'll see that all these are passed without you needing to display anything.

Now we'll alter it by changing some parameters. Be aware, however, that `wp_tag_cloud()` reads its parameters in what is commonly referred to as query style. That's a good thing, because having to type in all the 12 possible parameters when you really just want to change the font size unit from pt to px (pixels) wouldn't be very user-friendly. Instead, you can just write it in plain text:

```php
<?php wp_tag_cloud('unit=px'); ?>
```

Naturally, I didn't know that px was valid for the unit option; I found that on the description of the template tag (`codex.wordpress.org/Template_Tags/wp_tag_cloud`). Other possible font size units are em, %, and of course pt, which is the default.

If you want to pass more parameters, just add an ampersand (&) between them, within the parameter, with no spaces. Change the tag order to 'count' rather than 'name':

```php
<?php wp_tag_cloud('unit=px&orderby=count'); ?>
```

You can add even more by just separating the various parameters for the template tag with ampersands. Now randomize the order, changing the smallest tag to 10 px (because the default 8 is a bit small when you're using pixels rather than points) and the largest to 24 px:

```php
<?php wp_tag_cloud('smallest=10&largest=24unit=px&orderby=count&order=RAND'); ?>
```

The order value, RAND, is in capitals. That is intentional; it is just how you pass data to order (the other options are ASC for ascending and DESC for descending). Also, you probably noticed that both smallest and largest were placed before the unit option. It is good form to put the various parameters in the order they are described, as you'll be able to find them more easily whenever you need to edit the code or look something up.

More on Parameters

Since you'll be doing a lot of stuff with the template tags, understanding parameters is crucial. There are three types of template tags, which have been touched on already. The first kind takes no parameters at all, the second takes one or several parameters within quotation marks, while the third type is the one called *query style*, separating the various options with ampersands.

Naturally, not passing a parameter at all means that you just put the template tag wherever you need it, and this also goes for the other template tags since there is a default output. The problems come when you need to change that default output, and hence the parameters.

In the preceding examples, you have done all this. Remember, you passed just one piece of information in a parameter to the bloginfo() template tag:

```php
<?php bloginfo('name'); ?>
```

Then you passed a parameter in PHP function style, with the edit_post_link() template tag. Here, you told the template tag what the link text should be, and what should come before and after it, separating each instruction with a comma and putting the data within quotation marks:

```php
<?php edit_post_link('Edit this post', '<p>Admin: ', '</p>'); ?>
```

Finally, you passed a lot of options within a query-style parameter to output a tag cloud with wp_tag_cloud(). This method splits parameters with ampersands, and lets you change just the settings you want:

```php
<?php wp_tag_cloud('smallest=10&largest=24unit=px&orderby=count&order=RAND'); ?>
```

At this point, this section gets a bit technical. There are three ways to pass data to template tags, and although the template tag's definition (as stated in the WordPress Codex wiki) will tell you exactly how to pass data to that particular template tag, it may be a good idea to know what's behind it. You can't just pick one and go with it, you need to find out what the particular tags want.

First you've got *strings*, which are lines of text. The bloginfo('name') example is a string, because you tell it that 'name' is the parameter. Strings are found within single or double quotation marks (they do the same thing), although the single version is a lot more common and the one used in the examples in this book.

Integers are whole numbers, such as 55900 or -3 for that matter. You can pass them inside quotation marks if you want, but you don't need to. They are usually used whenever you need to fetch something that has an ID, which is a lot of things. You'll stumble onto template tags as well as conditional tags that do this later on.

Finally, there are the *boolean* parameters, which basically mean that something is either true or false. You can pass this information with all capitals (TRUE or FALSE), all lower case letters (true or false), or using numbers (1 being true and 0 being false). However, you cannot put boolean values within quotation marks; they always stand on their own. For example, the get_calendar() template tag only takes one instruction, and that is whether to display the full day, or just a one-letter abbreviation. True is the default value and displays the first letter in the name of the day (for example, M for Monday), so if you want to output Monday instead of M, you need to set get_calendar() to false:

```php
<?php get_calendar(FALSE); ?>
```

No quotation marks or anything are required, just plain text. You can also write false in lower case, or just put a 0 in there.

Another example of boolean instructions is the_date() template tag, usually used to output the date of a post. You may, for example, want to use that information in PHP instead, and display nothing. Reading up on the template tag reveals that you can change the output format of the date (the first string in the parameter), what goes before the outputted date (the second string), and after it (the third string). The fourth instruction you can pass, however, is a boolean that tells the system whether to output or not (true by default). Say you want to output a year-month-day date (Y-m-d says the PHP manual for date functions; WordPress can take them all) within a paragraph. It would look like this:

```php
<?php the_date('Y-m-d', '<p>', '</p>'); ?>
```

However, if you want to use this with PHP for some reason, outputting nothing, you can set it to `false` with the echo option that this template tag has. This goes last, is a boolean value, and hence you won't put it within quotation marks:

```
<?php the_date('Y-m-d', '<p>', '</p>', FALSE); ?>
```

This would give you the same result, being year-month-day within a <p> tag, but it would output nothing so if you want to use it you need to do something funky with PHP.

It may be good to remember that strings are text within quotation marks, integers are whole numbers, and Boolean parameters are true or false without any quotation marks. With this in mind, it'll be a lot easier to understand the template tags you'll use to build really cool WordPress sites later on.

Conditional Tags

Conditional tags are very handy. You use them in your theme's template files, and as the name implies they are for setting various conditions. In other words, you can use them to display different things depending on the situation. A very good example is the conditional tag `is_home()`, which checks if the page you're on is the homepage. Use it to output a greeting, since that is the polite thing to do:

```
<?php if (is_home())
{
    echo '<p class ="welcome">Hey you, welcome to the site. I love new visitors!</p>';
} ?>
```

This would output a paragraph with the class `welcome`, and the text within. So looking closer at this, you'll see it is a simple if clause asking if the page `is_home()`, and then an echo with the paragraph. Very straightforward, so let's try something else. Say you've got a specific category that should have a different sidebar than the rest of the site, for example. You can check that with the conditional tag `is_category()`, and then output another sidebar. Whenever it is another page within the site, use the traditional `get_sidebar()` include tag.

This code will replace the `get_sidebar()` PHP snippet in the theme's template files wherever it matters, which probably means files like index.php, category.php, single.php, and so on.

```
<?php if (is_category('very-special')) {
        get_sidebar('special');
} else {
        get_sidebar();
} ?>
```

29

So you're asking if the category is `very-special`, which is the category slug (used in perma-links and such) in this case. You could have asked for the category ID or the category name as well, and while an ID is pretty foolproof, the code is a lot easier to read if you use the slug because it is nicenamed, meaning it can't contain nasty special characters and such. So if the category is in fact the one with the `very-special` slug, then use the include tag `get_sidebar('special')`, where `'special'` is a parameter that tells you that you want sidebar-special.php. If you wanted to, you could have done a traditional PHP include, using the `TEMPLATEPATH` option to find the theme folder (see the section "The Include Tags" earlier in this chapter), but `get_sidebar()` does the work for you, so go with that.

Moving on, should the category not be the one with the `very-special` slug, move on to the `else` clause and that tells you to use the normal `get_sidebar()` include tag, which means you'll include sidebar.php.

This is all very simple stuff, but it clearly shows how conditional tags can be used to create dynamic pages. We'll do fun stuff with it later.

Summary

Now that you know that WordPress sites are built on themes, which in turn consist of template files containing different kinds of tags that do funky stuff, it's time to start manipulating the content. This is done with the loop, a snippet of PHP that is the heart and soul of WordPress. While understanding it may not be entirely necessary to do things with WordPress, you certainly have to understand it if you want to truly bend the platform to your will. It is with the loop that you can make posts show up in a different order and generally display things the way you want.

If that doesn't convince you that the loop is important and well worth the full chapter it has been awarded, maybe the mere fact that a lot of the things you'll want to do have to reside within the loop to actually be possible will. And that in turn means that you sometimes need multiple loops with custom outputs. Or, at the very least, you need to figure out where the loop begins and ends so that you can add the cool template tags and plugin features you no doubt will find or create on your own.

There's no way of getting around it, the loop is important. Better hop to it, then.

3

THE LOOP

Now that you have the basic WordPress installation as well as the theme concept under control, it is time to look at what really makes the system run. This chapter will teach you about the loop, which basically is a PHP query that talks to WordPress and makes it output the things requested. The chapter will start with some basic usage, and then branch out to multiple loops and some nice little trickery used within to achieve various effects.

You need to understand the loop to really create cool WordPress sites, and while you won't need to know it by heart, you should grasp what it does. That way, you can research the many functions and features available when you run into a solution that requires custom content output.

Understanding the WordPress Loop

The loop is the heart of WordPress, and it resides in your theme's template files. While you can in fact have a theme without the loop, it would make the fluidity of the content handling, like displaying the latest posts and browsing backwards, quite difficult to pull off. Some template files, for example 404 error pages, don't have the loop at all, but most do. If you want to look for it in a theme template file, open index.php; this is the fallback file as you'll recall, hence it needs the loop to display content listings and single posts as well as pages.

Some template tags only work within the loop, so you need to be able to identify it. This is easy, as you will see in the next section.

The Basic Loop

If you want to create sites using WordPress, you need to understand the loop. Luckily, the basic one is pretty easy. It starts with this:

```php
<?php if ( have_posts() ) : while ( have_posts() ) : the_post(); ?>
```

And ends with this:

```php
<?php endwhile; else: ?>
    <p>Some error message or similar.</p>
<?php endif; ?>
```

Actually, you don't need the error message part other than in template files that are used to output errors, but since a lot of themes do have it, it is included here. It can be a 404 page not found error, or a search result message telling the visitor that the query in question didn't return any hits.

What follows is a fully functional loop, with the common template tags for outputting post content. You'll find it, or something pretty similar to it, in the index.php file of most themes:

```php
<?php if ( have_posts() ) : while ( have_posts() ) : the_post(); ?>
    <div id="post-<?php the_ID(); ?>" <?php post_class(); ?>>
        <h2><a href="<?php the_permalink(); ?>" title="<?php the_title(); ?>"><?php the_title();
    ?></a></h2>
        <?php the_content(); ?>
        <?php get_comments(); ?>
    </div>
<?php endwhile; else: ?>
    <div class="post">
        <h2>Error!</h2>
        <p>Something went wrong! Please try again.</p>
    </div>
<?php endif; ?>
```

Naturally, you'd want a more comprehensive error message than that, but that's not the point right now.

The basic loop checks if there are any posts to return, and in turn the loop is controlled by the global blog settings (how many posts to display and such), and whereabouts on the blog you are. A single post would return just one post (the one you want presumably), while a category listing would return the number of posts specified in the WordPress settings, but only the ones that belong to that particular category.

If there are posts, a while loop is started, and as long as there are posts to return, as controlled by the situation and settings, posts will be returned and displayed. When the while loop is done (all posts that should be returned have been output), it ends with `endwhile`, and then the loop ends with `endif`.

Should there be no posts that match the criteria of the particular situation, the `else` clause is called, and that's when the error message (or similar) will be output. Or nothing at all, if there is nothing defined. After that, the loop ends.

So the loop actually loops content from the database, based on the WordPress settings and any criteria that the page you're on may bring. Makes sense, doesn't it?

A Few Words about WP_Query

`WP_Query` is the heart of the loop, even though you don't see it spelled out in the most basic code. It is really a class that handles all the loop magic, and you'll find it in wp-includes/query.php if you want to dig deep within the WordPress core files. Most of you will be happy with the Codex page (`codex.wordpress.org/Function_Reference/WP_Query`) explaining all the properties and methods that go with `WP_Query`.

The basic loop uses `WP_Query`, or rather it uses the default `$wp_query` object. This means that when you use necessities such as `have_posts()` and `the_post()` you'll in fact use `$wp_query->have_posts()` and `$wp_query->the_post()`. In other words, `have_posts()` and its friends take it for granted that you want to be using `$wp_query`. Whenever you go outside `$wp_query` by creating your own queries, as we'll do in the multiple loops section as well as in examples and adaptations further into the book, you'll have to create an object for it. Like this:

```php
<?php $brand_new_query = new WP_Query(); ?>
```

Here, you're loading everything into `$brand_new_query` instead of the default `$wp_query`, and that means that you can do stuff outside of the main loop.

Most things will connect to the `WP_Query` class, including templates and conditional tags. These should always be used if possible. You can tap into and alter things within the `WP_Query` class, but you should refrain from it if there is an available solution already. That's just common sense. Naturally, there may come a time when you want to do things that are truly out of the box, but that's a whole other matter.

Using the Loop

Now that you've established where you need the loop (in post listings, no matter if it is one or several), and that you can run several of them at once, the question becomes how to use it well rather than just use it. For one thing, maybe you don't want to display the full post in your category listings—maybe you just want an excerpt? This brings you back to the template tags, and the ones that control the output of the loop.

This section takes a quick look at the most frequently used tags. Chances are, you'll want to display and link the title of the various posts. This little code snippet is present in just about every theme's template files that list several posts, and sometimes in the ones that just display the one as well:

```
<h2><a href="<?php the_permalink(); ?>" title="<?php the_title(); ?>"><?php the_title(); ?></a></h2>
```

It's really simple: using the tags for outputting the post title, you display just that (and also use it for the title attribute in the link). Around the title is a traditional hyperlink, getting its href value from `<?php the_permalink(); ?>`, which of course is the permalink to the post in question. Nothing weird or anything there, so let's output some content. Here you have two options, using either one of these two template tags:

```
<?php the_content(); ?>
<?php the_excerpt(); ?>
```

The first one outputs the full post content, unless you're on a page listing several blog posts. In that case, it outputs the content until the point where the `<!--more-->` tag is inserted, which may not be used and then the full post is displayed. If you're a WordPress user you know all about that one; it is the More button in the HTML editor, inserting a Read More link. Incidentally, you can make that appear in any way you like. For example:

```
<?php the_content('Read more here, mate!'); ?>
```

This would change the default read more link text to "Read more here, mate!" instead. There are more options for this, and you can even put HTML code in it (or perhaps a graphic instead of text), but that's a discussion for another time. The important thing is that the template tag `the_content()` outputs the post content, and if it is a blog, listing it breaks it with a read more link if the `<!--more-->` tag is inserted.

Naturally, when you're on a single-post page, and `the_content()` is used (whether a custom read more text is defined or not), it won't output a read more link. You'll see the full post.

The second content template tag available is `the_excerpt()`. As the name implies, it only outputs an excerpt of the actual content, by default the first 55 words. All HTML, whether it

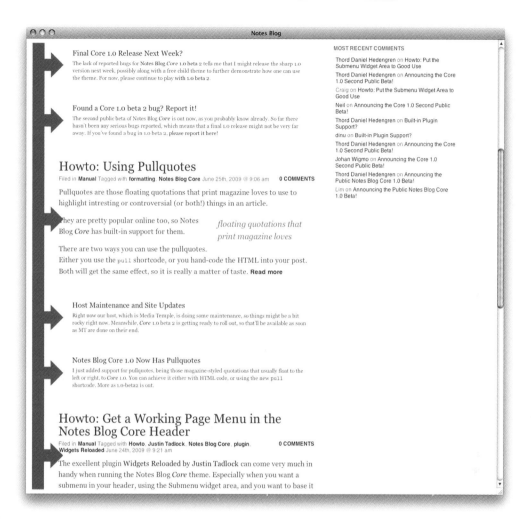

Figure 3-1: All these posts are output with the loop

is images or paragraph breaks or YouTube videos, is stripped from this excerpt, so it should really be used with caution. Neither are there any parameters, which is a bit weird, really: you would think that you'd be able to control the length of the actual excerpt, but there is no such setting.

However, the_excerpt() does fulfill a purpose. You know that excerpt box on the Write Post screen in WordPress (Figure 3-2)? If you put something there, the_excerpt() will output that instead of the first 55 words. So a simple "Hi, this is my post!" in the excerpt field for a post, and the usage of the_excerpt(), will result in a mere "Hi, this is my post!" output, despite it being a lot shorter than 55 words.

What good is the_excerpt(), then? It may be useful for lists where you don't want the blog posts to take up so much space, such as in search results or perhaps some kind of archive page.

Figure 3-2: The Excerpt box on the Write Post screen in WordPress admin

However, the most obvious usage would be as an alternative way of promoting a post. You can have a separate loop that would feature posts with a specific tag, and display their title as usual, but then just output `the_excerpt()` rather than the content. In fact, I'll show you how in just a little bit.

For clarity's sake, this is the default usage of `the_excerpt()`:

```php
<?php the_excerpt(); ?>
```

Remember not to use `the_excerpt()` on templates displaying just one post, like single.php, for example. You need `the_content()` to display the full content! And, yes, should you want to you can use them together.

TRY IT OUT List Excerpts Instead of Full Posts

1. Open the default theme that ships with WordPress from wp-content/themes/default. The file you want is index.php, and it contains the following code:

```php
<?php
/**
 * @package WordPress
 * @subpackage Default_Theme
 */

get_header(); ?>

 <div id="content" class="narrowcolumn" role="main">

 <?php if (have_posts()) : ?>

  <?php while (have_posts()) : the_post(); ?>

   <div <?php post_class() ?> id="post-<?php the_ID(); ?>">
    <h2><a href="<?php the_permalink() ?>" rel="bookmark" title="Permanent Link to
 <?php the_title_attribute(); ?>"><?php the_title(); ?></a></h2>
    <small><?php the_time('F jS, Y') ?> <!-- by <?php the_author() ?> --></small>

    <div class="entry">
     <?php the_content('Read the rest of this entry &raquo;'); ?>
    </div>

    <p class="postmetadata"><?php the_tags('Tags: ', ', ', '<br />'); ?> Posted in
 <?php the_category(', ') ?> | <?php edit_post_link('Edit', '', ' | '); ?>  <?php
 comments_popup_link('No Comments &#187;', '1 Comment &#187;', '% Comments &#187;'); ?></p>
   </div>

  <?php endwhile; ?>

  <div class="navigation">
   <div class="alignleft"><?php next_posts_link('&laquo; Older Entries') ?></div>
   <div class="alignright"><?php previous_posts_link('Newer Entries &raquo;') ?></div>
  </div>

 <?php else : ?>

  <h2 class="center">Not Found</h2>
  <p class="center">Sorry, but you are looking for something that isn't here.</p>
  <?php get_search_form(); ?>

 <?php endif; ?>
```

```
</div>

<?php get_sidebar(); ?>

<?php get_footer(); ?>
```

2. You want to change the_content to the_excerpt so that only excerpts are displayed. You'll find the following code snippet around line 20 in the file:

```
<?php the_content('Read the rest of this entry &raquo;'); ?>
```

3. Replace the code from step 2 with the following, so that the theme will output the excerpt rather than the full content:

```
<?php the_excerpt(); ?>
```

4. Save and upload index.php. Now you'll see the default excerpt (the first 55 characters from the post) rather than the full post view when visiting the site. Since the theme has its own single.php template, you don't have to worry about just showing excerpts when you read individual posts (see Figure 3-3).

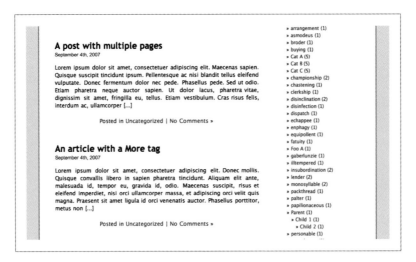

Figure 3-3: Two posts showing the excerpt rather than the full post; note the ellipsis ([. . .]) at the end of them

5. If you want to, you can fill out a custom excerpt in the appointed box found on the Write Post screen in WordPress admin (Figure 3-4). If you do, the excerpt will display instead (Figure 3-5).

Figure 3-4: Editing one of the posts in WordPress admin, adding an excerpt in the appointed box

Figure 3-5: The edited post now displays the custom excerpt rather than the automatic one

About Those Sticky Posts

WordPress added something called *sticky posts* back in version 2.7. People familiar with online discussion forums will recognize the lingo; it is basically something that sticks to the top at all times (see Figure 3-6). The idea is that, in the Edit Post screen, you set a blog post to sticky, hence making it stay on top at all times. If two posts are sticky, you'll end up with both on top, in chronological

Figure 3-6. A sticky post

order, and so on. When you remove the sticky setting from the Edit post screen, the post will automatically sort itself into place with the others.

There is a `sticky_class()` template tag to output the sticky post class, but with the addition of `post_class()` it really isn't very useful.

```
<div id="post-<?php the_ID(); ?>" <?php post_class(); ?>>
```

The lovely `post_class()` template tag will add a number of classes to the post, depending on the details of the post. This is very useful for a designer, so this book covers `post_class()` in more depth in Chapter 6.

If the post is marked as sticky, `post_class()` will add a CSS .sticky class. That way you can alter it in any way you want. Maybe you want it to have a light grey background, larger type, or something else? Just add the necessary styles to your stylesheet, applying them to the sticky class:

```
.sticky { padding: 15px; background: #eee; border: 1px solid #bbb; color: #444; font-size: 18px; }
```

That CSS code would put the sticky post in a light grey box with a slightly darker frame, and 18-pixel-sized default font size. Here it is in action, within a basic loop:

```
<?php if ( have_posts() ) : while ( have_posts() ) : the_post(); ?>
    <div id="post-<?php the_ID(); ?>" <?php post_class(); ?>>
        <h2><a href="<?php the_permalink(); ?>" title="<?php the_title(); ?>"><?php the_title();
 ?></a></h2>
        <?php the_content(); ?>
    </div>
<?php endwhile; else: ?>
    <p>Some error message or similar.</p>
<?php endif; ?>
```

Want to do more with sticky posts? The conditional tag is_sticky() will help you do some funky stuff. Maybe you really want to rub in the importance of this post above all others? Then why not say so:

```
<?php if (is_sticky()) echo 'Super important post! Read it! Now!'; ?>
```

A bit over the top, of course, but there may indeed be times when it is a good idea to output or change things if there is a sticky post involved. It all depends on how you use them, but the basic concept that they are important things that you really want your readers to see should be observed. Say you sell e-books on your blog; you could use sticky posts to promote your latest one:

```
<?php if (is_sticky()) echo 'The latest e-book release by yours truly'; ?>
```

Because of sticky posts being fairly new, both theme designers and users tend to forget about the possibilities that they offer. Be sure to have that in mind when it is time to emphasize the content.

Putting query_posts() to Good Use

Every WordPress loop hacker and ambitious theme designer should know about the nifty query_posts() tool. In essence, query_posts() represents a way to take the loop Word-Press wants to output (the latest posts being the most common usage) and do something else with it. Perhaps you want to limit the amount of posts, exclude a set number of categories, or change the order of things.

A few words of caution: the idea is to apply the query_posts() template tag on the main loop, not to use it to build multiple loops. That is possible, but things can get weird if you do, so it's best not to use it that way. See the "Multiple Loops" section later in this chapter to see how to create as many loops as you like.

To use `query_posts()` you apply it before your main loop, like this:

```
<?php query_posts(); ?>
<?php if ( have_posts() ) : while ( have_posts() ) : the_post(); ?>
 <!- Doing stuff here, styling the posts and so on. ->
<?php endwhile; else: ?>
 <p>Some error message or similar.</p>
<?php endif; ?>
```

Naturally you can tighten that code a bit; there is no need for separate PHP tags for `query_posts()` and the `have_posts()` part.

So what does this do to the loop? Nothing really, since you haven't passed any parameters to `query_posts()` yet. There are no default values; this would just return the standard loop according to your WordPress settings. What `query_posts()` does is alert the SQL query from the loop to fit your needs.

Now that you're acquainted with `query_posts()`, you can execute a few examples to get used to it. First of all, you need to know that there are tons of things you can do with this template tag: it really has a lot of settings, and combining it with conditional tags is the route to hundreds of possible combinations.

But first, start by removing all posts from a category from the listings; probably that asides category where you push out your short, nonsensical posts. The first thing you need to do is figure out what ID it has, which is easily done by logging in to the WordPress admin interface and find your way to the Edit category page. There you'll find the ID hidden at the end of the URL of the edit page:

```
http://notesblog.com/wp-admin/categories.php?action=edit&cat_ID=130
```

As you'll probably have gathered, `cat_ID=130` tells you that the ID is 130. Remember, category IDs (or any IDs really) don't relate to the each other in any other way than that they are all numerical values. Posts, categories, tags, and everything else are mixed, so you can have one category with ID 3 and the next may have ID 749.

Back to the example: we don't want to display posts from the asides category, which has the ID 130. The `query_posts()` page in the Codex (`codex.wordpress.org/Template_Tags/query_posts`) says that you can use a number of ways to pass category information to `query_posts()`, but in this case, use the `cat` parameter, which takes IDs:

```
<?php query_posts('cat=-130'); ?>
```

This, in front of the loop as stated previously, will exclude posts belonging to the category with the ID 130. Notice the minus sign in front of the ID: you really need that. If you forget about it, you would get the exact opposite result, which would be to show only posts from the category with

ID 130. There are a lot of times when a minus sign in front of an ID number will mean that you exclude that particular ID, so that's useful to know.

Next, display posts tagged with blue, green, or yellow. It is easy enough; just apply this before the loop:

```
<?php query_posts('tag=blue+green+yellow'); ?>
```

Here, you obviously use that particular tag parameter. There's a bunch of those as well, just as with categories. Other things you can do with `query_posts()` are fetch posts from a specific author, do time-based queries, and order whatever data you choose any way you like. You can even grab the custom fields data and do things with that, which means that posts suddenly can get even more parameters to be sorted with. You'll do a lot of these things later on when you're building cool WordPress-powered sites.

One snag you may run into when doing things with `query_posts()` is the number of posts being returned. This is still controlled by the main WordPress settings related to how many blog posts to display per page in fact. Luckily, you can control that as well. Say you want your front page to display just five posts, but all other listings should display 10. You can tackle this problem in two ways. You can either create a home.php template, and do the `query_post()` magic there, or use a conditional tag for your index.php template. Start with the home.php variant since it is the cleanest and easiest one. Using `query_posts()` and the `posts_per_page` parameter, you can control these things:

```
<?php query_posts('posts_per_page=5'); ?>
```

By placing that before the loop on your home.php template, you'll display five posts per page. Simple, huh? Now, put those conditional tags to use and add this functionality to the index.php page instead, because you really don't need a separate home.php for this. All you need to do is use the conditional tag `is_home()` in an `if` clause to check if you're on the home page. If not, nothing will happen, but if you are, the `query_posts()` statement will go through. By adding this before the loop in index.php you achieve the same thing as you did with the home.php template:

```
<?php
   if (is_home()) {
      query_posts('posts_per_page=5');
   }
?>
```

Now, since you can limit the number of posts, naturally you can remove the limit as well. Just set the `posts_per_page` parameter to −1 and you'll show all posts that fit the loop criteria. Beware of putting that on a blog with thousands of posts, since if you do that on the front page it will show all your posts, and that's not a fun SQL query to pass to the database at all. That being said, why not show all posts written by the author with the name TDH, published in 2009?

```
<?php query_posts('author_name=TDH&year=2009&posts_per_page=-1'); ?>
```

As you can see, `query_posts()` take its parameters in query string style. That means you can cram a lot of things into it without it being too complicated. We'll be doing a lot with `query_posts()` from now on, so get used to it.

Alternatives to the Loop

You may be tempted to create multiple loops or advanced loop queries in your theme's template files when you've figured out how it works. However, while that may be the solution to what you want to do in some cases, it probably isn't in all. Doing a lot of funky stuff with the loop, often utilizing `query_posts()`, is sometimes completely unnecessary. Here's why.

First of all, you really should ask yourself if it really is another loop you need. Often there are template tags that can do for you what you need accomplished, and that is almost always a better solution. Custom loop magic should be saved for actions that truly deserve and need them. The same goes for conditional tags; you can build pretty advanced pages that rely on the situation that could possibly get the result your want.

Second, are there any plugins that can do the work for you? The WordPress community is full of brilliant solutions to common problems, and while it may both seem and indeed be a lot cleaner to sort these things from within your own theme, a plugin may in fact enhance the functionality and be easier for you to manage. A lot of the plugins that do things with post listings are in fact doing stuff with the loop that you could do yourself, from within your theme. Normally I would recommend the latter solution, but what if you're not the one responsible for maintaining the theme in the long run, as is common when doing theme design work and then leaving it to the client to nurture? If the client is reluctant to pay more for customizations, or if they think that their in-house HTML skills are enough, then you're probably better off finding a plugin solution than one that will break when they do something with their template files. Granted, plugins come with their own issues, like suddenly not being developed anymore, or relying on WordPress functionality that isn't favored, but still, it is something to consider.

Finally, there is the possible strain on the server and database. Doing loop after loop means a lot of PHP and SQL queries and that will slow down the site. Simple is not always best, but keeping things as simple as possible while managing to get the required result is always a good idea. Both Web hosts and WordPress have come a long way since the early days, but that doesn't mean that you should make things more clunky or complicated than they need to be.

My point and advice is this: always question the need for that extra loop. It may save you some headaches in the future.

Multiple Loops

Sometimes you want several loops on a page. Perhaps you have a category for your extremely important posts, and want to run those by themselves on the front page, or maybe you just want the latest posts in the sidebar. Either way, whenever you need to fetch posts a second time, you'll want another loop. This is often essential when you want to break from the traditional blog mold, so you may as well master it.

Start with the most basic multiple loop solution, which is to just get another loop on the page. This is done with `rewind_posts()`, which just resets the loop's counter and lets you run it again:

```
<?php rewind_posts(); ?>
<?php while (have_posts()) : the_post(); ?>
<!- And then the basic loop continues... ->
```

Naturally, this would just output the exact same thing as your first loop, which would neither look good nor be particularly useful, so to actually do something with `rewind_posts()` you need to change something. Say you want a box at the bottom of the page showing the last five posts from the News category; this can be achieved by using `query_posts`, which was touched upon earlier:

```
<?php rewind_posts(); ?>
<?php query_posts('category_name=news&showposts=5'); ?>
<?php while (have_posts()) : the_post(); ?>
<!- And then the basic loop continues…. ->
```

This would then output the five latest posts from the News category, which we would put in the box mentioned in the previous paragraph.

Featured Posts with Multiple Loops

Another common usage for multiple loops is to display a featured post at the top of the page. This allows the WordPress theme to break from the traditional blog layout, and has become quite popular, especially with the so-called magazine themes that mimic their print counterparts.

Here's how to do this. First, you need a loop that fetches a single post—the latest one, naturally—from the Featured category. Then, you need a second loop that does the regular thing, listing the latest posts from all categories. To pull this off, you need to store the first loop query inside its own query object. Do that by calling the `WP_Query` object and storing it in a new query. `WP_Query` is the big huge thing that makes the loop tick. While you don't see it in the basic loop you actually use it with `have_posts()`, for example, which in essence is `$wp_query->have_posts()`; you just don't have to write it all out all the time. `WP_Query` is huge and somewhat complicated, so messing with it requires some decent coding skills or a lot of trial and error. As any experienced PHP coder will tell you, a little of both usually does the trick. Often, however, you'll interact with `WP_Query` by using the various template and conditional tags.

Recall the `query_posts()` template tag. The usage description says that it is intended to modify the main loop only, so you won't be using that for your new loop. Instead, pass the same variables to `WP_Query`. Here is the code:

45

```php
<?php $featured_query = new WP_Query('category_name=featured&showposts=1');
while ($featured_query->have_posts()) : $featured_query->the_post();
$do_not_duplicate = $post->ID; ?>
    <!- Styling for your featured post ->
<?php endwhile; ?>
    <!- Put whatever you want between the featured post and the normal post listing ->
<?php if (have_posts()) : while (have_posts()) : the_post();
if( $post->ID == $do_not_duplicate ) continue; update_post_caches($posts); ?>
    <!- Your normal loop post styling goes here ->
<?php endwhile; else: ?>
    <p>Some error message or similar.</p>
<?php endif; ?>
```

So, what happens here? Let's start with the first loop that kicks off with the first line, where you load `$featured_query` with a new `WP_Query` loop query. This query is served `query_post()`-like parameters, which means you're limiting it to the category `Featured`, and showing just one post: `<?php $featured_query = new WP_Query('category_name=featured&showposts=1');`.

Then, you move into a while loop (which naturally will only contain one turnaround; you said just one post after all) looking somewhat like the basic loop: `while ($featured_query->have_posts()) : $featured_query->the_post();`. Remember that `have_posts()` in the basic loop was actually `$wp_query->have_posts();` this is the same, but instead of the default `$wp_query` you're using the brand-new `$featured_query`. This means that we're doing the exact same thing as in the basic loop, but not in the default `$wp_query` object but rather in the new one, hence not affecting `$wp_query` at all. The third line is simple. You're loading the post ID into the `$do_not_duplicate` object. The idea here is to make sure that a featured post won't turn up both in the featured post section, and in the post listing below. If you've ever looked at an example of multiple loops doing this, you recognize this code snippet; it is featured in the Codex as well. You'll use it in your main loop, but for now the post ID is sorted in `$do_not_duplicate`. Of course, this would only work if you only have one featured post. If you had several, you would need to store them in an array instead.

```php
$do_not_duplicate = $post->ID; ?>
    <!- Styling for your featured post ->
<?php endwhile; ?>
```

After that you've got the typical post output section, usually an h2 heading with a linked title for the post, and then the content or an excerpt of the content. You may want to make it fancy with images and so forth, using custom fields (embellishing posts is covered later). For now, though, you can be satisfied that this will contain your output of the featured post.

Moving on, we've got a typical basic loop with an addition. Line 8 is an `if` clause checking if the post ID is the same as the ID stored in the `$do_not_duplicate` object. If it is, we continue and update the post cache, otherwise we output it as normal. In other words, when you get to the featured post in your main loop, you'll skip it and move on.

```
<?php if (have_posts()) : while (have_posts()) : the_post();
if( $post->ID == $do_not_duplicate ) continue; update_post_caches($posts); ?>
```

After that it is the basic loop all the way, with post output and all.

```
<!— Your normal loop post styling goes here —>
<?php endwhile; else: ?>
    <p>Some error message or similar.</p>
<?php endif; ?>
```

So, in other words, first you output the featured post in a loop of its own. Then you do the regular loop, checking the post ID to make sure that our featured post won't show up again.

Three's a Charm, But Four Loops Are Way Cooler

Using the knowledge you've gained thus far, in this section you'll put the multiple loop concept to the test. In this example you'll have three featured posts in one loop, then you'll imagine three columns underneath consisting of the latest posts from one category each. The idea is to mimic the front page of a non-bloggish site. In terms of template files, this would ideally be in the home.php template, which means that it would only be loaded when on the front page. Consider the following code:

```
<?php $featured_query = new WP_Query('category_name=featured&showposts=3');
while ($featured_query->have_posts()) : $featured_query->the_post();
$do_not_duplicate[] = $post->ID ?>
    <!— Styling for your featured posts —>
<?php endwhile; ?>
    <!— Now begins the first column loop —>
<?php query_posts('category_name=apples&showposts=10'); ?>
<?php while (have_posts()) : the_post(); ?>
if (in_array($post->ID, $do_not_duplicate)) continue; update_post_caches($posts); ?>
    <!— Category Apples post —>
<?php endwhile; ?>
    <!— Now begins the second column loop —>
<?php rewind_posts(); ?>
<?php query_posts('category_name=oranges&showposts=10'); ?>
<?php while (have_posts()) : the_post(); ?>
if (in_array($post->ID, $do_not_duplicate)) continue; update_post_caches($posts); ?>
    <!— Category Oranges post —>
<?php endwhile; ?>
    <!— Now begins the third column loop —>
<?php rewind_posts(); ?>
<?php query_posts('category_name=lemons&showposts=10'); ?>
<?php while (have_posts()) : the_post(); ?>
if (in_array($post->ID, $do_not_duplicate)) continue; update_post_caches($posts); ?>
    <!— Category Lemons post —>
<?php endwhile; ?>
```

What happened here? Start with the three featured posts. This is pretty much similar to the previous featured post loop example, but since you have three posts here and you don't want them to show up more than once, you need to store their IDs in an array. PHP-savvy readers will recognize the square brackets on the `$do_not_duplicate object`, which indicates that it is an array. If you're unfamiliar with the term *array*, it basically means that it is a series of stored information; in this case, three post IDs. These you'll check for in every loop that follows.

Moving on, every one of the three column loops, one per category, is the basic (main) loop using the `query_posts()` template tag to limit the output. You'll recognize the category sorting and the number of posts they'll show from previous examples.

Since you don't want to output any of the featured posts in the three category loops, you need to check the `$do_not_duplicate` object. You'll see that the if clause for this has changed a bit to reflect that it is an array.

Finally, after the first column loop, which is the main one, you'll need to use `rewind_posts()` to be able to use it again, but with different sorting thanks to `query_posts()`. Repeat as needed.

An optional solution for this would've been to create four different loops of your own, just like you did with the featured post example, thus sidestepping `$wp_query`. However, there really isn't any need here.

The following listing is the actual post code output stripped of everything that would go in the CSS file, but with the necessary IDs and classes.

```
<div id="featured">
    <?php $featured_query = new WP_Query('category_name=featured&showposts=3');
    while ($featured_query->have_posts()) : $featured_query->the_post();
    $do_not_duplicate[] = $post->ID ?>
        <div id="post-<?php the_ID(); ?>" <?php post_class(); ?>>
            <h2><a href="<?php the_permalink(); ?>" title="<?php the_title(); ?>"><?php the_title();
 ?></a></h2>
                <?php the_excerpt(); ?>
        </div>
    <?php endwhile; ?>
</div>
<div class="column left">
    <h2>Latest from <span>Apples</span></h2>
    <ul>
    <!- Now begins the first column loop ->
    <?php query_posts('category_name=apples&showposts=10'); ?>
    <?php while (have_posts()) : the_post();
        if (in_array($post->ID, $do_not_duplicate)) continue; update_post_caches($posts); ?>
        <li>
            <h3><a href="<?php the_permalink(); ?>" title="<?php the_title(); ?>"><?php the_title();
 ?></a></h3>
                <?php the_excerpt(); ?>
        </li>
```

```
    <?php endwhile; ?>
    </ul>
</div><div class="column left">
    <h2>Latest from <span>Oranges</span></h2>
    <ul>
    <!- Now begins the second column loop ->
    <?php rewind_posts(); ?>
 <?php query_posts('category_name=oranges&showposts=10'); ?>
    <?php while (have_posts()) : the_post();
        if (in_array($post->ID, $do_not_duplicate)) continue; update_post_caches($posts); ?>
        <li>
            <h3><a href="<?php the_permalink(); ?>" title="<?php the_title(); ?>"><?php the_title();
   ?></a></h3>
            <?php the_excerpt(); ?>
        </li>
    <?php endwhile; ?>
    </ul>
</div><div class="column right">
    <h2>Latest from <span>Lemons</span></h2>
    <ul>
    <!- Now begins the third column loop ->
    <?php rewind_posts(); ?>
    <?php query_posts('category_name=lemons&showposts=10'); ?>
    <?php while (have_posts()) : the_post();
        if (in_array($post->ID, $do_not_duplicate)) continue; update_post_caches($posts); ?>
        <li>
            <h3><a href="<?php the_permalink(); ?>" title="<?php the_title(); ?>"><?php the_title();
   ?></a></h3>
            <?php the_excerpt(); ?>
        </li>
    <?php endwhile; ?>
    </ul>
</div>
```

There you have it: four loops starting with one for featured posts, and then three more to display the latest from three different categories. This code can easily be implemented in just about any WordPress theme, but you would need to alter it to fit your category setup to make it work properly.

Custom Fields

Custom fields are always used within the loop, and they are database fields with content defined entirely by the user. If you take a look at the Write Post screen within the WordPress admin interface, you'll find a box for custom fields (see Figure 3-7). Here you can add one or several custom fields, and a value for each.

Custom fields always belong to posts, and consist of two things: a key and a value. You can add new keys whenever you want, and when you've used them once they show up in a drop-down box, which is nice since you may misspell or forget about them otherwise.

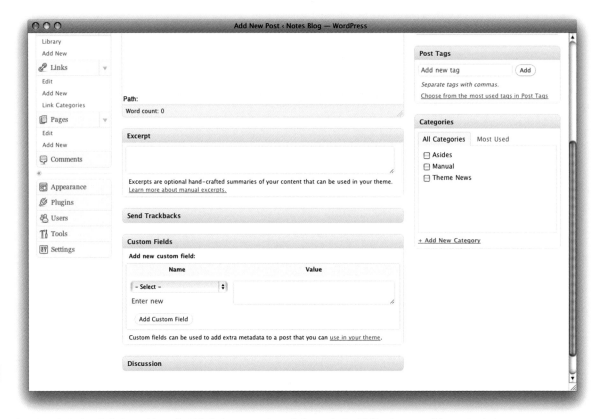

Figure 3-7: The Custom Fields box resides on the Write Post screen, underneath the regular Post Writing Box—yes, it is easy to miss!

Getting started with custom fields is easy: just write a post and add something in the key field, and then something in the value field, and click the Add Custom Field button to save. You've now stored your custom field data, although it won't show up anywhere unless you call it within the loop.

Before moving on and doing stuff with this, here's a quick recap. Each custom field (and yes you can have several per post) consists of a key and a value. The idea is to reuse the key across posts, in a way like a categorization of the kind of data you're storing, and just alter the value.

The template tag you use to make things happen with custom fields is the_meta(). By default it outputs an unlimited list (or a ul tag with list items; li's, in HTML speak) displaying the post's custom fields. That works great if you just store things such as how happy you are and what you're reading right now, or perhaps a grade for a review or something. The ul will have the class post-meta and then there's a li for each custom field, and within this li there is a span with the class="post-meta-key" that wraps around the key for that particular custom field. After that is the value in plain text.

Say you have a custom field with a key called "Actor" with the value "Harrison Ford." Then you have another custom field called "Director" with the value "Stephen Spielberg." Finally, you have a custom field called "Movie Title" with the value "Indiana Jones and the Raiders of the Lost Ark." All these custom fields and their values belong to a specific post, and if you put the template tag `the_meta()` somewhere within the loop, and this post shows, it will output this code:

```
<ul class='post-meta'>
    <li><span class='post-meta-key'>Actor</span> Harrison Ford</li>
    <li><span class='post-meta-key'>Director</span> Stephen Spielberg</li>
    <li><span class='post-meta-key'>Movie</span> Indiana Jones and the Raiders of the Lost Ark</
  li>
</ul>
```

As long as you just want to display simple stuff, that is enough and you can style it with CSS. Naturally, you'll want to do more, so let's move on.

Posting Header Images

One of the easiest and most popular uses of custom fields is attaching an image to a post, to spice up listings and such. First, you need to decide what to call your custom field key. Go with `post-image`, which will be easy to remember. When you see it in your code you'll instantly understand what it is, which is a good thing.

Next, you need some data to experiment with. Upload an image to your post using the WordPress image uploader, and then copy the image URL. It will be something like this:

```
http://notesblog.com/wp-content/2009/05/splashimage.jpg
```

Now, add that to the `post-image` key using the Custom Fields box on the Write Post screen. If you haven't used the `post-image` key before, you just type it in the key field; otherwise, you can choose it from the drop-down menu. Then, paste the image URL in the value field, and save. Now you have attached the URL with the post-image key for this particular post, which means that you can use it.

Find a place in your theme where you want this image to show, probably along with your posts on the home page or something. It all depends on how you shape the image: it can be anything from a thumbnail that goes to the right of your post's title, or a huge magazine-style photograph that sits behind it. This example shows you how to output the content in the custom field. Later on, this book will discuss more unique approaches.

Here's a simple example of putting the custom fields image above the h2 title tag, something a lot of magazine themes like to do, accomplished with just a few additions to the basic loop you've become accustomed to by now:

51

```php
<?php if ( have_posts() ) : while ( have_posts() ) : the_post(); ?>
<div id="post-<?php the_ID(); ?>" <?php post_class(); ?>>
 <?php $splashimg = get_post_meta($post->ID, 'post-image', $single = true); ?>
 <?php if($splashimg !== '') { ?>
  <img src="<?php echo $splashimg; ?>" alt="<?php { echo the_title(); } ?>" class="splashimg" />
    <?php } else { echo ''; } ?>
    <h2><a href="<?php the_permalink(); ?>" title="<?php the_title(); ?>"><?php the_title(); ?></
    a></h2>
    <?php the_content(); ?>
</div>
<?php endwhile; else: ?>
    <p>Some error message or similar.</p>
<?php endif; ?>
```

The third line is a PHP function where you store the variable $splashimg, created by you for this example, with the data from the get_post_meta() function. This is similar to the the_meta() template tag touched on previously, and you're getting three parameters from it. First, there is the post ID of course, which is needed for WordPress to figure out where to collect the custom field data from. Second, you need to request a custom field key and get the value of it, which in this case is post-image. Remember, you named the key just that, so now you'll get the value of the particular post's post-image key, which in turn is the image URL you saved. Finally, the third and last parameter you're passing is setting $single to true. You're doing this to tell get_post_meta() to pass the data as a string. If you set it to false, you would get an array of custom fields data, which of course can come in handy too, but not in this case. All this is stored in $splashimg.

Arriving at the third line, you're checking whether there is anything in the $splashimg function, and if there is, you're outputting an image with the source fetched from within the $splashimg.

```php
<?php if($splashimg !== '') { ?>
    <img src="<?php echo $splashimg; ?>" alt="<?php { echo the_title(); } ?>" class="splashimg" />
<?php } else { echo ''; } ?>
</CODE>
```

That is of course the data you got from get_post_meta(); in other words, the custom field data for post-image. Should there not be anything in $splashimg, which would mean that you haven't saved any custom field data for the key post-image, then you echo nothing at all. Maybe you want a default image there instead, in which case you would echo that.

After that it is the same standard loop, outputting the linked post title and the content, and so on.

Now You Get to Build Something

The loop can certainly feel tricky to work with at first. The basic one isn't too hard to identify, and that really is all you need to get started with WordPress for real. As you go along, it will be easier to understand its mechanics, and when you start to build your own themes to power your WordPress site, you'll soon find yourself fiddling with it. The mere fact that a lot of plugins and template tags that you will want to be using from here on out have to reside inside the loop makes it important, but the custom stuff, such as using multiple loops or specific content outputs, is of course just as important when pushing WordPress.

If you're having a hard time understanding the loop fully after reading this chapter, don't take it too hard. The more examples you read and the more you play with it, the easier it will become to alter the loop to your needs. And that's what you're going to do next: actually start to build stuff. First up are themes, which you'll work with for the coming three chapters. That means that you'll see a lot of the loop from now on, but you'll also delve deeper into template tags and other tools supplied by WordPress to control the content.

II

DESIGNING AND DEVELOPING WORDPRESS THEMES

4

THE WORDPRESS THEME ESSENTIALS

If you want to do more advanced stuff with WordPress, you need to understand theme essentials. Naturally, you can just start hacking the default theme, or download Notes Blog Core and go from there, but there are things that won't be obvious from just using and tinkering with the code. That's why we'll take a dive into the WordPress theme concept in this chapter to get acquainted with themes and how they work. After doing that, you'll be able to put your knowledge to good use in the coming chapters. The following two chapters will discuss more advanced usage, and then you'll take it from there.

This chapter will get you started with themes in the sense that you'll see how they work and see how you can alter them to fit your needs. You've already played with the loop, now lets put it to good use and start building stuff.

Theme Basics

You're probably familiar with WordPress themes and the premises under which they operate. In short, themes are a way to separate the design from the code, but in reality there is still a lot of coding happening in the more advanced themes out there.

A theme consists of a folder with template files and any other files that may be needed. The only two absolutely necessary template files are style.css and index.php. The former contains the header that identifies your theme, while the latter is the basic layout. In fact, even if you don't put in the sidebar.php template file, or the comments.php comments template, you'll get both sidebar and comment functionality served by WordPress automatically. If you're looking for a challenge, try to create a WordPress theme consisting of just the two necessary files, and see what you can do with it. It is an interesting exercise, but is not all that great an idea for more advanced sites, of course.

The style.css is not only a stylesheet, but also the theme's header file, so to speak. This is the file that identifies the theme, and it needs to start with some basic information:

```
/*
Theme Name: Your Theme Name
Theme URI: http://your-theme-homepage.com
Description: Oh what a lovely description of your theme you'll put here!
Author: Your Name
Author URI: http://your-website.com
Template: If this is a child theme, you'll set the template theme's folder name here
Version: A version number
.
Any general information, license statements, plugin requirements, or any other information you
  might want to share.
.
*/
```

Version numbering and template information is optional. Templates and child themes are covered later on, along with delving deeper into the concept.

Without this code on the top of the style.css, WordPress won't recognize your theme as a theme, and that in turn means that you won't be able to activate it. Not doing much good then, huh?

Like any properly coded Web site, you'll need a doctype heading and title tags and such. While you can rely on WordPress to serve the default headings needed with your `get_header()` call in index.php, it is a better idea to have your own header.php template file. Add a footer.php file while you're at it, and some proper comment handling with comments.php, and you're getting somewhere.

The Basic Theme

While you can get by with just style.css and index.php in your theme, it is generally not such a good idea to be so minimalist. At the very least, you should also have a header.php and a footer.php for your theme. These are called from within index.php, with the template tags `get_header()` and `get_footer()`. You'll also want a comments.php for commenting functionality, and you call that with `get_comments()`, also from within index.php. The same goes for the sidebar; you should have a template file for that too, and call it with `get_sidebar()`.

The header.php file consists of the doctype heading and everything related. We'll take a closer look at that in the following example section. Other things the header.php file generally does are basic stuff like getting the right favicon, generating proper title tags, and having the necessary keywords so that search engines can find the pages more easily. However, one thing it must have is a link to the stylesheet, and the `wp_head()` is also needed to start the whole WordPress shebang.

Moving on, footer.php should include `wp_footer()` to stop WordPress and, of course, all the necessary closing tags. You want to close the `body` and `html` tags, and anything else you may have opened in header.php.

Finally, comments.php needs the code for outputting comments, as well as the necessary forms so that people can actually post new comments. This is done with simple template tags these days, so comments.php files aren't as messy to work with as they once were, or at least appeared to be. The simplest file of them all is sidebar.php, which is just the stuff you want in the sidebar.

As you may have gathered, everything revolves around index.php. However, there are other template files that can replace index.php, depending on the situation. If you're on the front page, for example, home.php takes the top slot, and index.php will only be used if there isn't a home.php. The same goes for single post view, where single.php takes precedence above index.php, and for WordPress pages page.php goes before index.php. Actually, if you utilize every one of the possible template files, your index.php file will never load. The concept is the same, though, so leave things like that for a little while.

This is how it works.

Figure 4-1 is a common blog layout. At the top, spanning the full width, is the blog header, which in fact is the header.php file. Underneath is the actual blog area, with the content to the left (index.php) and the sidebar to the right (sidebar.php). Finally, there is a footer to wrap it up, using the footer.php template file.

This setup is not mandatory; you can change it, exclude parts of it, or expand it further. It is, however, a very common setup, one that the default WordPress theme as well as the Notes Blog Core theme adheres to. You'll see a lot of themes using template files in this manner if you look around, but it is in no way the only way to do things. It is just common, that's all.

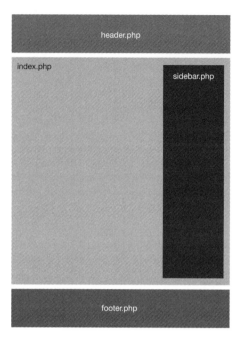

Figure 4-1: A Basic Blog Layout

A Few Words about the Code

There's a lot of code ahead. Most of it is pretty simple, and I'll be keeping things as conceptual and straightforward as possible. That way, the actual usage of the various template tags and functions come into play, rather than being obscured by other code that won't matter in the long run.

That being said, you should be aware that the following examples include localization tags and both template and conditional tags that you may not be entirely familiar with. Most of the latter two categories speak for themselves, but localization may be a bit harder to grasp. You'll get to the details of that later on, but for now you only need to know that when you localize, you either wrap the text/code within _e() or __(). You use __() within PHP code, while the former is more or less used anywhere. Add a textdomain and you've got the basics, like this:

```php
<?php _e('This text can be localized, mate!', 'the-textdomain'); ?>
```

Both _e() and __() rely on the premise that the text or code you can localize gets passed first, and then the textdomain that should be used. In the Notes Blog Core examples, the textdomain is called 'notesblog', so it would look like this:

```php
<?php _e('This text can be localized, mate!', 'notesblog'); ?>
```

Then, thanks to language files, users can fully localize the theme.

Now that the basics are out of the way, it's time to get our hands dirty!

A Closer Look at Notes Blog Core

We'll be touching on the Notes Blog Core theme frequently from now on, so this section demonstrates the basic theme by taking the Core theme and cutting it down a bit to illustrate what a minimal WordPress theme can look like. Sure, you can make it even smaller still—after all, you just need a style.css and an index.php to have a fully functional WordPress theme—but it is a lot more likely that you'll use at least the most common template files.

A few words about the Notes Blog Core theme are probably in order before you cut it to pieces. This theme is free to download from notesblog.com/core/ and is designed and maintained by yours truly. It is actually meant to be a host for child themes, which are covered later on, but like any good theme it works perfectly well by itself.

Remember, you have all your document heading stuff in header.php, the footer stuff in footer.php, and the sidebar content is in sidebar.php. Comment functionality is in comments.php, and, finally, the theme information is in the style.css file, along with any basic styling you may have. This will be a lot of code, even though I'll stick to the most important parts. Download the full thing from notesblog.com/core/ to get the complete picture.

The Stylesheet: style.css

The first thing any theme needs is the stylesheet. Not only does it have the actual theme information header at the very top, it is also where as much of the design as possible should be managed. If you can do something with CSS, you should put it in style.css.

First of all, you've got the theme's header, at the very top of the stylesheet:

```
/*
Theme Name: Notes Blog Core Theme
Theme URI: http://notesblog.com/
Description: The core for the Notes Blog theme. <a href="http://tdhedengren.com/">Made by TDH</a> and
   maintained at <a href="http://notesblog.com/">notesblog.com</a>. Requires WordPress 2.8 or higher.
Version: 1.0
Tags: two columns, fixed width, custom, widgets
Author: Thord Daniel Hedengren
Author URI: http://tdhedengren.com/

    Get support and services for the Notes Blog Core Theme:
    http://notesblog.com

    Created and managed by Thord Daniel Hedengren:
    http://tdhedengren.com

*/
```

Nothing weird or fancy there. Theme designers will be pleased to note that the description field supports some basic HTML code.

Moving on, I have a reset segment. I'm opposed to the popular practice of applying a margin and padding reset to everything, since far from every element has these settings. That being said, I'm breaking my own rule somewhat with the following border reset:

```
body, h1, h2, h3, h4, h5, ul#sidebar, ul.widgets, li, ul#sidebar li ul, ol.commentlist,
    ul.children, ul#footercol li ul,
div#submenu-nav ul, div#submenu-nav ol, form, img, table
    {
    margin:0;
    padding:0;
    border: 0;
    }
```

After that follows type and link styling, detailing which fonts and colors are used where. I'm skipping that part; it is just simple stuff. If you want to dive deeper into it, visit notesblog.com/core/ and grab the theme for yourself. It's all there, after all. Just open style.css and scroll down below the reset section (the one found above), and you'll find all the styling code.

The layout section (labeled "Layout" in a comment in the file) is more interesting:

```
.left { float:left; }
.right { float:right; }
.center { text-align:center; }
.aligncenter, div.aligncenter { display: block; margin-left: auto; margin-right: auto; }


div.widecolumn { width: 620px; }

div.column, ul.column, ul#sidebar
    { width: 320px; }

div#site { width: 100%; }

div#wrap
    {
    width: 960px;
    margin: 0 auto;
    background: #fff;
    }
    div#toplist { position:relative; width: 960px; }
        div#toplist div.feed { float:right; padding: 5px 0; }
            div#toplist div.feed a { padding: 5px; background: #444; color: #fff; }
                div#toplist div.feed a:hover { background: #000; }
```

I like to define a few basic things in classes for alignment; this comes in handy every now and then. I also define the columns and the `ul#sidebar` (which is only used in sidebar.php), along with centering the site using `div#wrap`.

After this is the code for the header, content, sidebar, footer, and even copyright areas. These are divs floating to the left and right, along with some styles to the elements within them. Nothing fancy, so I'll save some trees and pick out the comments part only:

```css
ol.commentlist {}
    ol.commentlist li { margin: 0 20px 10px 20px; padding: 0; list-style:none; border: 1px solid
 #e8e8e8; border-width: 0 0 1px 0; }
        ol.commentlist li div.comment-author, ol.commentlist li div.comment-meta { font-size:
 12px; line-height: 16px; }
            ol.commentlist li div.comment-author img.avatar { float:left; margin: 0 10px 0 0; }
            div.comment-author cite.fn { font-family: Georgia, "Adobe Garamond", "Times New Roman",
 serif; font-size: 16px; font-style: normal; font-weight:bold; }
                div.comment-author cite.fn a { text-decoration: none; }
            div.comment-meta { margin-bottom: 10px; }
    ol.commentlist li.even {}
    ol.commentlist li.odd {}
    ol.commentlist li.bypostauthor {}
    ol.commentlist li.pingback { font-size: 12px; color: #777; padding: 0 0 10px 5px; color: #777; }
        ol.commentlist li.pingback a { font-size: 12px; font-weight:normal; }
        ol.commentlist li.pingback p, ol.commentlist li.pingback span, ol.commentlist li.pingback
 div.comment-meta, ol.commentlist li.pingback div.reply { display:none; }
    div.reply { float:right; margin: -25px 0 0 10px; line-height: 12px; }
    ul.children { margin: 20px 0 20px 20px; }
        ul.children li { margin: 10px 0; padding-left: 10px; border: 1px solid #e8e8e8; border-
 width: 0 0 0 1px; }
div#respond { margin: 20px; }
    div#respond h3 {}
    table.commenttable { border:0; padding: 0; }
    table.commenttable tr td { font-size: 12px; line-height: 12px; text-transform: uppercase;  }
    form#commentform {}
        input#author, input#email, input#url { margin-bottom: 5px; padding: 2px; width: 250px;
 font-style: italic; }
        textarea#comment { width: 556px; height: 150px; padding: 10px; font-style: italic; }
        input#submit { float:right; }
```

This should be pretty self-explanatory. Comments are output within the `ol.commentlist` element, with each comment a list item in itself. After that is the `div#response` area with the necessary forms for posting a comment.

Take another long leap forward, skipping the `div#footer`, `div#copy`, and the `ul#sidebar` parts. These are just floating elements with some styling, you'll find them in the style.css file if you want to take a closer look. Instead, let's take a look at some elements I usually add at the end of the stylesheet:

```
p.right { text-align:right; }
p.admin { color: grey; font-size: 12px; }
p.nocomments { padding: 0 20px; font-style: italic; color: #777; }

div#content embed, .embedded { text-align:center; margin: 0 0 14px 0; } /* for movies */

div#content p span { background: #ffc; }

div.post ul li, div.page ul li, div.post ol li, div.page ol li { margin-bottom: 5px; color: #333; }

blockquote { margin: 0 0 14px 20px; padding: 0 15px; border: 1px solid #e8e8e8; border-width: 0 0
   0 1px; color: #777; font-style: italic; }
   blockquote.pullquote { width: 220px; padding: 5px 0; border: 0; font-size: 18px; line-height:
150%; }
       blockquote.pullquote p { margin-bottom: 0; }
ol.commentlist li blockquote { border: 0; padding:0; }

/* Images and aligns */
.alignleft, blockquote.alignleft { float:left; margin: 0 15px 15px 0; }
.alignright, blockquote.alignright { float:right; margin: 0 0 15px 15px; }
.frame { padding: 5px; border: 1px solid #e8e8e8; }
.wp-caption { padding: 10px 7px; border: 1px solid #e8e8e8; font-size: 12px; color: #777; font-style:
   italic; text-align:center; }
p.wp-caption-text { margin:10px 0 0 0 !important; padding:0; line-height: 14px !important; }
```

The only really important part of this is the image classes at the end (img.frame is my own addition; I put it in just about every theme for adding classy borders to images) as well as the wp-caption classes for image captions.

Not too fancy, right? Remember, Notes Blog Core is meant to be a simple theme to build upon, so a lot of the bling you may add normally is completely left out, as are images altogether.

Theme Top: header.php

When the active theme is loaded, it starts with the header.php file. This is where you put all the metadata, fire up WordPress with wp_head(), and usually put the top of your page:

```
<!DOCTYPE html PUBLIC "-//W3C//DTD XHTML 1.0 Transitional//EN" "http://www.w3.org/TR/xhtml1/DTD/
xhtml1-transitional.dtd">
<html xmlns="http://www.w3.org/1999/xhtml" <?php language_attributes(); ?>>
<head profile="http://gmpg.org/xfn/11">
<meta http-equiv="Content-Type" content="<?php bloginfo('html_type'); ?>; charset=<?php
   bloginfo('charset'); ?>" />
<title><?php if (is_single() || is_page() || is_archive()) { ?><?php wp_title('',true); ?> | <?php
   } bloginfo('name'); ?> </title>
<meta name="generator" content="WordPress <?php bloginfo('version'); ?>" /> <!-- leave this for
   stats -->
```

```
<link rel="stylesheet" href="<?php bloginfo('stylesheet_url'); ?>" type="text/css" media="screen" />
<link rel="alternate" type="application/rss+xml" title="<?php bloginfo('name'); ?> RSS Feed"
  href="<?php bloginfo('rss2_url'); ?>" />
<link rel="pingback" href="<?php bloginfo('pingback_url'); ?>" />
<link rel="shortcut icon" href="<?php bloginfo('template_directory'); ?>/favicon.ico" />
<?php wp_head(); ?>
</head>
<body <?php body_class(); ?>>

<div id="site">
<div id="wrap">
    <div id="toplist">
        <div class="feed"><a href="<?php bloginfo('rss2_url'); ?>" title="RSS">RSS</a></div>
    </div>
<div id="header">
    <h1><a href="<?php bloginfo('url'); ?>" title="<?php bloginfo('name'); ?>" name="top"><?php
bloginfo('name'); ?></a> <span><?php bloginfo('description'); ?></span></h1>
</div>
<?php if ( !function_exists('dynamic_sidebar') || !dynamic_sidebar('Submenu') ) : ?><?php endif; ?>
```

This is the top of the theme and it should be pretty self-explanatory. A lot of header stuff, naturally, but one of the more important parts is the title tag, which will adapt to where on the site you are, thanks to some conditional tags. Also, the stylesheet link is important, as is the RSS link, which tells the Web browser that there is a feed available. Actually, all link tags within the head area are important, except the favicon, which is just for show!

It is a good idea to put `wp_head()` just before you close the head tag; this is what initializes WordPress. Also note `body_class()` in the body tag, which more or less does what `post_class()` does for posts, which is to say it adds various CSS classes depending on where on the site the visitor is. Very handy for theme designers.

You may notice the absence of this row:

```
<meta name="generator" content="WordPress <?php bloginfo('version'); ?>" /> <!-- leave this for
  stats -->
```

That's because you don't want the wrong people to find out what version of WordPress you're running. Why make it any easier for hackers than it already is, eh?

Finally, there is a PHP snippet below the `div#header` area, where the blog title is output courtesy of `bloginfo()`. This is a widget area called Submenu, which will only display if it contains anything. We'll get to that later on.

The Main Template: index.php

The main template file, index.php, is used for single post view and in most other situations as well, where template files would be just as good. This is done by putting conditional tags to good use, and the reason is because it makes the Notes Blog Core theme a lot easier to use when it comes to child themes. After all, the fewer template files you need to overwrite by including them in your child theme the better, right? Here's index.php in full:

```php
<?php get_header(); ?>

    <div id="content" class="widecolumn">

    <?php
    if (is_category()) {
        echo '<h1 class="listhead">';
        _e("Category", "notesblog");
        echo ' <strong>';
        single_cat_title();
        echo '</strong></h1>';
    } if (is_tag()) {
        echo '<h1 class="listhead">';
        _e("Tag", "notesblog");
        echo ' <strong>';
        single_tag_title();
        echo '</strong></h1>';
    } if (is_search()) {
        echo '<h1 class="listhead">';
        _e("Your <strong>search result</strong>", "notesblog");
        echo '</h1>';
    }
    ?>

    <?php if (have_posts()) : while (have_posts()) : the_post(); ?>

            <div id="post-<?php the_ID(); ?>" <?php post_class(); ?>>
                <?php if (is_single()) { ?>
                    <h1><?php the_title(); ?></h1>
                    <div class="postmeta">
                    <span class="comments"><?php comments_popup_link(__('0 <span>comments</span>',
'notesblog'), __('1 <span>comment</span>', 'notesblog'), __('% <span>comments</span>', 'notesblog'),
", "); ?></span>
                    <span class="author"><?php _e("By", "notesblog");?> <a href="<?php
the_author_url(); ?>" title="<?php the_author(); ?>" class="author"><?php the_author(); ?></a></
span>
                    <span class="categories"><?php _e("Filed in", "notesblog");?> <?php
the_category(', '); ?></span>
                    <span class="tags"><?php the_tags(__('Tagged with ', 'notesblog'),', ',""); ?></
span>
                    <span class="timestamp"><?php the_time(__('F jS, Y', 'notesblog')) ?> @ <?php
the_time(); ?></span>
                    </div>
                <?php } else if (is_page()) { ?>
                    <h1><?php the_title(); ?></h1>
```

```
                <div class="postmeta">
                <span class="comments"><?php comments_popup_link(__('0 <span>comments</span>',
'notesblog'), __('1 <span>comment</span>', 'notesblog'), __('% <span>comments</span>', 'notesblog'),
'', ''); ?></span>
        <span class="author"><?php _e("By", 'notesblog');?> <a href="<?php the_author_url(); ?>"
title="<?php the_author(); ?>" class="author"><?php the_author(); ?></a></span>
                </div>
                <?php } else { ?>
                <h2><a href="<?php the_permalink() ?>" rel="bookmark" title="<?php the_title();
?>"><?php the_title(); ?></a></h2>
                <div class="postmeta">
                <span class="comments"><?php comments_popup_link(__('0 <span>comments</span>',
'notesblog'), __('1 <span>comment</span>', 'notesblog'), __('% <span>comments</span>', 'notesblog'),
'', 'Comments are closed'); ?></span>
                <span class="author"><?php _e("By", 'notesblog');?> <a href="<?php the_author_url();
?>" title="<?php the_author(); ?>" class="author"><?php the_author(); ?></a></span>
                <span class="categories"><?php _e("Filed in", 'notesblog');?> <?php
the_category(', '); ?></span>
                <span class="tags"><?php the_tags(__('Tagged with ', 'notesblog'),', ',''); ?></
span>
                <span class="timestamp"><?php the_time(__('F jS, Y', 'notesblog')) ?> @ <?php
the_time(); ?></span>
                </div>
            <?php } ?>

            <div class="entry">
                <?php the_content(__('Read more', 'notesblog')); ?>
            </div>
            <?php if (is_single() || is_page()) { edit_post_link(__('Edit', 'notesblog'), '<p
class="admin">Admin: ', '</p>'); } ?>
        </div>

        <?php comments_template('', true); ?>

    <?php endwhile; ?>

    <div class="nav widecolumn">
        <div class="left"><?php next_posts_link(__('Read previous entries', 'notesblog')) ?></div>
        <div class="right"><?php previous_posts_link(__('Read more recent entries', 'notesblog'))
?></div>
    </div>

  <?php else : ?>
    <!-- search found nothing -->
    <?php if (is_search()) { ?>
        <div class="post single">
            <h2>We got nothing!</h2>
            <p>Your search query didn't return any results. We're sorry about that, why don't
you give it another go, tweaking it a bit perhaps? Use the search box as you did before, maybe
you'll have more luck.</p>
```

```
                <h3>Something to read?</h3>
                <p>Want to read something else? These are the 20 latest updates:</p>
                <ul><?php wp_get_archives('type=postbypost&limit=20&format=html'); ?></ul>
                </div>
        <?php } ?>
        <!-- search found nothing -->
        <?php if (is_404()) { ?>
            <h1 class="listhead">This is a <strong>404 Page Not Found</strong></h1>
            <div class="post single">
                <h2>There's nothing here!</h2>
                <p>We're sorry, but there is nothing here! You might even call this a <strong>404
 Page Not Found</strong> error message, which is exactly what it is. The page you're looking for
 either doesn't exist, or the URL you followed or typed to get to it is incorrect in some way.</p>
                <p><strong>Why don't you try and search for it?</strong> Use the search box and
 try to think of a suitable keyword query, and you'll probably be fine.</p>
                <p>You're sure that it should be here, that page you were looking for? <a href="/
 contact">Then tell us about it!</a></p>
                <h3>Something to read?</h3>
                <p>Want to read something else? These are the 20 latest updates:</p>
                <ul><?php wp_get_archives('type=postbypost&limit=20&format=html'); ?></ul>
            </div>
        <?php } ?>
    <?php endif; ?>

    </div>

<?php get_sidebar(); ?>
<?php get_footer(); ?>
```

So, what do we have here? First of all, you're loading the header.php template with `get_header()`, then the content div starts. This one is floating to the left, says the stylesheet. You'll call the sidebar, which floats to the right, later.

This is what follows:

```
<?php
if (is_category()) {
    echo '<h1 class="listhead">';
    _e("Category", "notesblog");
    echo ' <strong>';
    single_cat_title();
    echo '</strong></h1>';
} if (is_tag()) {
    echo '<h1 class="listhead">';
    _e("Tag", "notesblog");
    echo ' <strong>';
    single_tag_title();
    echo '</strong></h1>';
```

```
} if (is_search()) {
    echo '<h1 class="listhead">';
    _e("Your <strong>search result</strong>", 'notesblog');
    echo '</h1>';
}
?>
```

These are conditional tags that check whether the visitor is on a category, tag, or search page, in which case it will output random headers before the actual loop starts. If you want to create template tags (category.php, tag.php, and search.php, respectively) for these pages, you can just delete this part. The _e() that wraps the wordings is for localization purposes. We'll get to that later as well. If you don't want that, just strip it out.

Moving on, you have the loop. It basically looks like the one we went through in Chapter 3, so I won't dig into it. However, when it comes to outputting the actual content, it gets a bit messier:

```
<?php if (is_single()) { ?>
    <h1><?php the_title(); ?></h1>
    <div class="postmeta">
        <span class="comments"><?php comments_popup_link(__('0 <span>comments</span>', 'notesblog'),
    __('1 <span>comment</span>', 'notesblog'), __('% <span>comments</span>', 'notesblog'), '', ''); ?></
    span>
        <span class="author"><?php _e("By", 'notesblog');?> <a href="<?php the_author_url(); ?>"
    title="<?php the_author(); ?>" class="author"><?php the_author(); ?></a></span>
        <span class="categories"><?php _e("Filed in", 'notesblog');?> <?php the_category(', '); ?></
    span>
        <span class="tags"><?php the_tags(__('Tagged with ', 'notesblog'),', ',''); ?></span>
        <span class="timestamp"><?php the_time(__('F jS, Y', 'notesblog')) ?> @ <?php the_time();
    ?></span>
    </div>
<?php } else if (is_page()) { ?>
    <h1><?php the_title(); ?></h1>
    <div class="postmeta">
        <span class="comments"><?php comments_popup_link(__('0 <span>comments</span>', 'notesblog'),
    __('1 <span>comment</span>', 'notesblog'), __('% <span>comments</span>', 'notesblog'), '', ''); ?></
    span>
        <span class="author"><?php _e("By", 'notesblog');?> <a href="<?php the_author_url(); ?>"
    title="<?php the_author(); ?>" class="author"><?php the_author(); ?></a></span>
    </div>
<?php } else { ?>
    <h2><a href="<?php the_permalink() ?>" rel="bookmark" title="<?php the_title(); ?>"><?php
    the_title(); ?></a></h2>
    <div class="postmeta">
        <span class="comments"><?php comments_popup_link(__('0 <span>comments</span>', 'notesblog'),
    __('1 <span>comment</span>', 'notesblog'), __('% <span>comments</span>', 'notesblog'), '', 'Comments
    are closed'); ?></span>
        <span class="author"><?php _e("By", 'notesblog');?> <a href="<?php the_author_url(); ?>"
    title="<?php the_author(); ?>" class="author"><?php the_author(); ?></a></span>
```

```
            <span class="categories"><?php _e("Filed in", "notesblog");?> <?php the_category(', ');
     ?></span>
            <span class="tags"><?php the_tags(__('Tagged with ', 'notesblog'),', ',"); ?></span>
            <span class="timestamp"><?php the_time(__('F jS, Y', 'notesblog')) ?> @ <?php the_time();
     ?></span>
         </div>
    <?php } ?>
```

This is to output an h1 title tag with just the page or post title, unlinked, if you're loading a page or post. That's what is_single (for posts) and is_page (for pages) check for. If they don't return true, it moves on to the else clause, which is an h2 linked title instead. That would be everything that isn't a post or a page. And again, you've got some localization, both the _e() variant mentioned previously, and the __() variant, which is used within PHP tags. Both of these can be stripped away.

Also, this part relates to the fact that you don't have templates for 404 errors (404.php) or a search. php template:

```
<?php else : ?>
    <!-- search found nothing -->
    <?php if (is_search()) { ?>
        <div class="post single">
            <h2>We got nothing!</h2>
            <p>Your search query didn't return any results. We're sorry about that, why don't you
     give it another go, tweaking it a bit perhaps? Use the search box as you did before, maybe
     you'll have more luck.</p>
            <h3>Something to read?</h3>
            <p>Want to read something else? These are the 20 latest updates:</p>
            <ul><?php wp_get_archives('type=postbypost&limit=20&format=html'); ?></ul>
        </div>
    <?php } ?>
    <!-- search found nothing -->
    <?php if (is_404()) { ?>
        <h1 class="listhead">This is a <strong>404 Page Not Found</strong></h1>
        <div class="post single">
            <h2>There's nothing here!</h2>
            <p>We're sorry, but there is nothing here! You might even call this a <strong>404 Page
     Not Found</strong> error message, which is exactly what it is. The page you're looking for either
     doesn't exist, or the URL you followed or typed to get to it is incorrect in some way.</p>
            <p><strong>Why don't you try and search for it?</strong> Use the search box and try to
     think of a suitable keyword query, and you'll probably be fine.</p>
            <p>You're sure that it should be here, that page you were looking for? <a href="/
     contact">Then tell us about it!</a></p>
            <h3>Something to read?</h3>
            <p>Want to read something else? These are the 20 latest updates:</p>
            <ul><?php wp_get_archives('type=postbypost&limit=20&format=html'); ?></ul>
        </div>
    <?php } ?>
<?php endif; ?>
```

Again, conditional tags check where you are, and then output content should they fall out as `true`. Naturally, `is_404()` only returns something if the page is indeed a 404 page not found result, and `is_search()` will only output the nothing found message if the loop doesn't return anything. Remember, you're in the else part of the loop.

Finally, you're closing the loop with the `endif`.

The index.php template ends with calling first the sidebar.php template with `get_sidebar()`, and then the footer.php template with `get_footer()`.

Side Order: sidebar.php

Moving on, you've got sidebar.php, which is loaded to the right in the Notes Blog Core theme, as you've probably already gathered from the style.css file:

```
<ul id="sidebar" class="column">

    <?php if ( !function_exists('dynamic_sidebar') || !dynamic_sidebar('Sidebar') ) : ?>
        <li id="search">
            <h2><?php _e("Search", "notesblog"); ?></h2>
            <?php get_search_form(); ?>
        </li>
        <li id="tag_cloud">
            <h2><?php _e("Tag Cloud", "notesblog");?></h2>
            <?php wp_tag_cloud('smallest=10&largest=20&unit=px'); ?>
        </li>
        <?php wp_list_categories('title_li=<h2>' .__('Categories') . '</h2>'); ?>
        <?php wp_list_pages('title_li=<h2>' .__('Pages') . '</h2>'); ?>
        <?php wp_list_bookmarks(); ?>
    <?php endif; ?>

</ul>
```

This is really simple. The sidebar is in an unlimited list, and each item in it is a `li` (list item). The PHP code checks if there's any widget content in the Sidebar named `'Sidebar'`. If there is, it will output that and ignore anything else found in the sidebar.php template up until the PHP code is ended with `endif`. However, should there be no widgets, it will output what you've got here.

We'll come back to widgets later on.

Soapboxing: comments.php

The comment functionality is controlled by comments.php, and while you can opt to rely on the default theme's comments.php, you're probably better off creating your own. That being said, the most up-to-date comment functionality is the default theme's comments.php, so that's why Notes Blog Core's comments.php file is based on that.

However, there are some minor differences between the default theme's comments.php and the one in Notes Blog Core, with the most obvious one being further localization. The comments.php in Notes Blog Core looks like this:

```php
<?php
// Do not delete these lines
    if (!empty($_SERVER['SCRIPT_FILENAME']) && 'comments.php' == basename($_SERVER['SCRIPT_FILENAME']))
    die ('Please do not load this page directly. Thanks!');

    if ( post_password_required() ) { ?>
        <p class="nocomments"><?php _e("This post is password protected. Enter the password to
view comments.", "notesblog"); ?></p>
    <?php
        return;
        }
?>


<!-- You can start editing here. -->

<?php if ( have_comments() ) : ?>
    <h2 id="comments"><?php comments_number( __('No comments posted yet', 'notesblog'), __('One single
    comment', 'notesblog'), __('% comments', 'notesblog') );?> <a name="comments"></a></h2>

    <div class="navigation">
        <div class="alignleft"><?php previous_comments_link() ?></div>
        <div class="alignright"><?php next_comments_link() ?></div>
    </div>

    <ol class="commentlist">
        <?php wp_list_comments(); ?>
    </ol>

    <div class="navigation">
        <div class="alignleft"><?php previous_comments_link() ?></div>
        <div class="alignright"><?php next_comments_link() ?></div>
    </div>
 <?php else : // this is displayed if there are no comments so far ?>

    <?php if ( comments_open() ) : ?>
        <!-- If comments are open, but there are no comments. -->

      <?php else : // comments are closed ?>
        <!-- If comments are closed. -->
        <!-- <p class="nocomments"><?php _e("Comments are closed.", "notesblog");?></p> //-->

    <?php endif; ?>
<?php endif; ?>


<?php if ( comments_open() ) : ?>
```

```
<div id="respond">

<h3><?php comment_form_title(__('Post a comment', 'notesblog'), __('Post a comment to %s', 'notesblog'));
   ?> <a name="respond"></a></h3>

<div class="cancel-comment-reply">
    <?php cancel_comment_reply_link(); ?>
</div>

<?php if ( get_option('comment_registration') && !is_user_logged_in() ) : ?>
<p><?php e_("You must be logged in to post a comment.", "notesblog");?> <a href="<?php echo
   wp_login_url( get_permalink() ); ?>"><?php _e("So log in!", "notesblog");?></a></p>
<?php else : ?>

<form action="<?php echo get_option('siteurl'); ?>/wp-comments-post.php" method="post"
   id="commentform">

<?php if ( is_user_logged_in() ) : ?>

<p class="commentloggedin"><?php _e("Logged in as", "notesblog");?> <a href="<?php echo get_
   option('siteurl'); ?>/wp-admin/profile.php"><?php echo $user_identity; ?></a>. <?php _e("Not you?",
   "notesblog");?> <a href="<?php echo wp_logout_url(get_permalink()); ?>" title="Logout"><?php
   _e("Then please log out!", "notesblog");?></a></p>

<?php else : ?>

<table width="100%" class="commenttable">
    <tr>
        <td><label for="author"><?php _e("Name", "notesblog");?> <?php if ($req) echo
   _e("(required)", "notesblog"); ?></label></td>
        <td align="right"><input type="text" name="author" id="author" value="<?php echo esc_
   attr($comment_author); ?>" size="22" tabindex="1" <?php if ($req) echo "aria-required='true'";
   ?> /></td>
    </tr><tr>
        <td><label for="email"><?php _e("Email", "notesblog");?> (never published, <?php if ($req)
   echo _e("required", "notesblog"); ?>)</label></td>
        <td align="right"><input type="text" name="email" id="email" value="<?php echo esc_
   attr($comment_author_email); ?>" size="22" tabindex="2" <?php if ($req) echo "aria-required='true'";
   ?> /></td>
    </tr><tr>
        <td><label for="url">URL</label></td>
        <td align="right"><input type="text" name="url" id="url" value="<?php echo esc_attr($comment_
   author_url); ?>" size="22" tabindex="3" /></td>
    </tr>
</table>

<?php endif; ?>

<!--<p><small><strong>XHTML:</strong> You can use these tags: <code><?php echo allowed_tags();
?></code></small></p>-->
```

73

```
<p><textarea name="comment" id="comment" cols="100%" rows="10" tabindex="4"></textarea></p>

<p><input name="submit" type="submit" id="submit" tabindex="5" value="<?php _e('Submit Comment',
  'notesblog');?>" />
<?php comment_id_fields(); ?>
</p>
<?php do_action('comment_form', $post->ID); ?>

</form>

<?php endif; // If registration required and not logged in ?>
</div>

<?php endif; // if you delete this the sky will fall on your head ?>
```

That's a lot of code, so the following discussion breaks it down into pieces. First there's the part that the WordPress developers don't want you to edit. You can, but you shouldn't unless you know what you're doing:

```
<?php
// Do not delete these lines
    if (!empty($_SERVER['SCRIPT_FILENAME']) && 'comments.php' == basename($_SERVER['SCRIPT_
    FILENAME']))
        die ('Please do not load this page directly. Thanks!');

    if ( post_password_required() ) { ?>
        <p class="nocomments"><?php _e("This post is password protected. Enter the password to
    view comments.", "notesblog"); ?></p>
    <?php
        return;
    }
?>
```

Moving on, you've got something of a comment loop that checks if there are any comments, and then outputs them. If you've worked with WordPress in the past, you may not recognize this. Thanks to `wp_list_comments()`, the comments.php template is a lot easier to work with these days:

```
<?php if ( have_comments() ) : ?>
    <h2 id="comments"><?php comments_number( __('No comments posted yet', 'notesblog'), __('One single
    comment', 'notesblog'), __('% comments', 'notesblog') );?> <a name="comments"></a></h2>

    <div class="navigation">
        <div class="alignleft"><?php previous_comments_link() ?></div>
        <div class="alignright"><?php next_comments_link() ?></div>
    </div>

    <ol class="commentlist">
```

```
        <?php wp_list_comments(); ?>
    </ol>

    <div class="navigation">
        <div class="alignleft"><?php previous_comments_link() ?></div>
        <div class="alignright"><?php next_comments_link() ?></div>
    </div>
 <?php else : // this is displayed if there are no comments so far ?>

    <?php if ( comments_open() ) : ?>
        <!-- If comments are open, but there are no comments. -->

     <?php else : // comments are closed ?>
        <!-- If comments are closed. -->
        <!-- <p class="nocomments"><?php _e("Comments are closed.", "notesblog");?></p> //-->

    <?php endif; ?>
<?php endif; ?>
```

Finally, there's the response section. This is basically a form, which in Notes Blog Core is presented in a table for clean and sober listing. It starts with a check to see if commenting is enabled at all, and then it checks to see if the person is in fact a user that is logged in or not. Then there's the form, and some wrapping up:

```
<?php if ( comments_open() ) : ?>

<div id="respond">

<h3><?php comment_form_title( __('Post a comment', 'notesblog'), __('Post a comment to %s', 'notesblog'));
  ?> <a name="respond"></a></h3>

<div class="cancel-comment-reply">
    <?php cancel_comment_reply_link(); ?>
</div>

<?php if ( get_option('comment_registration') && !is_user_logged_in() ) : ?>
<p><?php e_("You must be logged in to post a comment.", "notesblog");?> <a href="<?php echo
  wp_login_url( get_permalink() ); ?>"><?php _e("So log in!", "notesblog");?></a></p>
<?php else : ?>

<form action="<?php echo get_option('siteurl'); ?>/wp-comments-post.php" method="post"
  id="commentform">

<?php if ( is_user_logged_in() ) : ?>

<p class="commentloggedin"><?php _e("Logged in as", "notesblog");?> <a href="<?php echo get_
  option('siteurl'); ?>/wp-admin/profile.php"><?php echo $user_identity; ?></a>. <?php _e("Not you?",
```

```
"notesblog");?> <a href="<?php echo wp_logout_url(get_permalink()); ?>" title="Logout"><?php
_e("Then please log out!", "notesblog");?></a></p>

<?php else : ?>

<table width="100%" class="commenttable">
    <tr>
        <td><label for="author"><?php _e("Name", "notesblog");?> <?php if ($req) echo
_e("(required)", "notesblog"); ?></label></td>
        <td align="right"><input type="text" name="author" id="author" value="<?php echo esc_
attr($comment_author); ?>" size="22" tabindex="1" <?php if ($req) echo "aria-required='true"; ?>
/></td>
    </tr><tr>
        <td><label for="email"><?php _e("Email", "notesblog");?> (never published, <?php if ($req)
echo _e("required", "notesblog"); ?>)</label></td>
        <td align="right"><input type="text" name="email" id="email" value="<?php echo esc_
attr($comment_author_email); ?>" size="22" tabindex="2" <?php if ($req) echo "aria-required='true";
?> /></td>
    </tr><tr>
        <td><label for="url">URL</label></td>
        <td align="right"><input type="text" name="url" id="url" value="<?php echo esc_attr($comment_
author_url); ?>" size="22" tabindex="3" /></td>
    </tr>
</table>

<?php endif; ?>

<!--<p><small><strong>XHTML:</strong> You can use these tags: <code><?php echo allowed_tags();
?></code></small></p>-->

<p><textarea name="comment" id="comment" cols="100%" rows="10" tabindex="4"></textarea></p>

<p><input name="submit" type="submit" id="submit" tabindex="5" value="<?php _e("Submit Comment",
"notesblog");?>" />
<?php comment_id_fields(); ?>
</p>
<?php do_action('comment_form', $post->ID); ?>

</form>

<?php endif; // If registration required and not logged in ?>
</div>

<?php endif; // if you delete this the sky will fall on your head ?>
```

The `cancel_comment_reply_link()` is only displayed if threaded comments are enabled within WordPress admin. It is the link that lets you cancel a reply should you change your mind. The actual reply link that goes with every comment, however, is output by default so you don't need to put a specific template tag in for that to work.

Most of the time, this basic comments.php template will do the job. However, sometimes you want something more, such as Facebook Connect integration and things like that. Sometimes those special cases are managed by plugins, but not always, so it is a good idea to get acquainted with the comments.php file.

Wrapping Up: footer.php

Finally it's time to close the whole thing, with the footer.php template file. This one wraps up all the tags from header.php, and adds some copyright information and such. But it also features two widget areas, named Footer A and Footer B, both with default text that tells the user to add something to them:

```
<div id="footer">
    <ul id="footercol" class="a widgets">
        <?php if ( !function_exists('dynamic_sidebar') || !dynamic_sidebar('Footer A') ) : ?>
            <li>This column is a widget area.<br /><span class="alert">Add widgets to
<strong>Footer A</strong> for this one to rock!</span></li>
        <?php endif; ?>
    </ul>
    <ul id="footercol" class="b widgets">
        <?php if ( !function_exists('dynamic_sidebar') || !dynamic_sidebar('Footer B') ) : ?>
    <li>This column is a widget area.<br /><span class="alert">Add widgets to <strong>Footer B</
strong> for this one to rock!</span></li>
        <?php endif; ?>
    </ul>
</div>
<div id="copy">
    <div class="copycolumnwide">
        <p>Copyright &copy; <a href="<?php bloginfo('url'); ?>"><?php bloginfo('name'); ?></
a><br /><em><?php bloginfo('description'); ?></em></p>
    </div>
<div class="copycolumn">
        <p class="right"><?php _e("Built on", "notesblog");?> <a href="http://notesblog.com"
title="Notes Blog">Notes Blog</a> <em><a href="http://notesblog.com/core/" title="Notes Blog
Core">Core</a></em><br />Powered by <a href="http://wordpress.org" title="WordPress">WordPress</
a></p>
    </div>
</div>

    <div id="finalword"><span>&uarr;</span> <a href="#top" title="To page top"><?php _e("That's it -
back to the top of page!", "notesblog");?></a> <span>&uarr;</span></div>

</div>
</div>

<?php wp_footer(); ?>
</body>
</html>
```

Obviously each one of those `ul` lists is floating so they can fit beside each other. Underneath is a simple copyright notice, and then a link back to the top of the page. It's a pretty basic footer, wrapping up the page. If you glance back at then the basic theme layout dummy (Figure 4-1) at the beginning of this chapter, you'll find that all template tags are now accounted for.

Wait, There's More!

But hang on, that's not the whole story. Notes Blog Core contains a couple of other files as well, such as functions.php, along with a favicon (you saw the inclusion of it in the header.php file), and some other small things.

Here's the functions.php file:

```php
<?php
load_theme_textdomain("notesblog");
$content_width = 580;
// widgets
    if ( function_exists('register_sidebar') )
        register_sidebar(array('name'=>'Sidebar'));
        register_sidebar(array('name'=>'Footer A'));
        register_sidebar(array('name'=>'Footer B'));
        register_sidebar(array(
            'name' => 'Submenu',
            'id' => 'submenu',
            'before_widget' => '<div id="submenu-nav">',
            'after_widget' => '</div>',
            'before_title' => false,
            'after_title' => false
    ));
// ends ---
// pullquote shortcode
function pullquote( $atts, $content = null ) {
    extract(shortcode_atts(array(
        'float' => '$align',
    ), $atts));
    return '<blockquote class="pullquote ' . $float . '">' . $content . '</blockquote>';
}
add_shortcode('pull', 'pullquote');
// ends ---
// admin page
add_action('admin_menu', 'nbcore_menu');
function nbcore_menu() {
  add_theme_page('Notes Blog Core', 'Notes Blog Core', 8, 'your-unique-identifier', 'nbcore_options');
}
function nbcore_options() {
  echo '<div class="wrap"><h2>Notes Blog Core</h2>';
  echo '<p>This is a placeholder for upcoming admin options for the Notes Blog Core theme. These
  things aren\'t due yet, in fact, they are pretty far away, so just forget about this page for
```

```
    now huh?</p><p>Get the latest Notes Blog and Notes Blog Core news from <a href="http://notes-
    blog.com" title="Notes Blog">http://notesblog.com</a> - it\'s that sweet!</p>';
    echo '<h3>Pullquote shortcode</h3><p>Notes Blog Core has support for pullquotes. Either you
    use the <em>pullquote</em> class on a <em>blockquote</em> tag along with the <em>alignleft</
    em> or <em>alignright</em> tags, or you use shortcode to do the same.</p><p>Usage is simple:
    <code>[pull float="X"]Your pullqoute text[/pull]</code> will output att pullquote aligned ei-
    ther to the left or right. The key is <em>float="X"</em>, where X can be <strong>either</strong>
    <em>alignleft</em> or <em>alignright</em>. Simple huh?</p>';
    echo '</div>';
}
// ends ---
?>
```

The `textdomain` load that you're starting everything off with is for localization of the theme. We'll get to that later in the book. Then you've got the default content width, and the initialization of the four widget areas (first the Sidebar area, then Footer A and Footer B), and finally the Submenu area, which is displayed a little differently and hence is passed as an array.

After that follows a custom pullquote shortcode (which we'll get to later), as well as an admin page for Notes Blog Core that shows up in the WordPress admin interface. As you can see, you can do a lot with functions.php; consequently, it has grown more and more important over the years. These days, a lot of things you can do with a plugin can theoretically be done from within functions.php.

Template Files

Template files can be used in a wide variety of ways. Exact use depends on what you put in them, of course. You can make them behave in almost any way you want by changing the loop or leaving it out altogether, and you can use template tags to generate a specific behavior. Likewise, you can make pages a lot more dynamic by using conditional tags, and if you really want to shake things up you can always use plugins to extend WordPress beyond any of the built-in functionality.

There are a few things you need to know about template files. First, you need to know which ones are necessary for the basic functionality. Second, you have to work out which template file is used when. Third, you should figure out which template files are necessary for what you want to achieve.

A good example of knowing which template files help you achieve a particular result would be to have both an index.php and a home.php template, without any other difference than an image or welcome text. It would be a lot more convenient to put that in index.php and use the `is_home()` conditional tag to output this on the front page only. The same goes for single posts: if you just don't have all that much that is different between single post view and the front page, you can use `is_single()` to alter the parts that need to be different (like not linking the post title, for example).

Which Template File is Used When?

There are a bunch of possible template files, and remember, a theme doesn't need them all. In fact, you shouldn't use more of these than you really need to, since that only means that you'll have more files to maintain should WordPress change or if you want to alter something in your design.

The following table tells you what each of these templates can be used for.

Template	Function
archive.php	Template for archives based on author, category and date, overridden by respective individual template
attachment.php	Template for any post attachment, usually images but any mime type will do; custom styling is done with [mime-type].php, for example image.php or video.php
author.php	The author template
category.php	Template for category view listings, where category-X.php can be used for the category with the ID or slug X; slug support was added in 2.9
comments.php	Comment display and posting template; if not available, the default comment template will be loaded
comments-popup.php	Comments in a popup; almost nobody uses this one anymore
date.php	Template for any date-based listing (per year, per month, and so on)
404.php	Page not found 404 error message template
home.php	The front page template
index.php	The main template; must be included as a fallback to every page should it not have a template file, should most likely include the loop
page.php	The template for page view, with support for individual page templates; also, from 2.9, support for page-X.php where X is either the ID or the slug of the page
search.php	Search result/error message template
single.php	Single post view template
style.css	Stylesheet file; must be included with a theme info header at top, put everything CSS here
tag.php	List display for a tag, tag-X.php will be used for the tag with the slug or ID X; support for ID was added in 2.9

The category template may be confusing. By default, the category.php template will be used to display the post listing from any given category. However, should there be a category-X.php template, where X is the ID of the category in question, that template file will be used rather than the category.php template. The same goes for tags: tag-X.php is displayed before tag.php, with the exception that X here isn't the ID but the slug of the particular tag.

When it comes to page.php and Page templates, these are actually two different things. You may have noticed that you can set a template when creating WordPress Pages. These are Page templates, and not controlled by page.php but rather sporting their own header information much like style. css. They can be very useful, so we'll play with them in a little while.

Template Hierarchy

Now that you know what the template files are, you need to know which one is loaded when, and what is happening if there is no template at all. As you know, index.php is the fallback template for everything, and you can settle for using only that. Figure 4-2 illustrates the hierarchy of the template files.

Page Templates

WordPress Pages are meant for static content, less time-dependent than your average blog post (which probably is static, after all). The Pages can have subpages, and are usually used for information about the site, contact forms, and so on. However, you can take it way beyond that if you want. First of all, you can give the page.php template a nice styling that fits the kind of content you want to display on your Pages (rather than just have them mimic your blog posts). Second, you can create Page templates that you can apply to individual Pages from the Write page section in WordPress admin.

These Page templates are basically normal template files, with the difference that they need a little code snippet at the top of the file before the actual code begins so that WordPress can find them. (Much like your theme's style.css, in other words.)

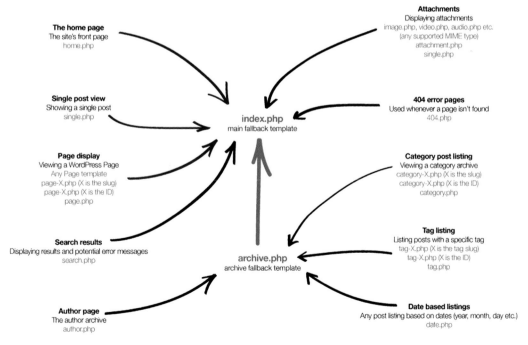

Figure 4-2: The hierarchy of template files

Just put this on top of the Page template file, which you can name whatever you like as long as it is suffixed with .php:

```php
<?php
/*
Template Name: My Page Template
*/
?>
```

This one , for example, could be named mypagetemplate.php. It may be a good idea to name Page templates page-<something>.php for semantic reasons, but that's entirely up to you.

With that code snippet on top, and then any kind of template file content you like, the Page template will show up in the Page template box in the Write page section in WordPress admin. Just pick it, save, and there you go.

A common usage is an archive page. Maybe you want to have a link to your archives that displays all authors, categories, tags, and the 50 latest posts using template tags. This just won't work with a normal Page, since you can't put template tags within the post itself through WordPress admin (at least not without using plugins that open up the editor), so a Page template is needed. Like this one, page-archives.php from Notes Blog Core, designed for use with simple blog archives:

```php
<?php
/*
Template Name: Archives
*/
?>

<?php get_header(); ?>

<div id="content" class="widecolumn">

    <?php while (have_posts()) : the_post(); ?>

        <div id="post-<?php the_ID(); ?>" <?php post_class(); ?>>
            <h1><?php the_title(); ?></h1>
            <div class="postmeta">
                <?php if (comments_open()) : ?><span class="comments"><?php comments_popup_link(__
    ('0 <span>comments</span>', 'notesblog'), __('1 <span>comment</span>', 'notesblog'), __('%
    <span>comments</span>', 'notesblog'), '', ''); ?></span><?php endif; ?>
                <span class="author"><?php _e("By", "notesblog"); ?> <a href="<?php the_author_url(); ?>"
    title="<?php the_author(); ?>" class="author"><?php the_author(); ?></a></span>
            </div>
```

```
        <div class="entry">
            <?php the_content(); ?>
            <h2><?php _e("Browse by Month:", "notesblog");?></h2>
            <ul>
                <?php wp_get_archives('type=monthly'); ?>
            </ul>
            <h2><?php _e("Browse by Category:", "notesblog");?></h2>
            <ul>
                <?php wp_list_categories('title_li='); ?>
            </ul>
            <h2><?php _e("Browse by Tag:", "notesblog");?></h2>
            <?php wp_tag_cloud('smallest=8&largest=28&number=0&orderby=name&order=ASC'); ?>
        </div>
    </div>

    <?php endwhile; ?>

</div>

<?php get_sidebar(); ?>
<?php get_footer(); ?>
```

Other common uses are Pages created just to display a specific loop. You can take your index.php template file, for example, and make a Page template out of it (put the code snippet on top), and then change the loop to output whatever you want using `query_posts()`. You can also have a Page containing multiple loops, or perhaps not do WordPress stuff at all.

Putting Page templates to good use is a huge step toward creating the site you want using WordPress.

The 404 Template

The 404.php template differs a bit from the other template files. It is only displayed when someone either clicks a faulty link to your WordPress powered site, or when someone misspells something. In other words, 404.php is used when stuff isn't working, and nothing can be returned.

That means that the 404.php template won't use the loop unless you want it to. A good 404 page, no matter what system you're running, should be informative and offer the lost visitor a way to get back on track. That can be a quick link to the site's front page, a search form, or a list of the 20 latest updates. Or all that, as it were.

What follows is the 404 error message from the Notes Blog Core theme. The theme actually doesn't have a 404.php template, to make it easier to style your child themes, so I have adapted the code somewhat as it would look in a template file. As you'll see, it does all the things you may want it to, to help the visitor on their way. You can spice it up even more if you like.

```php
<?php get_header(); ?>
<div id="content" class="widecolumn">
    <h1 class="listhead">This is a <strong>404 Page Not Found</strong></h1>
    <div class="post single">
        <h2>There's nothing here!</h2>
        <p>We're sorry, but there is nothing here! You might even call this a <strong>404 Page Not
  Found</strong> error message, which is exactly what it is. The page you're looking for either
  doesn't exist, or the URL you followed or typed to get to it is incorrect in some way.</p>
        <p><strong>Why don't you try and search for it?</strong> Use the search box and try to
  think of a suitable keyword query, and you'll probably be fine.</p>
        <p>You're sure that it should be here, that page you were looking for? <a href="/
  contact">Then tell us about it!</a></p>
        <h3>Something to read?</h3>
        <p>Want to read something else? These are the 20 latest updates:</p>
        <ul><?php wp_get_archives('type=postbypost&limit=20&format=html'); ?></ul>
    </div>
</div>
<?php get_footer(); ?>
```

If there's no 404.php template to call, the index.php template will be used. In fact, you'll see the error message from the loop that was so painstakingly included in just about every loop example in Chapter 3. You can style those individually using conditional tags; is_404() is the one you want if you need to output something only if someone got something wrong. Such as this code, taken from the index.php template file from Notes Blog Core and found in its full glory earlier in this chapter:

```php
<?php if (is_404()) { ?>
    <h1 class="listhead">This is a <strong>404 Page Not Found</strong></h1>
    <div class="post single">
        <h2>There's nothing here!</h2>
        <p>We're sorry, but there is nothing here! You might even call this a <strong>404 Page Not
  Found</strong> error message, which is exactly what it is. The page you're looking for either
  doesn't exist, or the URL you followed or typed to get to it is incorrect in some way.</p>
        <p><strong>Why don't you try and search for it?</strong> Use the search box and try to
  think of a suitable keyword query, and you'll probably be fine.</p>
        <p>You're sure that it should be here, that page you were looking for? <a href="/
  contact">Then tell us about it!</a></p>
        <h3>Something to read?</h3>
        <p>Want to read something else? These are the 20 latest updates:</p>
        <ul><?php wp_get_archives('type=postbypost&limit=20&format=html'); ?></ul>
    </div>
<?php } ?>
```

Personally, I prefer to manage 404 errors through a 404.php template, but obviously you don't have to. Just make sure you make it a good error message; just displaying 404 Page Not Found will certainly let the lost visitor know that something went wrong, but it won't be much help to them in finding the correct destination either.

Using functions.php

One theme template file you haven't touched very much yet is functions.php. It is a bit mysterious, and most people take a brief look at it and then shy away. Not all themes have functions.php files, but the ones that do usually support widgets and may even have their own options page inside WordPress admin. This is all possible thanks to the functions.php file.

What, then, does functions.php do? Basically, it does whatever you want it to, since it more or less acts like a plugin that is called within the WordPress initialization, both when viewing the public site and when loading the admin interface. Because of that, you can add admin functionality to functions.php.

You'll look at widgets and how to set up widget areas in a little while, but first, add a simple function to functions.php:

```php
<?php
    function $hellomate() {
        echo 'Hello mate, how are you doing?';
    }
?>
```

If you put that simple little code snippet in functions.php, and then call the function somewhere within your theme, it will output the "Hello mate, how are you doing?" text. You call the function like you would call any PHP function:

```php
<?php hellomate(); ?>
```

So that would echo the text. Not very useful, perhaps, but it does show you something functions.php can do. If you have code snippets you use all the time, and want them easily accessible, this is your solution.

Many themes use admin options pages to let the user set their own color schemes, font styles, or perhaps change the header. This is all managed with functions.php. You'll get to create your own theme options pages later on.

Setting the Default Width

A commonly forgotten feature that has been around since WordPress 2.5 is the content width setting. Content width, which is a simple little snippet added to functions.php, will tell WordPress the maximum width that the theme can manage, which in turns means that the theme will resize the image accordingly. Sure, you have Media Settings in the WordPress admin interface, where you can control the size of images (Figure 4-3), but the user may forget to change these things when changing themes.

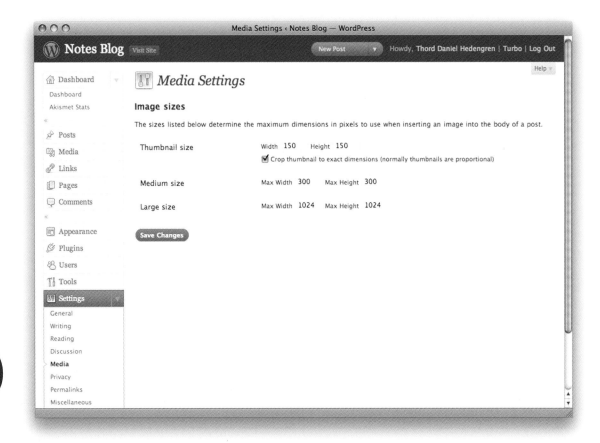

Figure 4-3: The Media Settings in WordPress admin isn't the only way to control image width

This is where $content_width comes in. It sets the width for large-sized images. Remember, when uploading an image to WordPress you get a total of four images; the ones listed above, and the original one. And with $content_width, the large image will fit perfectly with your theme.

It is easy to add. Just put this snippet in functions.php (within the PHP tags of course):

```
$content_width = 580;
```

580 is the width in pixels, so you need to change that to whatever is the maximum width for content in your theme.

Inserting Promotions with functions.php

A lot of blogs and sites show promotional elements after the post, usually to get people to subscribe to the RSS feed. This is easily done in the theme's template files, of course, but it can also be handled by your functions.php file and some action hookery.

Say you want to encourage your readers to subscribe to your RSS feed. You want to output a `div` with the class `promotion`, and within it an h4 header and a line of text. Thanks to the magic of CSS you can style it graphically any way you want just by applying styles to the `div`. Maybe something like this:

```css
div.promotion { background: #eee; border: 1px solid #bbb; padding: 10px; }
div.promotion h4 { color: #f00; font-size: 14px; margin: 0 0 5px 0; padding: 0; }
div.promotion p { font-size: 12px; color: #444; margin-bottom: 0; }
```

That would probably look decent. To really bling it up you should add a background image featuring a nice RSS graphic or something to the `div`, but forget about that for now. This is the full HTML you want to output after your marvelous posts:

```html
<div class="promotion">
    <h4>Never miss a beat!</h4>
    <p>Our smashing <a href="http://notesblog.com/feed/">RSS feed</a> keeps you up-to-date!</p>
</div>
```

How, then, do you get this thing to output itself without hacking the template files? Easy enough: you can use functions.php and attach it to the `the_content()` template tag. (You know, the one that outputs the actual content, after which you want to add it.) Here's the functions.php code:

```php
function Promotion($content) {
        if(!is_feed() && !is_home()) {
                $content.= '<div class="promotion">';
                $content.= '<h4>Never miss a beat!</h4>';
                $content.= '<p>Our smashing <a href="http://notesblog.com/feed/">RSS feed</a> keeps
  you up-to-date!</p>';
                $content.= '</div>';
        }
        return $content;
}
add_filter ('the_content', 'Promotion');
```

The function creates a variable called `Promotion`, which you're storing with the HTML code. Naturally, you can just as easily write the whole HTML in one long string, rather than having four lines of `$content`, but this way makes it a bit simpler to write. Then you return `$content`, which means that `Promotion` is now stored with the HTML you want to output. Finally, you use `add_filter` to add it after `the_content`.

And there you have it; whenever it is not a home or a feed listing (the `if` clause—you may want to add more conditions there by the way), you'll output the promotional box that asks the reader to subscribe to the RSS feed.

So why would you do this rather than just hack the template files? The only real reason for this is that this method is pretty theme independent, so you can copy and paste it between your themes and just add the necessary CSS to the stylesheet. Having a set of functions for the most common content you want to output, and even hooking them onto template tags when possible, is a way to streamline your WordPress themes even more.

As you can see, functions.php can be very handy, and it is certainly a lot more than just the widget declarations that just about every theme has these days. That being said, the widgets are the most commonly used feature originating from functions.php, so we'll look at those next.

Widgets, and When to Use Them

Widgets add drag-and-drop functionality that allows the administrator to add features to a WordPress site from within the admin interface. This can be anything from a simple text block in the sidebar, to category listings, recent comments, or the latest updates from RSS feeds. That is just core widget functionality built into WordPress; add widget-ready plugins and you get a lot more.

When used right, widgets can be a great asset for a site administrator, since the hands-on way you use and alter them makes them really easy to work with. In the coming chapters you'll see how you can use widget areas for various things other than just displaying a lot of clutter in the sidebar of typical blog 1A. In fact, you may remember that Notes Blog Core has a widget area called Submenu in the header, in which users easily can add a simple menu should they want to. That's just a small taste of what widget areas can do for you.

Declaring Widgets

It is easy to make your theme widget-ready. Do so using functions.php within your theme, where you declare the widget areas, and then you add the necessary code in your various theme files (usually sidebar.php) where you want the widget area to show up.

This is the simplest way of doing it, just creating the default sidebar widget in functions.php:

```php
<?php
if ( function_exists('register_sidebar') )
    register_sidebar();
?>
```

Then, add this to the part of sidebar.php where you want the widgets to show up. It should go within the `ul` tags:

```
<ul id="sidebar">
<?php if ( !function_exists('dynamic_sidebar')
    || !dynamic_sidebar() ) : ?>
    <li id="about">
```

```
        <h2>About this site</h2>
        <p>Welcome to this most excellent site!</p>
    </li>
    <li id="search">
        <h2>Search</h2>
        <?php get_search_form(); ?>
    </li>
<?php endif; ?>
</ul>
```

The widget area starts with this:

```
<?php if ( !function_exists('dynamic_sidebar')
    || !dynamic_sidebar() ) : ?>
```

And it ends with this:

```
<?php endif; ?>
```

Everything that goes in between will be displayed when there are no widgets chosen for the widget area. So if you look at the sidebar.php code above, and you haven't added any widgets in WordPress admin, then you'll see the `li` with the "Add widgets here" text. Naturally, when you add widgets, anything within the widget area code won't show. As you can see in the previous example, you can put both traditional HTML content in there, like the "about" `li` with a `p` and so on. However, you can also use template tags, like the `get_search_form()` tag used in the `li` in the following section. That template tag fetches the searchform.php content, incidentally.

For a more detailed example of how the sidebar.php can look with default content within, see the "Side Order: sidebar.php" section of "A Closer Look at Notes Blog Core" earlier in this chapter.

Multiple Widget Areas

Some themes have more than one widget area. This is achieved by declaring the widget areas in functions.php a little differently. If you want two sidebar areas, a header area, and a footer area that are widget ready, you can accomplish these goals in the following manner, adding the code to functions.php:

```
if ( function_exists('register_sidebar') )
    register_sidebar(array('name'=>'Sidebar 1'));
    register_sidebar(array('name'=>'Sidebar 2'));
    register_sidebar(array('name'=>'Header'));
    register_sidebar(array('name'=>'Footer'));
    ));
```

Speaks for itself, right? It is basically the same declaration as for one (default) widget area, but with the names of every area defined. This will have to carry on to the code that defines the actual areas in the template files. This isn't very fancy, just add the widget area name to the first PHP tag for defining an area, like this:

```php
<?php if ( !function_exists('dynamic_sidebar') || !dynamic_sidebar('The-Widget-Area-Name') ) :
    ?><?php endif; ?>
```

So the footer area would look like this:

```php
<?php if ( !function_exists('dynamic_sidebar') || !dynamic_sidebar('Footer') ) : ?><?php endif; ?>
```

Simple and straightforward enough. Naturally, anything that goes for single widget areas can be used when you have multiple widget areas, so if you need them to behave differently by all means go for it.

Customizing Widgets

Sometimes you may not want the widgets to output the way they do by default. Maybe you want to enclose them in div tags, for example. Assuming you have a good reason to be doing this, you can register them in functions.php using an array:

```php
<?php
if ( function_exists('register_sidebar') )
    register_sidebar(array(
        'before_widget' => '',
        'after_widget' => '',
        'before_title' => '',
        'after_title' => '',
    ));
?>
```

The wrapping code goes inside the single quotation marks at the end of each line.

Now, wrap the widget in a div with the class customwidget, and enclose the title in a div with the class customtitle:

```php
<?php
if ( function_exists('register_sidebar') )
    register_sidebar(array(
        'before_widget' => '<div class="customwidget">',
        'after_widget' => '</div>',
        'before_title' => '<div class="customtitle">',
        'after_title' => '</div>',
    ));
?>
```

You should use this custom stuff with caution. After all, most themes and widgetized plugins are created with the unlimited list in mind.

Now that you've gotten deep into the theme's template files, and have looked into how to widgetize areas, you can do something about those comments. Yes, you did indeed look at the comments.php template file earlier in this chapter, but there is more to them than just getting the functionality working. They need to look good.

Making Comments Look Good

Not all sites need comment functionality, but chances are that a lot of the sites you'll be building with WordPress will. Most, if not all, blogs allow readers to comment on the posts, and the same goes for the vast majority of editorial sites out there, from newspapers to magazines. It is just a good way to connect with the readership, and while the sites in question may have completely different motives for doing this, and may have different comment policies, the basic functionality remains the same.

From a WordPress theme designer's point of view, comments can be a bore, mostly because making them look good can be a problem. The actual code isn't all that hard, though, and if you like the default comment view (as featured in the default WordPress theme) you won't even have to create the comments.php template file. We looked closer at such a file in the "A Closer Look at the Notes Blog Core" section earlier in this chapter, so we'll gloss over that part for now and look at the comments from a less technical point of view for a little while.

These are the most important things to consider when designing the comments section of a site:

- It needs to be obvious where the comment section begins. You don't want the readers to mix up comments with the editorial content.
- The comments need to be easy to read, just like the rest of the site.
- Proper spacing between comments, along with alternating colors or dividing lines, helps to separate them from each other. Any way that accomplishes this separation is a good way.
- It has to be obvious who the comment author is.
- The post comment form should be obvious to use, properly tabbed, and use a readable font in a decent size. Think about it: if you want the readers to write long and insightful comments, you should make it as easy on them as possible to do so.

A few other things comes to mind as well, not as important design-wise but still in need of a decision and possible proper placing within the comments area:

- What's the comment policy? You should link to it or put it in small print along with the Post Comment button.
- Do you allow HTML code? If so, which tags are acceptable?
- Do the comments go into moderation before publication? If they do, you should probably let the readers know, or at the very least output a big note when a posted comment goes into moderation.
- Do you require signup and/or login to comment? Then make that process as simple and obvious as possible.

Think the comment functionality through and you'll be fine. You'll also have a much easier time designing it, and possibly altering the functionality as well.

Threaded Comments

Threaded comments were introduced in WordPress 2.7 and require activation from within the WordPress admin interface, under Settings → Discussion. Any theme that uses the proper template tag for listing the comments, which is `wp_list_comments()`, supports threaded comments should you want them. See the "Soapboxing: comments.php" section of "A Closer Look at Notes Blog Core" earlier in this chapter for more on how the actual comment output code looks.

If you activate threaded comments you'll get a reply link at the end of each comment. Clicking it will alter the post comment section somewhat and add a Cancel Reply link as well. This is all built-in stuff, so you needn't worry about it.

What you do need to consider, however, is the following:

- How deep will the threaded comments go? This is an admin setting, and you need to make sure you support it within your design.
- You need to ensure the Reply link is properly styled.
- You need to ensure the Cancel Reply link is properly styled.

Replies to comments end up within that particular comment's `li`, inside a `ul` with the class `children`. The comment hierarchy is basically like this (lots of stuff cut out to illustrate the point):

```
<li>
    [The top level comment content]
    <ul class="children">
        <li>
            [First level reply]
            <ul class="children">
                <li>
                    [Second level reply]
                </li>
            </ul>
        </li>
    </ul>
</li>
<li>
    [Next comment on the top level]
</li>
```

How many `ul`'s with the `children` class are allowed is determined by the threaded comment depth setting in admin. Five is the default, so your themes should support that many at least. The whole concept of threaded comments is built on hierarchy, so you should probably set the margin or padding for the `children` class to 10 pixels or so. It all depends on your theme, but you should make every reply indent a bit.

Styling the Reply link is easier. The link resides in a `div` with the class `reply`, so just style that any way you want. You can make it float to the right and in a font size of 12 pixels easily enough by adding this to the stylesheet:

```
div.reply { float:right; font-size: 12px; }
```

The same applies to the Cancel link that is output just below the Post a Comment header in the Respond section of the comment area. Again, this all depends on how your comments.php template looks, of course, but usually you'll find it here. It is in a `div` with the `cancel-comment-reply` class by default. You can make that bold just as easy as you managed the Reply link:

```
div.cancel-comment-reply { font-weight:bold; }
```

If you want this link somewhere particular, you can control it by placing the `cancel_comment_reply_link()` template tag wherever is suitable for your theme. Naturally, it should be close to the respond form, since that is where the link will be output. The default `div` listed above needs to be in the template too, so this is what you'll be moving around:

```
<div class="cancel-comment-reply">
    <?php cancel_comment_reply_link(); ?>
</div>
```

Threaded comments are a great way to make longer conversations more manageable, so do consider using them if the topics on the site in question spark debates.

Author Highlighting

Highlighting the post author's comments is a good idea, especially if the site is of the teaching kind. Say, for instance, you're doing tutorials. The readers may have questions, in which case it is a good idea to be very clear about which comments are the author's. This used to be accomplished by using plugins (and conceivably still could be), but now there's a better way.

Examine the code from comments.php that outputs the actual comments.

```
<?php if ( have_comments() ) : ?>
    <h2 id="comments"><?php comments_number( __('No comments posted yet', 'notesblog'), __('One single
comment', 'notesblog'), __('% comments', 'notesblog') );?> <a name="comments"></a></h2>

    <div class="navigation">
        <div class="alignleft"><?php previous_comments_link() ?></div>
        <div class="alignright"><?php next_comments_link() ?></div>
    </div>

    <ol class="commentlist">
```

```
        <?php wp_list_comments(); ?>
    </ol>

    <div class="navigation">
        <div class="alignleft"><?php previous_comments_link() ?></div>
        <div class="alignright"><?php next_comments_link() ?></div>
    </div>
<?php else : // this is displayed if there are no comments so far ?>
```

The comments are basically an ordered list (ol) with a list item (li) for each comment. You can see the former in the code, but not the latter since it is generated by the wp_list_comments() template tag.

This is where you can make a difference, since wp_list_comments() applies some CSS classes to each li. Among those classes is bypostauthor, if it is in fact the post author who wrote a comment. That means that the post author needs to be logged in when commenting, of course, otherwise WordPress won't recognize him or her.

Give the post author comments a yellow background by adding this to style.css:

```
li.bypostauthor { background: yellow; }
```

Now, all comments by the author of the original post will have a yellow background. Naturally, you should do something more fancy than that, but changing the background of the comment is a good idea, as is upping the font size and/or color a bit. And if you want, you can take it really far because everything related to the particular comment is found within the li.bypostauthor tag. That means that you can change the way the avatar is displayed (img.avatar is the CSS class you're looking for), or alter the comment metadata (div.comment-author and div.comment-meta) as well as the actual comment text. Set the comment text font size to 18 pixels, just for the fun of it, and keep the comment background yellow:

```
li.bypostauthor { background: yellow; }
li.bypostauthor div.comment-body p { font-size: 18px; }
```

Use post author highlighting with caution. After all, it is not always all that important that the post author's comments are highlighted this way. A smaller note, however, will never hurt.

Custom Fields

Custom fields open up even more advanced options to the theme and plugin designer. They are a way to store custom data in the database, and that in turn means that they can open up new functionality. See the "Custom Fields" section in Chapter 3 for hands-on examples on how custom fields work; in this section we'll look instead at what you can do with them as a designer.

Common Usage

Custom fields were initially thought of as a way to store metadata for a post, and that's still the way it is presented in the Codex, as well as how the default output (which we'll get to) is behaving. However, that is not the most common usage for custom fields these days. Far more often custom fields are used to apply an image to a post, and use it in listings, or to achieve what is often referred to as magazine-style headlines. This is obviously good, although maybe not the ideal solution when it comes to usability.

However, custom fields needn't be limited to managing magazine-style headlines or showing off post thumbnails in listings. You can use custom fields for a number of things, such as applying custom CSS styles depending on the post, as a way to add further unique styling to the posts. Or you use custom fields to create and identify a series of posts (the key would be Series and the value would be the various series' names), and then create a Page template with a custom loop that limits the output to posts with a specific Series value.

Another image-based custom fields implementation would be to not only apply headline and listing images for the post, but also alter the complete body background!

Custom fields can be taken pretty far, and whenever you need to step outside the boundaries of traditional WordPress template tags and functions, custom fields are where you should look first.

95

The Usability Factor

My main gripe with custom fields is that they look so messy. Just look at that custom fields box in WordPress admin; it isn't at all as user-friendly as the rest of the interface. Just the "key" and "value" nomenclature, and then the whole design of the box. . . . No, it just isn't something I'd trust a client with.

This is the most serious issue with custom fields, I think. After all, when you've used it once it is easy enough to pick the key you need and copy and paste the image you want in the value field, for instance. But while that may not seem daunting to you, a client may feel differently.

This is something you need to consider when doing work for clients. Is it feasible to assume that the person(s) updating the site can handle custom fields? The most common usage of custom fields is, after all, headline images and things like that, and they almost always involve finding a URL to the image and copying and pasting it to the value field of the appropriate key. Can the client handle that?

Custom fields are great, don't get me wrong, but until they are presented in a more user-friendly way, they are limited to the more Web-savvy crowd that isn't afraid to do some manual inputting. You probably fall into that category, but whether or not your clients (or partners, collaborators, or whatever) do is up to you to decide. If not, you are probably better off finding another solution.

Developing a Core Theme

If you're a theme designer, or just an aspiring one, and you want to develop WordPress-based sites, then you really need a basic core theme. Here's why:

1. **It is a time saver.** Every time you need to start a new WordPress project, you have a basic and easy to edit/alter/break theme to begin with.
2. **It is familiar.** When you've spent hours and hours hacking a theme, possibly for several different projects, then you'll feel right at home when going at it again and again.
3. **It is easy to keep up-to-date.** If you keep your core theme up-to-date, you won't have to struggle with new functionality all the time: just update once, and there you have it.
4. **It may make client updates easier.** Assuming you're building your sites as child themes standing on your core theme's shoulders, updating client sites with new functionality shouldn't be a problem.

As you will discover in Chapter 5, child themes are your friends here. If you set up a solid core theme that you build your WordPress sites on, you'll make everything easier on yourself.

In this book you're using the Notes Blog Core theme (by yours truly) as an example. You can use it as your own basic core theme to build upon, whether you do this by hacking the theme directly to fit your needs, or by applying the child theme concept to it; this is up to you. The theme is free to use in just about any way you like, from personal sites to a basis for commercial projects.

Should you not want to use Notes Blog Core you can either create your very own basic core theme from scratch (or copy and paste your way, with sensibility of course), or find a theme framework that fits you. There are several to choose from online, and a quick search will give dozens of promising hits. What you do need to be wary of is the license, since you want to be able to use your basic core theme any way you like without paying for every setup or something like that. If your core theme of choice is a premium theme, there is most likely a developer's license that gives you these rights, but if you're reading this book, chances are you're better off spending some time creating your very own core theme.

So what should the core theme do then? Well, everything you think you need on a regular basis, and absolutely nothing more. The last thing you want is a bloated core theme that may look good in itself, or perhaps suit one kind of WordPress site, but be entirely overkill for others. It is a better idea to keep an extras library with stuff you won't need all the time, from custom code to small code snippets and template files, and deploy these things only when needed. After all, you want the final theme to be as tight as possible, without being hard to maintain.

To sum up:

- Analyze your needs, and set up a basic core WordPress theme based on those needs.
- Use an existing theme framework, if possible, to save time.
- Be wary of theme licenses!

Say you're the generous kind and want to share your brilliant core theme, or a variant of it at least, with the general public. Good for you, that's very much in line with the open source spirit. But if you're gonna do it, then let's make sure you do it right!

Releasing a Theme

Releasing a theme to the WordPress community is always appreciated. As of WordPress 2.8, the official theme directory offers theme installation from within the WordPress admin interface, which makes it all the more interesting to host your theme there. That way, the WordPress site will also make sure that sites use the latest version of the theme, and should they not the option to upgrade automatically through the admin interface will present itself. That is assuming you keep your theme up-to-date in the directory, of course.

When you release a theme, it should, of course, be fully functional, preferably validated, and not a complete copy of someone else's work. See the theme checklist below for more on what you should consider before releasing your theme.

It may be tempting to sell your theme. Commercial (or premium, as they are sometimes called) themes are a reality, and there are licenses for sale with support programs, as well as other solutions that work around the GPL license that WordPress carries. Why should that matter to you and the theme you want to sell? Well, since WordPress is licensed under GPL, that means everything relying on WordPress is also covered. This is rocky ground to say the least, and you should consider how you license your theme carefully. It may also be good to know that the directory on `wordpress.org` only accepts themes compatible with the GPL license, which has sparked a mass conversion of premium themes to GPL.

Theme Checklists

When releasing a WordPress theme, and to some extent also when delivering one to a client or rolling out one of your own projects on a theme, there are some things that just have to be there. Naturally, the theme needs to work, that's the first thing, and that means you need at the very least the style.css file with the theme information at the top, as well as the index.php file, and whatever other template files you may want to use.

But that's not all. There are a bunch of other things, outlined in this section, that you should make sure are in your theme and have been properly considered. This checklist can help you avoid the unnecessary mistake of releasing a theme and then having to patch it right away.

Development Issues

- Does the theme validate?
- Is there a proper doctype in the header?
- Do you call `wp_head()` and `wp_footer()`? (Because you really should!)
- Is there a RSS feed link in the header declaration? Web browsers need that to see the feed and add that pretty little icon to the right of the URL.
- Have you gotten rid of everything from your local development environment? This can be anything from local image references, to things relating to your svn.
- Are you using JavaScript properly? Remember, a lot of themes are shipped with WordPress and there is even a `wp_enqueue_script()` function for this purpose, available at `codex.wordpress.org/Function_Reference/wp_enqueue_script`.

- Are the widget areas working as they should, and do they display default content? If they are, make sure it matters, otherwise they shouldn't output anything at all.

- Have you added Edit links to posts, Pages, and possibly even comments that display only when administrators are logged in? This is very handy so you should use it.

- Make sure the gravatars work properly.

- Remember to add CSS for threaded comments, even if you don't think you'll use it. It should support three, preferably five, comments in-depth at the very least.

- Is your theme ready for localization? Should it be?

- Are all the dates and times displaying properly? Try to not code this into the template files by passing parameters to `the_date()` and `the_time()`; it is a lot better than having the user controlling these things in the WordPress admin settings.

- Have you set the content width variable in functions.php? You really should; it helps a lot.

- If you have built-in support for plugins, make sure that the theme works even when the plugins aren't installed.

- Are your readme.txt and the theme information in style.css up-to-date? Do you fulfill whatever demands your license of choice puts on the theme?

- Have you done the basic tests to make sure that the correct posts are displayed in listings, posting comments works, and things like that? Don't forget the most basic stuff: you can break a lot of WordPress functionality with your theme, so test it from the ground up!

Things the User Will Notice

- Is there proper 404 error handling?

- Is there a search form, and is the search results page actually usable?

- Are all the archive templates in your theme, or have you considered them in any other way? Make sure that archives for categories, tags, author, dates, and so on work in the way you want.

- Do nested categories and Pages display correctly when used? If there are widget areas where they should not be used at all, have you made sure the user is aware of this?

- Have you styled the single post view properly?

- Have you styled the Page view properly?

- Make sure you're not using `the_excerpt()` anywhere you should be using `the_content()`.

- Do you have pagination working? Previous/later posts on post listing pages, and possibly previous/next post links on single posts.

- Does the author name display the way you want?

- Make sure attachments (images, videos, and so on) are displayed properly. You may need to make a template file for this if your design is limiting in any way.

- Do image galleries look good?

- When comments are turned off, what happens? Make sure that it looks good and displays a message the way you'd like it to.

Formatting

- Have you styled every element from the visual editor in WordPress admin to display properly? This includes block quotes, tables, and both ordered and unordered lists.
- Do block quotes, lists, and so on work within the comments?
- Are you styling comments and trackbacks differently? And do you highlight author comments?
- Have you put in special styling for sticky posts? Is special styling needed?
- Make sure headings 1 to 6 look good, even if you think that fewer is more than enough (which it is).
- Do images inserted from within WordPress display properly? This includes images floating to the left and right as well as centered images.
- Do image captions work?
- What happens if an image that is too wide gets published? Does it break the design?

Naturally, there is a ton of things that are directly related to your theme that you need to test out as well. Things like working menu links and readability will have to be put to the test too. The previous checklists are to help you avoid common WordPress-related mistakes with your theme. Add to the checklists anything that is related to your design and code, and you'll find they'll grow even more.

Commercial Themes and the GPL License

Commercial GPL themes, or premium themes as they are also called, cannot be submitted to wordpress.org at this time. However, if you're a theme reseller you can get featured on the commercial themes page, which currently is just a links page containing screenshots of some popular themes, but no hosting. In other words, that means that the commercial GPL'd theme you're selling won't work with automatic updates from within the WordPress admin interface, since wordpress.org won't let you host it there unless you let it be free for all to download. Naturally, if you do that hosting may be approved, and you can make money on providing support or customizations to the design, or whatever your theme business is all about.

This is a new addition to wordpress.org, and the debate on how commercial GPL themes should be managed, is more or less raging all the time. That's why you should probably take a look at what the situation is right now and, if you intend to profit from commercial GPL themes in any way, you should keep up-to-date. Read more at wordpress.org/extend/themes/commercial/.

Submitting to wordpress.org

If the theme checklist wasn't an obstacle, and your theme is licensed under a GPL compatible license, you can submit it to the wordpress.org theme directory. This is good for several reasons, the most prominent being the ability to reach WordPress users through the official channel, which incidentally now also resides within the admin interface. It also brings version control and hosting, as well as nice linkage with the wordpress.org support forums.

Your theme needs to be complete and saved in a single zip file. This should contain all the theme's template files, where style.css is extremely important. This is where the version is listed, along with the tags that are used to sort your theme. You also need to include a screenshot.png file, which has to be a screenshot of your theme in action, not a logo or similar. Other rules include `Gravatar.com` and widget support, exposed RSS feeds, showing the blog title and tagline, as well as listing both categories and tags by default.

Remember the Tags label in the top of style.css? That's where you define how your theme will be sorted on `wordpress.org`, should it be approved. Tags are separated by commas, like this (from the Notes Blog Core theme's style.css):

```
Tags: light, two-columns, right-sidebar, fixed-width, threaded-comments, sticky-post, translation-
   ready
```

That would obviously go in the top of the style.css file, along with the other things that define the theme. For clarity's sake, here's the full theme declaration top of the Notes Blog Core's style.css file. Notice the Tags line showing what the theme supports:

```
/*
Theme Name: Notes Blog Core Theme
Theme URI: http://notesblog.com/
Description: The Notes Blog Core theme is meant to work both as a framework to build child
   themes on, as well as a stand-alone clean theme for your perusal. <a href="http://tdhedengren.
   com/">Made by TDH</a> and maintained at <a href="http://notesblog.com/">notesblog.com</a>.
   Requires WordPress 2.8 or higher.
Version: 1.0.1
Tags: light, two-columns, right-sidebar, fixed-width, threaded-comments, sticky-post, translation-
   ready
Author: Thord Daniel Hedengren
Author URI: http://tdhedengren.com/

   Get support and services for the Notes Blog Core Theme:
   http://notesblog.com

   Created and managed by Thord Daniel Hedengren:
   http://tdhedengren.com

*/
```

Here are the tags currently used for sorting your theme on `wordpress.org` (a definitely up-to-date version is available at `wordpress.org/extend/themes/about/`):

Colors

- Black
- Blue
- Brown
- Green
- Orange

- Pink
- Purple
- Red
- Silver
- Tan
- White
- Yellow
- Dark
- Light

Columns

- One-column
- Two-columns
- Three-columns
- Four-columns
- Left-sidebar
- Right-sidebar

Width

- Fixed-width
- Flexible-width

Features

- Custom-colors
- Custom-header
- Theme-options
- Threaded-comments
- Sticky-post
- Microformats

Subject

- Holiday
- Photoblogging
- Seasonal

Those are the currently available tags used to sort your theme when submitting it to `wordpress.org`. You should take good care to make them as accurate as possible, because it is via these tags that people will find your theme in the `wordpress.org` theme directory, no matter if they're browsing it from the `wordpress.org` Web site or from within their WordPress install (under Appearance and then Add New Themes). Make the tags count is all I'm saying.

Submit your theme at `wordpress.org/extend/themes/upload/`.

Moving Onward with Themes

Now you know how the WordPress syntax is constructed (Chapter 2), how the loop works (Chapter 3), and also how a theme is built from the ground up. The Notes Blog Core theme is meant as a framework for you to build on, so you should definitely get acquainted with it. We'll be using it for our adaptations in Part 4 as well, proving that it is good to build upon.

At this point you may even have started to consider creating your own core theme, tuned to your needs. By all means go for it, and be sure to pick the best from the themes you like as well as altering the code to fit your needs. There is no reason for you not to start fiddling with themes now, although the following two chapters may open up some more doors for you.

Next up are child themes, a way for you to build upon a theme without actually altering it. Think about that, and the possibilities, for a while, or just turn the page and get on with it.

5

THE CHILD THEME CONCEPT

As a WordPress designer, one of the things you need to keep in mind is the addition of new features with new versions of WordPress, and in turn the deprecation of old ones. A theme created a few years ago will probably still work, but it will definitely be lacking some of the newer functionality of more modern themes. And the further question is, will it still work in another few years? The backwards compatibility in WordPress is pretty extensive, but there's a line to be drawn, of course.

Compatibility is one of the many reasons why you create core themes to build on, and why using child themes to extend them is such a great idea. In a way, the child theme concept is all about moving the individual styling for the sites you create another step from the code, since the child theme will consist mostly of visual enhancements and changes to the core theme. That means that the user can update the core theme without breaking anything.

This chapter is dedicated to the brilliance of child themes and how you can use them for your own gain and projects.

The Brilliance of Child Themes

Child themes are a fairly new concept that started blooming with WordPress 2.7, where the support for them was greatly improved. Basically, you create themes that rely on other themes as templates (mother themes, if you will), and that in turn means that you'll only have to change the things you dislike in the child theme (see Figure 5-1).

For example, say you love a particular theme, but dislike the fonts and colors. You may also think that it needs a few Page templates to meet your needs. There are two ways to tackle this problem. The most obvious is also the direct route: just open the theme's files and edit them to your heart's content. In this case, that would mean doing some changes in style.css (for the fonts and colors), and adding a couple of Page templates. No big deal, right?

Wrong. What happens when the theme author updates the theme with brand-new functionality, and you, giddy with joy, upload the new version and see all your edits go away? Obviously, your edits, with the colors you changed and your Page templates, aren't included in the original author's theme, so now you'll have to recreate all your adaptations so that the theme fits your needs again. You can of course keep notes of what you change, and back up your altered files, but the new version of the theme may have several changes and (re)applying your edits will be at best a bore, at worst tricky and time consuming.

Hacking a theme may be a simple solution, but if you want to be able to upgrade it with new versions with your edits intact, there is a better way. What you do is create child theme, using the original

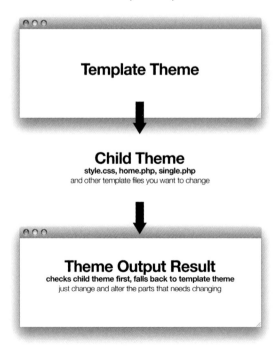

Figure 5-1: The child theme concept

theme as the mother theme (or template, as it is called when defining it). The child theme sits in its own folder, and so do all its associated files, so when you upload the new version of the original theme that you've built your site upon, you'll only overwrite that theme's files, and not your child theme, which contains all your changes. In other words, none of your edits will go away on updating the main theme. The whole idea is to separate the main theme functionality, code and content from your own edits and adaptations. And since those will reside in your child theme's area they are safe from the template theme's updates.

How Child Themes Work

Any theme can be the mother of a child theme. The only thing that is really important is that the theme is located in your wp-content/themes/ folder (because otherwise you can't use its files), and that the child theme is in its own folder, just like a regular theme. So if you want to use the Notes Blog Core theme as a mother template theme, you need to have it in the wp-content/themes/ folder, and then you can have your very own Small Notes child theme (or whatever you want to call it) in its own folder, also in wp-content/themes/.

If child themes are in wp-content/themes/ just like ordinary themes, then how do you use them and what do you need? Basically, all you need is a style.css file to tell WordPress that it is a theme, and in fact a child theme, as well as point to the mother theme. Whenever a template file is called for, WordPress will look for it within the child theme, and if it isn't there, it'll load up the one in the original mother template theme. The lingo may be a bit hard to follow, by the way, because the community really hasn't decided on what to call this relationship between themes yet.

All you need is a style.css:

```
/*
Theme Name: Your Theme Name
Theme URI: http://your-theme-homepage.com
Description: Oh what a lovely description of your theme you'll put here!
Author: Your Name
Author URI: http://your-website.com
Template: If this is a child theme, you'll set the template theme's folder name here, otherwise
    remove
Version: A version number
.
Any general information, license statements, plugin requirements, or any other information you
    may want to share.
.
*/
```

That's the basic style.css for just about any theme. Now, you'll need the Template part if you want the stylesheet to declare that it is a child theme, otherwise you'll just leave that out. So if you want to create that Small Notes child theme built on Notes Blog Core, you need to add the Template row.

However, you don't just write the mother template theme's name in the child theme's style.css header, you write the folder in which it resides. The default WordPress theme is located in wp-content/themes/default/ so if you wanted to use that as your template for your child theme, you'd write "default." Now, you wanted to use the Notes Blog Core theme, which is located in wp-content/themes/notesblog-core/, hence the folder you want to pass along in your child theme style.css is notesblog-core.

Or like this, filled out with dummy content to fit the hypothetical Small Notes child theme for Notes Blog Core:

```
/*
Theme Name: Small Notes
Theme URI: http://notesblog.com/core/small-notes/
Description: This is Small Notes, a child theme for Notes Blog Core.
Author: Thord Daniel Hedengren
Author URI: http://thedengren.com
Template: notesblog-core
Version: 1.0
.
You need to have both Child Notes and Notes Blog Core in your wp-content/themes/ folder for this
   theme to work.
.
*/
```

Remember, this is the child theme's style.css file. You can activate it just like a normal theme from the Appearance page in WordPress admin.

Now that you have your stylesheet for the Small Notes child theme, you can change those fonts and colors. First, you need to decide whether you want to completely replace the mother theme's style.css file (Notes Blog Core in this case), or build upon it. Most likely the latter is the case, so you need to import the stylesheet from Notes Blog Core. You can do that with the @import tag:

```
@import url("../notesblog-core/style.css");
```

Just add that below the style.css theme header information, and anything you want to alter below it. Change some colors and some fonts, just for the sake of things:

```
@import url("../notesblog-core/style.css");

div#content { font-family: Georgia, Times New Roman, serif; }
ul.sidebar ( color: #444; }
```

Nothing fancy there, but you will have the font-family starting with Georgia on everything in the div with id="content", and the color of type in the ul.sidebar tag will be dark grey. This will be read *after* everything in the stylesheet from Notes Blog Core is read; that's why you put the `@import` as high as possible in the style.css.

So the full style.css for the Small Notes child theme, just changing the things mentioned so far, would look like this:

```
/*
Theme Name: Small Notes
Theme URI: http://notesblog.com/core/small-notes/
Description: This is Small Notes, a child theme for Notes Blog Core.
Author: Thord Daniel Hedengren
Author URI: http://thedengren.com
Template: notesblog-core
Version: 1.0
.
You need to have both Child Notes and Notes Blog Core in your wp-content/themes/ folder for this
   theme to work.
.
*/

@import url("../notesblog-core/style.css");

div#content { font-family: Georgia, Times New Roman, serif; }
ul.sidebar ( color: #333; }
```

Remember the Page templates you wanted? Creating them is easier. Just create them like you would if you hacked the Notes Blog Core theme, and put them in the Small Notes child theme folder. Now they are available for use whenever the Small Notes child theme is activated, just like with a regular theme.

Every file in the child theme is ranked higher than its equivalent in the mother template theme. That means that even though there is a sidebar.php in Notes Blog Core, the mother theme, your sidebar.php from Small Notes will be loaded instead of it. And vice versa, if you don't want to do any changes to the sidebar.php file as compared to the mother template theme, then just don't add that file to the child theme.

The great part is that only changes go in your child theme, and that whenever the original template theme is updated, you can update your mother theme too, knowing that your changes are intact in the child theme. Better yet, your child theme will reap the benefits of the mother template theme update, while otherwise remaining untouched.

Event Child Themes

One of the cooler, albeit not as groundbreaking, usages of child themes is the possibility of short-term event themes. Think about it: if you have a theme that you're happy with, but suddenly want it full of snow and reindeers and such to celebrate that cold time of the year, then why not just create a child theme that swaps out the colors, background images, and even the graphics?

Or, to be blunt, say you want to make money by selling parts of your design to a company for promotion. Background images, slightly altered header files, that's all a breeze using child themes. Site-wide ads and roadblock-like functionality is easily implemented in this way.

Using child themes for minor events, promotions, and other custom hacks is a great way to keep the main theme clean of such things. Any good theme designer will be doing this in the future, and some are probably employing it already.

A Few Words on Theme Semantics

Child themes can certainly spin things around. Say that you love a particular theme, and it has a class called `column-right`, which is used to place the ever-present sidebar to the right side of the main content, in a suitable column. Fair enough. Problem is, you want it on the left side, which you can easily fix by just applying `float:left` in the style.css file of your child theme, possibly altering some other stuff as well, but you get the idea.

It works, but it is ugly to have an element named `column-right` positioned to the left.

This may seem a bit nerdy, even trivial, but writing code that makes sense is important when several people are collaborating on a project, and also good form in general. While you may not care much about the latter (which sometimes is more than warranted), the former can prove to be a real issue for the best of us. The whole point of naming elements in design after what they actually are supposed to be is that you, and the people you work with, will have an easier time finding your bearings in the design.

So `column-right` should really be on the right side. That's where you'll look for it, thanks to the name.

Another popular example of this is the sidebar. A lot of people think that the sidebar.php template, or at least the actual term "sidebar" should be retired. It is something of a relic from the past, from the time when WordPress was about blogging only. Today it is a CMS, and you use it for a lot more than just publishing blog posts. Why call it sidebar, why not sidecolumn? You can take the reasoning another step; what says that it will be on the side of things at all? Single column designs often position the sidebar.php content at full width below the main content, above the footer. There's nothing wrong with that, other than that the sidebar obviously isn't to the side.

Now, perhaps that's taking it a bit too far. WordPress will probably keep using the sidebar lingo for quite some time, but that doesn't mean that you need to name things `column-right`. It is something to think about when designing themes, because while a certain name may make a lot of sense in the present context, there's nothing to say that you won't be moving that `column-right` to the left side. And if someone were to take your theme as a mother template theme for a child theme, that is even more likely to happen.

So think about the semantics. It'll make things easier on everyone.

Also, if you're one of those people that think that this is a load of nonsense, or if you're on the other side of the fence, being very vocal about correct semantics, feel free to pick the Notes Blog Core theme to pieces. Personally, I think it is a fairly usable compromise, but it could be better in both ways. It just proves that these are hard things to agree upon.

The Flipside of Inheritance

You already know that every file in a child theme takes precedence over its mother template theme's counterpart. A child theme's style.css trumps the style.css of the mother theme, and so does the child theme's index.php compared to the mother theme's index.php, and so on.

The child theme inherits the contents of the template theme, but only if it needs it.

This brings up some issues, the most obvious probably being "what if they don't match, design-wise?" Well, the whole idea with child themes is to make customizations to themes you like. In other words, if you create a child theme based on a mother template theme that you end up changing altogether, with new template files for just about everything, one may wonder what the point is. After all, that is just like taking the original theme and making a new version of it, which may not bring us back to square one, but it certainly means that you're missing out on the smooth upgrading perks that child themes can claim.

A child theme is most warranted for when most of your changes go in style.css and possibly in functions.php. The former can alter the look and feel of the theme, while the latter can change the necessary functionality.

So what's the verdict, are child themes a good idea? In most cases, yes. Just don't end up creating a brand-new theme rather than making stand-alone changes to an existing one. If you do, you're better off creating what you need from scratch, or rather, from that core theme you may have ended up creating by now.

Common Issues to Observe

There really are just two things with child themes that can cause confusion. The first is purely user-based, and it is the fact that the child theme just won't work unless the mother template theme is in the wp-content/themes/ folder. This is pretty obvious when you think about it, but most users are used to just uploading a theme and then activating it, and that just won't work unless the template theme is there. Or, rather, it may work but it will definitely look awful and behave awfully too.

So the first issue to observe is the fact that the whole child theme concept, with one theme acting as the mother template and another just adding to/altering the functionality/design of said theme, may be hard to grasp.

The second issue with child themes is technical, and it involves the template path. Most of the time when you want to point to the theme directory, say to display an image, you'll use `bloginfo()`

and pass the `'template_directory'` parameter. That won't work in a child theme, because the template directory is in fact the mother template theme's directory! Hence this code, to display an image, would point to the mother theme's theme folder rather than the child theme's folder:

```
<img src="<?php bloginfo('template_directory'); ?>/images/the-image.gif" alt="My image" />
```

Luckily, there is a solution to this. By passing the parameter `'stylesheet_directory'` rather than `'template_directory'` in your child theme, WordPress will look in the folder with the theme's stylesheet instead. And guess what? That's your child theme! So the code above would have to be altered to this to work in a child theme:

```
<img src="<?php bloginfo('stylesheet_directory'); ?>/images/the-image.gif" alt="My image" />
```

This is a common issue, with images suddenly not working or perhaps the wrong one being displayed because of it existing in the mother template theme as well.

Managing Several Sites Using Child Themes

If you're one of those people running your very own blog network, or just a series of sites built on the same basic design, then child themes are just right for you. Think about it: you can put more resources into creating features and deploying new functionality in the mother template theme, and store all the custom stuff for the various sites in child themes. That way, you'll speed up development and make upgrades easier.

First of all, what you have got to do is find the common elements in your design. Granted, since most people don't launch a series of sites built on the same basic look, but rather pilfer themes and designs left and right, it may even be a better idea to start from scratch and create a basic design to build upon and customize. There are several big-name blog networks that employ this method today, so look around.

Second, after finding all the common elements your sites will need, you should wireframe the main mother theme design. Make room for everything, think about what may go where, and things like that.

Third, create the mother theme. This should be as simple and stripped down as possible, only containing the things that all your sites will use. After all, there is no point in including code or graphics that you'll just replace. If an element isn't a general one that goes across the board, ignore it and define it in the child themes instead when needed. A common mistake is to style the mother template theme too much because it just looks bland and boring otherwise. Don't do that; you'll just end up over-riding your own code in the child theme's template files, and that is code that has already been read once. Why make your themes slower to load, after all?

After these three steps, things get a bit more fluid. Start creating child themes that fit the various sites in your network and roll them out. When your network is built completely on child themes, and you want to add a feature, you only have to do this to the main mother template theme. Upgrade it across the network, and suddenly all the sites will have this new feature. Compare that to having to actually implement it in every theme, which is at best a tedious copy-and-paste exercise, and you'll understand that there is time and potentially money to be saved here.

Don't Forget about functions.php

It is not just on the design front where you can benefit from using one main mother template theme and any number of child themes across your network: pure functionality can gain from this too. Remember, you can have your very own functions.php file for every theme, both the main one and the child themes, which means that you can, if you're PHP-savvy, create plugin-like functionality on the theme side of things.

Another of the things people running multiple sites need to tackle is the maintenance of plugins. Granted, this is a lot easier these days, with upgrade functionality from within the WordPress admin interface, but some of the things you use plugins for can in fact be done just as well from within your themes. And while you can have those cool things in your theme's template files, whether it is a mother or child theme, it just isn't all that convenient. Besides, the whole idea with themes in the first place is to separate design from code, so filling the template files with more PHP snippets than usual kind of works against that purpose.

This is where functions.php may be an acceptable middle ground. After all, it is a template file outside of the design part of the theme, existing purely to add extra functionality through PHP coding. So maybe it is a better idea to write general functions in the functions.php file of the main mother template theme rather than maintaining plugins that do the same thing across all sites?

It is a thought worth considering to further ease the maintenance of several sites within a network.

What about Theme Frameworks?

There's been a lot of recent buzz regarding theme frameworks within the WordPress community. You may wonder how child themes fit with that notion, and the answer is, of course, perfectly well. Most so-called theme frameworks are semi-blank themes that are designed for you to modify, using either child themes or similar concepts. Some want you to put custom code in folders within the theme, for example, so it pretty much depends on how the theme designer envisions the usage of the creation.

However, that doesn't mean that you're limited to doing it the way the designer intended. Any theme is really a theme framework, and any theme can be used as the mother template theme for a child theme. In other words, just because a particular theme framework author thinks that you should do things in a particular way, that doesn't mean you have to. You can always just use the theme as the template theme, and then create your own child theme.

Some of the functionality in these themes designed to be used as frameworks for your own creations rely on *action hooks*. This is basically a way for the theme to pass implementation and data to the theme using functions.php. Then, your child theme (or pseudo-functions file within the theme framework if that's the solution of choice) can do things with these action hooks, including removing them should they not be wanted. We'll get to action hooks in the next chapter.

So any theme is a theme framework, and the themes that try to pass themselves off as theme frameworks are basically just creations more suited for being used as the basis for new designs. That is worth keeping in mind, I think.

Taking Themes to the Next Level

Understanding child themes is the first step in taking WordPress theme development to the next level, or at least bringing it up to a wider scale. You don't have to use child themes, obviously, but as a designer and developer it is a great concept to play with. After all, just the fact that you can put all your core functionality in one theme, everything you usually put into themes anyway, and then lean on that one theme by using a child theme that builds on it, certainly is food for thought.

Whether or not you want to use child themes in your projects is a matter of personal preference. I'm a firm believer in saving time and making updating easier, so I think child themes are a great idea in most cases, albeit not all. For example, a very traffic-heavy blog would want to cut down on everything that adds bandwidth, and in such a case you should consider as tight a theme as possible. Every project has its own requirements that you need to take into account.

And with that we'll move on to more advanced things that you can do with themes to make them even cooler and more adaptive to the goals you set.

6 ADVANCED THEME USAGE

To step further from traditional WordPress sites, which build upon the platform's blog basics, you need to be aware of some of the more advanced features that are available to the theme developer. Most of them build upon the template tags and conditional dittos that you have been using thus far, but the usage may differ. Some techniques, however, will change or add to the functionality of WordPress from within your theme, which may not always be such a good idea if you're looking to release it for general use, but may be a good fit for the project you're working on right now.

That's what it all boils down to, really: taking WordPress and putting it to good use for the task at hand. Building a WordPress theme and releasing or even selling it is one thing, but building a fully-fledged WordPress-powered site is something completely different. This chapter is all about taking that extra step and putting WordPress to good use.

Outlining the Theme

The first things you should do when you're starting a new WordPress project is consider what functionality you need from the theme. Simple blog designs usually aren't very complicated—you just start from the top and go from there—but if you want to build a newspaper-like site using WordPress there are more things to consider. One of the most obvious ones is how you make the site look customized, because, although we all love WordPress, one of the reasons for developing your own themes is to make your site look the way you want, otherwise everyone would just build everything on the default theme and be happy with it.

Before actually starting to design and code a site, you need to figure out some basic things, outlined in the following list. When you have, you can start mocking up, doing paper sketches, playing around with code snippets, and whatever else is in your workflow when creating fabulous Web sites.

- **The main Web site layout.** What sections, pages, and major elements are there to make room for, and how will you populate these with content from WordPress? This usually involves multiple loops and what template files are needed where.
- **Sorting the content.** This is usually all about what categories to choose, and which parts of the site are static enough to be Pages. Also, will there be a need for public tagging? If not, you can use that to do custom stuff.
- **The small stuff.** Will you need living elements in this site, where you can drop poll widgets and special promotions? These areas should probably be widgetized.
- **Commenting.** Most, but not all, modern Web sites with editorial content have commenting functionality these days, so you need to decide if it is the right way to go for this project.
- **Special functionality.** Is there anything you need that WordPress can't do out of the box? If there is, you need to figure out if there is a plugin that can help (or develop your own), or perhaps even find an external service to integrate into the site.

Knowing what you want to pull off is essential to outlining the perfect theme for the job. This is very important if you're doing advanced stuff, though not so much when it is a more straightforward production. Either way, the more you know about what you want and need to accomplish, the better.

My Three Steps

I've been developing WordPress sites on a professional basis since version 1.5, and I've been a user since before that. My sites range from simple blogs to magazines to things entirely different. Later in this book we'll create completely different things using WordPress, showing that it can be a framework as much as it is a CMS, but for now all you need to know is that I'm constantly trying to push it to do new things.

When I start up a new project, I always consider what it needs and how I can accomplish meeting those needs. This usually involves presenting various types of content in different ways. These next three sections outline my top three tips for doing this, which may not be universal and most likely won't fit everyone or even every project, but is as good a start as any.

Style by Category, Sort by Tag

Categories are great for rough sorting, like a category for Music and another for Books, but they should never be too niche. Tags, on the other hand, can be as precise as needed, which means that a book review may belong to the category Books, and have the author as a tag, along with the genre, the book title, and so on. The purpose of this isn't just nomenclature, there's also technical gains to the decision. First of all, it is easy to create custom looks for category listings using the category.php and even category-X.php (X is the ID) template files. These can let you list one kind of content in one way, and the other in another.

Tags, on the other hand, are niched in themselves and should be viewed partly as search keywords that get grouped together, and partly as descriptions of the content. They can be useful as both, especially when you want to collect all those J. K. Rowling book reviews without having to force a traditional (and not so exact) search. By carefully considering how you set up categories and tags, and how they relate to each other, you can achieve a great deal.

Carefully Consider Custom Fields

Custom fields are very useful. They can store data as well as images, and they can fill in the blanks when you need more than just a title, a slug, the content, and an excerpt, or when you want to side-step the categories and tags. That's great. They are not, however, very user-friendly as I've already argued, and that means you need to be wary. A lot of funky WordPress-powered sites need to rely heavily on custom fields, but if they do you need to educate the people running them. A plugin, which can do the same thing but just not show it, may in fact be a better idea.

Build with Pages

Pages have a great strength in that you can have just about as many as you want, and each and every one of them can have its own Page template if you like. That means that anything you can do with WordPress can be accessible at the address of your choosing. Hence, most of my Page templates don't include the actual Page's content or the traditional WordPress loop. Rather, they do other things, and while they may be a bit rough to manage by themselves—you have to hack the template file since there's nothing more than a title and a slug in WordPress admin—they can step outside the box.

Think about it. Say you need to show off your work stored at another service. You can include it by using the service's own JavaScript widget code, and you can even have it exist in itself that way; all functionality is included. Unfortunately, WordPress wouldn't let that code through. The solution is to just create a Page template and put the code there. The same goes for Google Custom Search Engine result listings, for showing off RSS feed content or your lifestream.

The Page template is a powerful tool. Use it wisely.

Individual Styling Techniques

Adding some individual styling can make both posts and Pages more interesting. At first glance this may seem hard, especially when it comes to posts since they are all governed by one single template file: single.php. Luckily, there are great methods to add a little extra flair to the posts, thanks to the excellent addition of the `post_class()` template tag, and some nifty little CSS.

But first, you need to understand the more obvious individual styling technique. I'm talking about Pages, which can be easily styled to act in any way you like, since all you really need to do is create a Page template that behaves in the way you want. You can take it even further than is possible with blog posts by loading different sidebars, headers, footers, or whatever you want, really. The strength of the Page template is that it can be set up any way you want, and all you need to do is create it and choose it for your Page.

The same applies to category and tag listings. If you want a header graphic for a specific category, for example, all you need to do is alter that particular category's template file. You may remember that category-X.php takes precedence over category.php (which in turn beats first archive.php and then index.php), and that X is the category ID. So category-37.php would be the template file whenever a listing of posts in the category with ID 37 is called for. And hence you can just edit the category-37.php template file to reflect how you want that listing to look.

In short, it is easy enough to add a little extra styling to the parts of your site where there are template files to control that style. You should consult Chapter 4 for more information on which template file is loaded when, and take that information into account when shaping up your site.

Styling the Posts

Styling the individual posts may be a bit trickier, however. They are all governed by single.php, which means that you need other means of making them stand out when needed.

Enter the `post_ID` and `post_class()` template tags, which go in your `div.post` container, like this (code snippet from Notes Blog Core, as so many times before):

```
<div id="post-<?php the_ID(); ?>" <?php post_class(); ?>>
<!- The post output stuff goes here ->
</div>
```

You'll find this (or something similar, at least) in most WordPress themes. The `the_ID()` template tag obviously returns the post ID, giving the `div` container the ID of post-X, where X is the returned ID. That means that this is a way to catch a specific post and make it behave the way you want. ID 674 would hence give you a `div` with `id="post-674"` to play with. Style it any way you like.

Most of the time, however, you don't want to style individual posts per se, but rather posts belonging to a certain category. You can check for this using a conditional tag and a short PHP snippet, of course, but `post_class()` already has you covered. The template tag returns a line of classes for you to style any way you want, depending on where the post belongs, and so on.

First of all, you'll get the post ID as a class as well, so your post with `id="post-674"` will also have the class `post-674`, actually. You'll also get every category that the post belongs to, with `category-` in front of the category slug. So a category called *Website news*, which usually gets the slug website-news, would return the class `category-website-news` from `post_class()`. The same goes for tags: if you tag something with "funny" you'll get that returned as the class `tag-funny`.

You'll also get the classes `post` and `hentry`, the former making sure that `post_class()` is compatible with older WordPress themes, which usually describe the `div` containers for posts with the post class. In fact, that usage is still there too.

So what good does this do? First, you can change the category styling, which is probably the most common usage for these things. Say you've got a news category called News, with the slug news; hence you'd get `class="category-news"` from `post_class()` whenever it was used. And say you want the links in this category to be green, and why not put a green border line to the left side as well, to really make it obvious? This can be easily achieved:

```
div.category-news { padding-left: 20px; border: 5px solid green; border-width: 0 0 0 5px; }
div.category-news a { color: green; }
```

Now every post belonging to the News category would get green links and a green border line to the left. This is great, since categories can be used to control design elements, and tags in turn should be used to further sort the posts. For example, you may have a tag for My Fave, a feature you're running. Every post that is one of my faves will get a My Fave graphic in the top right; not clickable or anything, just a marker so that people know it is one of my favorites:

```
div.tag-my-fave { background: url(myfave.gif) top right no-repeat; }
```

This would output a background image, myfave.gif, in the top right corner (and not repeat it) every time `post_class()` returns the tag with the slug `my-fave`. Naturally, it is no lucky coincidence that that is the actual slug for my My Fave tag, now is it?

Finally, you can pass a specific class to `post_class()`, which may be useful at times. Maybe you want to add the class single to single posts? If so, you'd just edit your `post_class()` code in the single.php template to this:

```
<div id="post-<?php the_ID(); ?>" <?php post_class('single'); ?>>
```

As you can see, adding a class to `post_class()` is as easy as adding a parameter. A similar solution is used when you need to retain post-specific styling through `post_class()`, but it acts outside the loop. Then, you need to tell `post_class()` to return the ID, which is done by altering the code to this:

```
<?php post_class('',$post_id); ?>
```

As you can see, `post_ID()` can let you add pinpointed style to one particular post, but `post_class()` is more useful because it lets you style sets of posts, and also that one post should you need to. In fact, one can question if the `post_ID()` part is still needed, but as long as it is in the default theme it obviously is, and it may be useful in the future.

Body Class Styling

Another way to apply some styling to various parts of a WordPress site is the `body_class()` template tag, introduced in version 2.8. Basically, it is to the body tag what `post_class()` is to the blog post div container. This is how you use it:

```
<body <?php body_class(); ?>>
```

Depending on where you are on the site, the body tag will get different classes. Say you're reading a post with the ID 245, and you're logged in. That would return this body tag:

```
<body class="single postid-245 logged-in">
```

A category listing would return other classes, and a tag listing another set again. The various different types of pages in WordPress will all return more or less different classes for your body tag.

Why is this good for you? Say you want a different size for your h2 headings depending on whether they are loaded in a listing, or in a single post. You can define this by adding classes to the various template files, or you can do it in CSS with the classes output by `body_class()`.

First of all, you need to find out what classes are returned and when. See the class listing later in this chapter for a detailed in-depth description of that, but for now it is enough to know that the class single is passed to the body tag when viewing a single post, and archive is passed universally for all listings pages (much like the template tag archive.php, which is called for both category and tag listings should category.php and tag.php not be present in the theme). That means you'll work with them. This is the code you may want to put in your stylesheet:

```
body.single h2 { font-size: 48px; }
body.archive h2 { font-size: 36px; }
```

Obviously it would mean that whenever `body_class()` returned the `single` class, which is in single post view, you'd get 48-pixel h2 headings, whereas whenever `body_class()` returned `class="archive"` you'd get 36-pixel h2 headings.

This can be taken a long way, actually, since the addition of body classes depending on whereabouts on a site you are is placed so high up in the hierarchy. Most themes designed prior to the addition of the `body_class()` template tag won't be able to truly put this to good use, but if you reconsider your CSS code you'll see that you can control more of your design from the classes passed to body, rather than by adding classes to every element in the template files.

The following classes are available (and are listed in order of importance), depending on where you are on the site. Most likely you don't have to style them all.

- `rtl`
- `home`
- `blog`
- `archive`
- `date`
- `search`
- `paged`
- `attachment`
- `error404`
- `single postid-X` (where X is the post ID)
- `attachmentid-X` (where X is the attachment ID)
- `attachment-MIME` (where MIME is the MIME type)
- `author`
- `author-USER` (where USER is the author's nicename)
- `category`
- `category-X` (where X is the category slug)
- `tag`
- `tag-X` (where X is the tag slug)
- `page-parent`
- `page-child parent-pageid-X` (where X is the Page ID)
- `page-template page-template-FILE` (where FILE is the template file name)
- `search-results`
- `search-no-results`
- `logged-in`
- `paged-X` (where X is the page number, refers to listings)
- `single-paged-X` (where X is the page number, refers to listings)
- `page-paged-X` (where X is the page number, refers to listings)

- `category-paged-X` (where X is the page number, refers to listings)
- `tag-paged-X` (where X is the page number, refers to listings)
- `date-paged-X` (where X is the page number, refers to listings)
- `author-paged-X` (where X is the page number, refers to listings)
- `search-paged-X` (where X is the page number, refers to listings)

Utilizing the classes output by `body_class()` is a great way to add more precise visual control to the various sections of a site. A lot of template files in older themes have become redundant because of minor visual tuning now being easily managed by the classes output by `body_class()`. That's a lot better than resorting to template file specific classes.

Sticky Posts

When sticky post functionality was introduced in WordPress 2.7, you needed to add the `sticky_class()` template tag to your post `div` containers. That added the class `'sticky'`, which could then be styled accordingly. Thing is, you don't need it anymore thanks to `post_class()`, which among all the things mentioned previously also applies the `'sticky'` class to posts that are marked as sticky from within WordPress admin.

Making the sticky posts stand out a bit is easy enough; just add something to div.sticky in your stylesheet. This is from Notes Blog Core:

```
div.sticky { padding: 20px 20px 8px 20px; background: #f8f8f8; border: 1px solid #e8e8e8;
  border-width: 1px 0; }
```

Nothing weird or fancy there, as you can see. The only thing you need to keep in mind when it comes to sticky posts is that you don't know how many of them will be used. If there are two sticky posts, the most recent one will end up on top, and then the next newest one below. That means that several sticky posts need to look good when placed together.

So what, then, can those sticky posts be good for? Well, the most obvious thing would of course be a traditional bloggish site, nailing the larger, important posts at the top using the sticky feature, and un-stickying them whenever there's something new to lift to the top. Something of a limited headline area, so to speak.

Another obvious usage would be announcements. If you're selling e-books, for example, you can stick the "Please buy my e-book for $9 so that I can pay the rent" post up on top (see Figure 6-1). More traditional announcements, like new site launches or a call to action for an important cause would also work well.

Finally, you can take it another step further by using the `is_sticky()` conditional tag. Naturally, you can query WordPress (using a loop, and `query_posts()` to get the desired effect) for your sticky posts and manage them separately. An idea would be to have a headline area outside the normal loop, and just include a set number of sticky posts in it, excluding everything else. In fact, you can use sticky posts to manage a full headline, but the same effect can be achieved with both custom fields and a specific tag, and since the sticky post checkbox is more or less hidden away, that may be a better call.

Figure 6-1: When this book comes out you may see this on notesblog.com

Want to insert content in other places in your design, without actually hacking the theme's template files? You can also hook things on to WordPress using what are called action hooks, and they're covered next.

Mastering Action Hooks

Action hooks are all the craze these days, just like theme frameworks. Actually, they are probably so hot because of the theme frameworks, because they are littered with these babies. But I get ahead of myself. First you need to understand what an action hook is.

Your theme, even if you've created your own in the past, is most definitely already using action hooks. The familiar `wp_head` and `wp_footer` calls in the header.php and footer.php template files are action hooks. They are there so developers can hook in and add stuff to the beginning of

WordPress, or after it has finished loading. Plugin developers use these all the time, and I'd imagine that any of the Web statistics plugins utilizing Google Analytics, pMetrics, Woopra, or whatever hook on to the `wp_footer` action hook and add their tracking code at the very end. That makes sense, since that particular tracking code usually should go just before the closing of the body tag, and that in turn is exactly where `wp_footer` should be if the theme is properly designed.

You can add your own hooks as well, which is the primary way theme framework designers use them. They basically add a number of hooks to various parts of the theme, and then let the user or child theme developer alter the looks by hooking onto them. This can be anything from populating a menu or advert spot with proper coding, to actually removing elements from the design. In a sense, it is a good way to make a very complete design, and then let the users decide which parts of it should be used. Add an admin options page that does this for you, and you don't have to worry about hacking functions.php as a user, as naturally that's where all the action is.

I tend to lean the other way, though. While it may be tempting to just add everything imaginable and then have the users check or uncheck boxes to decide what should be displayed, I find it is bloating the theme. In my opinion, a good framework is something to build on, not to cut away from. It is not a tree waiting to be made into a chair, it is a chair being used to reach the top shelf. Or something like that.

Either way, with action hooks you can add functionality, either by adding your own (we'll get to that in a little bit), or by freeloading the WordPress ones. There are a lot of piggyback possibilities within WordPress, way too many to list here, so I'll just point you to the (hopefully up-to-date) Action Reference page in the WordPress Codex: `codex.wordpress.org/Plugin_API/Action_Reference`.

Hooking On

If you want to hook onto one of WordPress's action hooks, say by adding some Web statistics code to the `wp_footer` hook, you do it in functions.php. What you need to do is write a PHP function containing the stuff you want to add, and then you add it to the hook.

Let's start with the function. The analytics code is just nonsense, so if you want to use this particular hook you should, of course, swap the code for your own. After all, even if I did put mine in it would just mess up things, now wouldn't it?

```php
<?php
function my_webstats()
{ ?>
    <script for your web statistics tracker />
<?php } ?>
```

This gives you the `my_webstats()` function to use, loaded with the (obviously faulty) script tag. This is what you want to hook onto `wp_footer`. Notice how I cut the PHP tag to make it easier to manage the HTML. You do that by using the `add_action` function, and it should go before the actual function:

```
add_action('wp_footer', 'my_webstats');
```

You're telling `add_action` that you want to add to `wp_footer` (first parameter), and then you tell it to add the function `my_webstats`, which you define below. The full code would be like this, in your functions.php file:

```php
<?php
    add_action('wp_footer', 'my_webstats');
    function my_webstats()
{ ?>
    <script code for your web statistics tracker />
<?php } ?>
```

That would add the script at the end of your theme when loaded. Some excellent WordPress hookery right there.

Creating Your Own Action Hooks

Creating your own action hooks is easy. First, you just create your PHP function like you did before. It can be anything, really: a simple echo, or something way more advanced. The only difference between creating and using your own action hooks, compared to the built-in ones, is that you need to add them to your theme. Remember, `wp_head` and `wp_footer` already sit there, so no need to add them, but your brand-new action hook won't be so lucky.

The code for adding action hooks is simple:

```php
<?php do_action('the-name-of-the-function'); ?>
```

Just put in your function's name (which would be `my_webstats` if you wanted to use the one from the previous example), and put the code wherever you want it in your theme. If your function is named `'welcome_text'`, that means you'll put this wherever you want to output the contents of the `welcome_text` function:

```php
<?php do_action('welcome_text'); ?>
```

No need to use the `add_action()` function since you have the `do_action()` snippet in the theme telling WordPress to run the function for you. It's as simple as that: a custom action hook is created. Naturally, you now need to hook onto it so it actually displays something. In the previous example, an options page within the WordPress admin interface where you can save your welcome text would be prudent. Then you'd just hook on to the `'welcome_text'` hook like you normally would.

The next section moves on to taxonomies, which let you play even more with how things are sorted and listed using additional tag structures for more precise control.

Using Taxonomies

Taxonomies are really cool, and as of WordPress 2.8 they are getting pretty useful, too. Basically, what they do is let you create your very own versions of categories or tags. That means you can have several different sets of tags, for example (see Figure 6-2).

What you do is add more ways to categorize and tag your posts. You could say that the default categories and tags are both taxonomies that are there by default, so you have one taxonomy called Categories and one called Tags to start with. Now you may want more, say a separate way of tagging posts, called Topics, and then you'd add that, which would give you two tagging taxonomies that can each take their own set of tags, independently of each other. And finally, you may want a third one called Frequently Asked Questions, which would leave you with three tagging boxes: the default one and the two new ones.

Naturally, there is a template file for taxonomies, called taxonomy.php. Create it and treat it like any other archive, which means that it needs the loop of course, and it will be used for post listings generated by a click on a taxonomy link. You cannot, however, create a taxonomy-X.php template file for a specific taxonomy tag, like you can with tag.php or categories.php. So if you want some

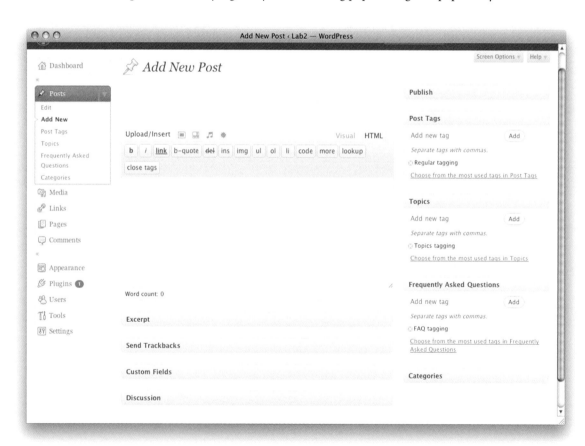

Figure 6-2: Multiple tag taxonomies

special treatment for a particular custom taxonomy tag, you need to write a PHP snippet to check for it, and then output according to the result.

An example is the best way to describe how this works. Say you want to create a site about videogames, focusing on Xbox 360, PlayStation 3, and Wii. You'll have news, reviews, and previews, which will be your categories. This lets people view the latest news without worrying about the platform. There are a lot of things you can take into account here, but this example will focus on what most gamers are most interested in: the games themselves.

TRY IT OUT The Videogame Site

Games can be more or less the same across platforms, but sometimes they are not. In fact, some games are only available on a specific platform, like the Super Mario games from Nintendo only being released on the Nintendo platform (which is the Wii in this example). This means that you may want to make something of a games database in tag form, but since the same game can be available for several platforms and you want to be able to tell them apart, you can't use regular tagging.

1. Start by creating a tagging feature for each of the video game platforms: one for Xbox 360, one for PlayStation 3, and one for Wii, using taxonomies. That way, you can tag on a per-platform basis, which also means that you can output individual tag clouds. And, since tags are the way tags are, it means that The Super Game can be a tag for both PlayStation 3 and Wii, without them being mixed up. (See Figure 6-3.)

125

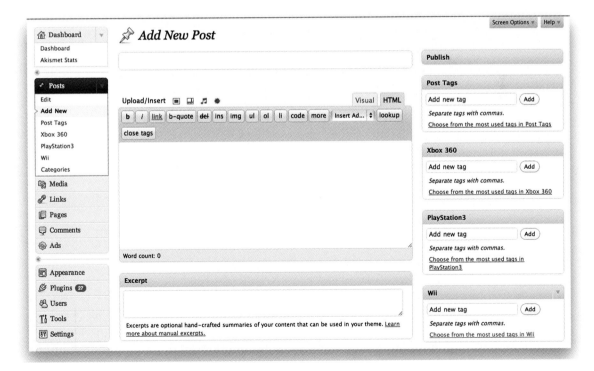

Figure 6-3: The taxonomies in action on the Write Post page in WordPress admin

You create your own taxonomies using functions.php, within the necessary PHP starting and closing tags as usual:

```
add_action( 'init', 'videogames', 0 );
function videogames() {
    register_taxonomy( 'xbox360', 'post', array( 'hierarchical' => false, 'label' => 'Xbox 360', 'query_var' => true, 'rewrite' => true ) );
    register_taxonomy( 'playstation3', 'post', array( 'hierarchical' => false, 'label' => 'PlaySta-tion 3', 'query_var' => true, 'rewrite' => true ) );
    register_taxonomy( 'wii', 'post', array( 'hierarchical' => false, 'label' => 'Wii', 'query_var' => true, 'rewrite' => true ) );
}
```

The first thing that happens is a simple action, added to the initialization and done so at first (the zero). It's called `'videogames'` here, but it could just as well have been `'new_taxonomies'` or something else.

Then you need to create the `'videogames'` function and register your new taxonomies. Take a closer look at the first one, for Xbox 360:

```
register_taxonomy( 'xbox360', 'post', array( 'hierarchical' => false, 'label' => 'Xbox 360', 'query_var' => true, 'rewrite' => true ) );
```

I'm sure you can figure out what `register_taxonomy()` does, so you'll move straight to the actual parameters. First, you've got `'xbox360'`, which is the name of the taxonomy (for internal purposes). Second, you've got `'post'`, which tells `register_taxonomy()` what kind of content this particular taxonomy is for. For now, only posts work (hence `'post'`), but later on WordPress will most likely support Pages and possibly links as well.

After that comes an array, which first needs to be passed a value for hierarchical. In this case, it is set to `'false'`, which means that the taxonomy will behave like tags. If you set it to `'true'` it would in fact be hierarchical, and thus would work like categories instead. However, in the current version of WordPress (2.8) the hierarchical listing doesn't work, so hopefully it will be added by the time you're reading this.

Moving on within the array, you set the label, which is the way the taxonomy will be presented within WordPress admin, to `'Xbox 360'`, which just looks a lot better than the taxonomy name `'xbox360'`. After that follows `'query_var'`, which is set to `'true'` here and hence will return the taxonomy name (`'xbox360'`, remember?) as the query variable for use with tags like `wp_tag_cloud()`, but you can set any text string here. Maybe you want it to be just `'360'`, in which case it would be presented exactly like that, as a parameter within single quotes, and not as `'true'` passed right now.

Finally, you've got `'rewrite'`, which tells WordPress whether to try and make a pretty permalink out of the taxonomy URLs or not. In other words, if you've got a The Super Game tag in the Xbox 360 taxonomy, it can either be the default `domain.com/?xbox360=the-super-game`, or it can be a pretty `domain.com/xbox360/the-super-game`. In other words, you probably want to have `'rewrite'` set to `'true'` because using permalinks is a good idea.

2. Right, that's basically it. Now, assuming you've tagged your posts with these new taxonomies, which will show up as boxes along with the default tag box, you can start using these new taxonomies. For single posts, you'll want to use `get_the_term_list()`, which will return a list of tags, linked and all, just like the `the_tags()` template tag would do. It is, however, a bit trickier to use:

```php
<?php echo get_the_term_list( $post->ID, 'xbox360', 'Xbox 360 games: ', ', ', " " ); ?>
```

As you can see you need to echo it. The first part in the `get_the_term_list()` function is passing the actual post you're on, so that you have something to start from, and then you pass the taxonomy to be used (the `'xbox360'` one), then you've got the actual printed text before the list, which is `'Xbox 360 games: '` which is what you were going to use these custom taxonomies for in the first place, remember? You'll recognize the setup: first you've got what goes before the list (again, the `'Xbox 360 games: '` text), then the separator, which is a comma and a space, and then what goes after, which is nothing at all passed.

You may say that `the_tags()` and echoing `get_the_term_list()` in the way shown above are the same thing. If the default tagging feature were named `'tags'`, you could put it in instead of `'xbox360'` and get the same result.

You can also use `the_terms()` to do this, but then the tags belonging to the taxonomy won't be linked.

3. Now spice up your site by outputting a tag cloud (Figure 6-4) for the **'xbox360'** taxonomy, displaying 25 tags (meaning 25 games in this example). To do this you would use **wp_tag_cloud()**:

```php
<?php wp_tag_cloud( array( 'taxonomy' => 'xbox360', 'number' => 25 ) ); ?>
```

You need to put things in an array to properly pass all the data to the `'taxonomy'` parameter, which along with `'echo'` are new additions for `wp_tag_cloud()` as of WordPress 2.8. Here, you're passing `'xbox360'` which is the name of the taxonomy in question, and then the number of tags to be shown.

127

The Xbox 360 Cloud ↓

Banjo & Kazooie **Bioshock Blue Dragon** Crackdown Eternal Sonata Fifa 08 Fifa 09 **Final Fantasy XI** Final Fantasy XII Gears of War **Gears of War 2** Guitar Hero 5 Guitar Hero II Guitar Hero III Guitar Hero World Tour Halo 3 **Halo 3 ODST NHL 10** Pro **Evolution Soccer 7** Project Sylpheed Pure **Rock Band Rock Band 2 Virtua Tennis 3**

Figure 6-4: A simple tag cloud Output from the Xbox 360 taxonomy using **wp_tag_cloud()**

4. Finally, you may want to put the taxonomy to good use in a loop. This is somewhat similar to `wp_tag_cloud()`, but you'll use `query_posts()` instead.

```php
<?php query_posts( array( 'xbox360' => 'the-super-game', 'showposts' => 25 ) ); ?>
```

Here you're querying for posts tagged with `'the-super-game'` in the `'xbox360'` taxonomy, and you'll display 25 of them.

That's it, now you've got an additional tag taxonomy that you'll use to input the game titles. This way you can get nice game archives without cluttering the regular tags with this content. As well as that, it also means that you can build more specific solutions for the tag taxonomy, which in the preceding example would mean that you show information about each game (for example, the taxonomy tag) in a way that differs from how your regular tags behave when someone clicks on them. It goes without saying that being able to add new taxonomies, essentially new separate sets of tags, can come in handy. Sites looking to work with data in almost database style can definitely put it to good use, as shown in the previous example, but it can also be a different way to tackle the sorting of content. In particular, the addition of more taxonomies can make it possible to further push the categories to a design-driven feature within the site. After all, tagging offers so much more focused control where it matters, and you get that when you add your own taxonomies as well. You can have a taxonomy for design tagging only, for example. The tags in this taxonomy would only be used by the theme, by adding classes to the post div or perhaps the body tag. There's no default support for this, but it can be used nonetheless by adding it to the theme using a few snippets of code.

You can also imagine some taxonomies overlapping with custom fields, since some usage of this feature is all about sorting posts. Taxonomies are better suited for this by nature. It is, however, when larger amounts of content need to be controlled that taxonomies reach their full potential. Taxonomies are, after all, a sorting feature and that means they work best when there is actually something to sort.

At first it can be a bit daunting to wrap your mind around the possibilities that custom taxonomies offer. This freedom can be put to good use, and with the ease of adding new taxonomies that comes with WordPress 2.8, I'm sure there will be several WordPress-powered sites putting taxonomies to useful work soon. You, as an end user, may not see it, but the developer may not have to write a bunch of plugins or strain the not so user-friendly custom fields to achieve the content sorting and presentation needed. So don't forget about taxonomies just because the documentation on them is limited and it isn't a function that is widely used yet; it is still a feature to be considered.

Sometimes you just need one place to provide the necessary data to make the site behave like you want it to. This data can obviously be coded into the theme's template files, but a popular alternative to having to hack the templates is to have an options page instead.

Theme Option Pages

A theme option page is a page in the WordPress admin interface containing information or options for your theme. You add it by adding code to your theme's functions.php file, and actually build the whole thing from there. Theme option pages have been around for quite some time, and the default WordPress theme uses the technique to offer color customizations to the rounded header, along with other things.

What you want your theme options page to do, if you feel you need one, depends on the kind of theme you've built. Some themes let the user alter the design by changing default font sizes and things like that, while others let you save custom code that will be output somewhere in the theme through action hooks. Either way, you should make sure you know why you may want an options page, and what you need it to do.

Creating a Simple Admin Page

The admin options pages can more or less be used to do just about anything. You kick it off in functions.php, but then you can call other files or just put the whole thing there. Keep it somewhat sane, though, since functions.php is part of your theme and it may slow things down if you cram it too full of cool functionality that needs to run a ton of things at once.

As an example we'll take a look at the Notes Blog Core placeholder page, output by functions.php just to say "hi," more or less.

First of all, you need to add the menu item to the WordPress admin. That means you need to add an action, and define the theme's option page:

```php
add_action('admin_menu', 'nbcore_menu');

function nbcore_menu() {
    add_theme_page('Notes Blog Core', 'Notes Blog Core', 8, 'your-unique-identifier', 'nbcore_options');
}
```

Remember, all this is in between PHP tags within functions.php.

The first line adds an action, the `admin_menu` one actually, and then you're adding the `nbcore_menu` function to it. Next, you define the `nbcore_menu()` function and load it with `add_theme_page`. This in turn consists of the name of the page, the title of the page (obviously identical in this case), the user level needed to see the page, and then a nonexistent unique identifier (which can be a file as well as some identifying string), and finally the function for the actual page HTML content, which we'll get to next:

```php
function nbcore_options() {
  echo '<div class="wrap">';
  echo '
        <h2>Notes Blog Core</h2>
        <p>This is a placeholder for upcoming admin options for the Notes Blog Core theme.
  These things aren\'t due yet, in fact, they are pretty far away, so just forget about this page
  for now huh?</p>
```

```
           <p>Get the latest Notes Blog and Notes Blog Core news from <a href="http://notesblog.
  com" title="Notes Blog">http://notesblog.com</a> - it\'s that sweet!</p>
    ';
  echo '</div>';

}
?>
```

Here, you basically just store the `nbcore_options()` function with the page you want to output in the admin interface. By putting a containing `div` with the `'wrap'` class around it all, you get the WordPress admin interface look, so you probably want to be doing that. The three `echo` statements are simple enough; it is all normal HTML code, with backslashes in front of single quotation marks to avoid it breaking the echo string. Nothing fancy, it is just a placeholder theme options page after all.

Here is the full code:

```
<?php
add_action('admin_menu', 'nbcore_menu');

function nbcore_menu() {
    add_theme_page('Notes Blog Core', 'Notes Blog Core', 8, 'your-unique-identifier', 'nbcore_
  options');
}

function nbcore_options() {
    echo '<div class="wrap">';
    echo '
        <h2>Notes Blog Core</h2>
        <p>This is a placeholder for upcoming admin options for the Notes Blog Core theme. These
  things aren\'t due yet, in fact, they are pretty far away, so just forget about this page for
  now huh?</p>
        <p>Get the latest Notes Blog and Notes Blog Core news from <a href="http://notesblog.com"
  title="Notes Blog">http://notesblog.com</a> - it\'s that sweet!</p>
    ';
    echo '</div>';
}
?>
```

Want to save stuff and add cool functionality? We'll dig deeper into that in the following chapters, dealing with WordPress plugin development. That's basically where you're at when you've gotten this far: you're doing a WordPress plugin, but in your theme's functions.php file.

Issues with Theme Options

Besides the obvious issues faulty code can cause, there's really just one big thing you need to consider when it comes to theme option pages and using functions.php this way: speed.

Remember, functions.php always gets loaded, and if it is big and does a lot of things, then loading it will take time, and an otherwise snappy site may be sluggish for a short while. That's not good, of course, and is why I personally recommend keeping things as clean as possible in functions.php.

That being said, using functions.php is a great way for small options settings. More advanced things should be handled outside, by calling other files, or in a plugin. It is all a matter of what you want to do, so the only really good advice here would be that you have to consider if you're executing your actions the right way, and if you can, move the code (or at least parts of it) somewhere else if your functions.php is growing too much.

One thing you shouldn't cut down on, though, is localization, at least not if you plan on releasing your theme. We'll tackle that next.

Multiple Language Support

Just like you can get WordPress in your language thanks to language files, you can do the same for your theme, and plugins as well for that matter. And just like with WordPress, you need to provide a .mo file that is tailored for your theme, which in turn is created from a POT file via the .po file. It is all a pretty messy business actually, since a lot of the tools used to generate these files are pretty clunky to use, but using the software is worth it.

First of all, you need to understand why a certain language file gets loaded if it is available to WordPress. There is (usually) no menu setting for what language you want a specific theme of plugin to be in; rather, WordPress looks for the one defined in the installation, which is to say the one you added to WPLANG in wp-config.php (see Chapter 1 for more). So that means that if your WordPress install is in German, then a localized theme containing German language files will use those if possible.

A little history lesson is in order before you get your theme ready for internationalization efforts. First of all, there's the POT (Portable Object Template) file. This is basically a file created by a program by analyzing your theme or plugin. The software of your choice (see the "Working With Language Files" section for links) will parse your theme and build a POT file containing all the words and phrases you have marked for translation.

Step 2 would be to create a .po (Portable Object) file from your POT file. What this does is save the original language (usually English), and the translated language in one file. This is where you do your translation.

The third and final step in the translation process would be the .mo (Machine Object) file. This file is created from the .po file, so that it becomes machine-readable, and that makes the translation a lot faster to read and hence output. The .mo file is the file used by WordPress and your theme.

So that's that! But how does the software that generates the POT file know what should be made available for translation?

This is where you come in, as the theme (or plugin) author. You need to mark the parts of your theme that should be up for translation, and you do that by wrapping the word or phrase in a PHP snippet, and then applying it to a domain. The domain is really just a translation set, and that in turn will be defined in functions.php.

Say you want to make the text "Hello you!" available for translation. That would look like this:

```
<?php _e('Hello you!', 'mydomain'); ?>
```

That would output "Hello you!" as if written in plain text, but if there is a translation available and mydomain is defined in functions.php, you'll get that instead. If not, you'll just get "Hello you!" in plain old English.

You can also write it like this:

```
<?php __('Hello you!', 'mydomain'); ?>
```

Same result, just two underscores before the opening parenthesis rather than one and the e.

Call up the trusty Notes Blog Core theme for an example. In the index.php file you'll find the following result output (within PHP code tags, so skip them) whenever a search result is called for:

```
_e('Your search result:', 'notesblog');
```

That would output "Your search result:" if there was a defined domain called notesblog.

Sometimes you want these translations within tags. This is how you've done it with the the_content() template tag, to make the "read more" link output by the <!-more-> code snippet in posts available for translation:

```
<?php the_content(__('Read more', 'notesblog')); ?>
```

A double underscore, and then the translation, does the same as _e(). So why the double underscore method? Well, the _e() is an echo statement, while the double underscore, or __(), is a return statement. Doing echo within PHP functions can create some weird results.

So how, then, do you tell the theme to use the translation file in the first place? Just dropping translation file in the theme won't do it; you need to declare that a specific text domain should be used ("notesblog" in the examples earlier). Just add this in the functions.php file:

```
load_theme_textdomain('notesblog');
```

Within the PHP tags of course, just like almost everything else in the functions.php file.

Now, what does this tell you?

1. That the theme is localized, otherwise there's not much point in using the `load_theme_text-domain` functionality.
2. That every translation string with the domain `'notesblog'` is considered.
3. That you still need a translation.

The actual translation should be in a .mo file, and that in turn comes from a .po file, which you created from a POT file. And the POT file is generated by your chosen software (again, see the "Working with Language Files" section for links and suggestions), which in turn has parsed your theme looking for your translation strings, the `__()` and `_()`.

Working with Language Files

There are several ways to work with the portable language files. One of the most popular programs available is PoEdit (`www.poedit.net/`), which is available across platforms. You can easily open and edit available .po files in PoEdit, and then save them as .mo files to be used with your theme or plugin.

Other software and services for working with .po files include GNU's very own gettext (`www.gnu.org/software/gettext/`) and LaunchPad (`translations.launchpad.net/`). However, neither of these are as easy to use as PoEdit and most often PoEdit is recommended.

When you release a theme or a plugin with a language file, be sure to also make the original .po file available so that the users can translate it into their own language as well. It is a good idea to encourage that, since others may benefit as well.

The Naming Issue

While it may not be entirely within your theme or plugin translation scope, a weird error arises when a widget area gets called, and it can't be found because of it being changed by the translation. That is (or hopefully was, by the time you read this) the case with WordPress and the Swedish translation of "Sidebar," a widget area located in sidebar.php no less. The translators translated "Sidebar" (to "Sidomeny," which somewhat misses the mark, but still) and by doing so the themes that made direct calls to the "Sidebar" widget area failed because it was translated incorrectly.

Messy? Yes, it is. The point is, be wary so that you don't end up translating things that are used for calling up various features, functions, or whatever. At least not without making sure that the actual call for whatever it is is also altered accordingly.

Next up is conditional design, which is basically all about names, be they category or Page names. While those won't be translated without quite a bit of fiddling, it is a good idea to consider their names regardless.

Conditional Design

Conditional tags are great, since they let you create a more dynamic design that aligns itself with whatever situation the visitor is in. This means that you can serve up different things depending on the condition, hence the title.

The most obvious usage of conditional tags is to check where the visitor is on your site, and output something accordingly. This is used in the index.php template file in the Notes Blog Core theme to keep it from having to have all the various archive template files (better you create them in your child themes, after all). This code checks where the visitor is and outputs something suitable:

```php
<?php
if (is_category()) {
    echo '<h1 class="listhead">';
    _e("Category", "notesblog");
    echo ' <strong>';
    single_cat_title();
    echo '</strong></h1>';
} if (is_tag()) {
    echo '<h1 class="listhead">';
    _e("Tag", "notesblog");
    echo ' <strong>';
    single_tag_title();
    echo '</strong></h1>';
} if (is_search()) {
    echo '<h1 class="listhead">';
    _e("Your <strong>search result</strong>", "notesblog");
    echo '</h1>';
}
?>
```

The code goes above the loop, and just outputs various h1 heading messages depending on where you are, using the conditional tags is_category(), is_tag(), and is_search(). These perform exactly as you may imagine: returning true if it is a category page, a tag page, or a search result. So when that is the case, the code will print the correct header.

And yes, _e() is used for localization, as you know by now.

So conditional design can be pretty useful, as you can probably tell. You can make more distinctive alterations to the design as well, such as including different headers depending on where on the site you are, and so on. Or you can build a menu that highlights the Page or category you are on. We'll do that next.

TRY IT OUT Building a Conditional Menu

A good way to put conditional tags to use is in menus. In this example you'll see how to build a simple one, and apply a specific class to the one menu item that is relevant, meaning the one that represents the page you're actually viewing.

1. Start with some basic markup for the menu:

```
<ul>
    <li>a menu item</li>
</ul>
```

This is obviously an unordered list, and the idea is to have a menu item per list item. So adding more menu items would only mean more list items.

2. Next, add some links:

```
<ul>
    <li><a href="/">Home</a></li>
    <li><a href="/category/music/">Music</a></li>
    <li><a href="/category/books/">Books</a></li>
    <li><a href="/category/games/">Games</a></li>
    <li><a href="/about/">About</a></li>
</ul>
```

Nothing fancy so far, just some plain links. The first link, Home, is obviously to the site's root. The Music, Books, and Games links are all to category archives, and About is to the About page. You probably read that from the links already.

3. Now, you want to add the `class="activemenu"` to the list item when the user is in that particular place. That way, you can style the class in your stylesheet and make it stand out. Maybe like this:

```
li.activemenu { background: yellow; }
```

That would give the active list item a yellow background. Probably a bit too hardcore for most of you, but you get the point. It could just as well be a background image showing an arrow, or a bottom border, or whatever really.

4. Next, add the conditional tags. The concept is easy enough, just check if you're in the place in question: if you are, output the class, otherwise don't. First, start by checking if you're on the homepage. The conditional `is_front_page()` is your choice here. You probably could have used `is_home()` too, but there are some cases when that would return differently, so go with the front page here:

```
<li <?php if (is_front_page()) echo 'class="activemenu"; ?>><a href="/">Home</a></li>
```

If it is the homepage, PHP will echo the class. Otherwise, it won't—it's as simple as that.

5. **Finally, complete the menu:**

```
<ul>
    <li <?php if (is_front_page()) echo 'class="activemenu"; ?>><a href="/">Home</a></li>
    <li <?php if (is_category('music')) echo 'class="activemenu"; ?>><a href="/category/
 music/">Music</a></li>
    <li <?php if (is_category('books')) echo 'class="activemenu"; ?>><a href="/category/
 books/">Books</a></li>
    <li <?php if (is_category('games')) echo 'class="activemenu"; ?>><a href="/category/
 games/">Games</a></li>
    <li <?php if (is_page('about')) echo 'class="activemenu"; ?>><a href="/about/">About</a></li>
</ul>
```

Most of these conditional tags take several types of parameters, from ID to the slug (used above) to actual Page and category naming. And whenever the glove fits, so to speak, the PHP code will apply the `class="activemenu"` on the list item. Simple as that!

Checking whether the visitor is on a specific Page or in a particular category can be very handy, since you can return what fits for your site. In the preceding example, you're just echoing a CSS class to mark a specific menu item differently using the `activemenu` class, but you can output anything you like. Maybe you want to have a category with beginner content, which would then output information on how to subscribe to the RSS feed, whereas the non-beginner would just get a traditional RSS feed icon and a brief text link.

Working with RSS Feeds

RSS feeds are a great way both to deliver and to subscribe to content. WordPress supports both the old 0.91 version, the 1.0 version, and, more up-to-date, the 2.0 version. There is also Atom support, but keep in mind that you need to activate Atom from the settings page should you want to use it.

Most themes have feed links built-in, and while the Web browser will tell your visitors discretely that there is a feed available, you really want to push it a bit harder than that. Take a look at just about any successful professional blogger and you'll see nice RSS graphics, often incorporating the feed icon, and promoting the subscription services in premiere positions.

You should, too, if you want to gain subscribers. That's lesson 1 on RSS really: position it well on your site, otherwise people will neither see it nor use it.

Lesson number 2 is to seriously consider full feeds. You can choose whether you want to send out a full feed or one just featuring excerpts. Feeds containing just excerpts *will* have fewer subscribers, since people using RSS prefer to get the whole story. You'll find that a large number of these readers will click the links and visit your site anyway, but they may just opt out if you're not publishing full feeds. Then again, if you really, truly, definitely have to get people to your site, and having them read the content in a feed reader is a disaster, then fine. Just make sure you know what you're doing, and why, if you're strapping your feed.

The third and final lesson is to offer alternative subscription methods. The most popular one would be e-mail subscriptions, usually delivered by Feedburner (`feedburner.com`), which is owned by Google. What it does is put together a daily digest from your RSS feed, delivering it to subscribers via e-mail. This is good because RSS feeds are still something mainly used by the technical crowd. Offering other subscription options is a good idea.

The WordPress Feeds

WordPress outputs a bunch of feeds by default. You can get them easily enough, using the `bloginfo()` template tag:

```php
<?php bloginfo('rdf_url'); ?>
<?php bloginfo('rss_url'); ?>
<?php bloginfo('rss2_url'); ?>
<?php bloginfo('atom_url'); ?>
```

These are for the 0.91, 1.0, and 2.0 RSS feed versions, respectively, and then there's the Atom feed as well.

You can also get the feed for your comments, as well as an individual post's comments. Naturally, you'd want to use these tags in your theme:

```php
<?php bloginfo('comments_rss2_url'); ?>
<?php comments_rss_link('RSS 2.0'); ?>
```

The second one is for a specific post's feed.

However, I personally prefer to keep the PHP calls at a minimum. All these feeds can be found by directly inputting the URL. Since you understand the necessities of permalinks (or will, when you've finished reading this chapter), you've got your blog set up to use these. That means that these URLs will work for you:

- `mydomain.com/feed/`
- `mydomain.com/feed/rss/`
- `mydomain.com/feed/rss2/`

137

- `mydomain.com/feed/rdf/`
- `mydomain.com/feed/atom/`

The first one is the default; you'll even find it in some themes, although that is a bad idea since it requires permalinks to be set up and not all hosts support that. The following, however, will always work, but don't look as pretty:

- `mydomain.com/?feed=rss`
- `mydomain.com/?feed=rss2`
- `mydomain.com/?feed=rdf`
- `mydomain.com/?feed=atom`

But there's more! These are just for the main feeds, but there are actually feeds for just about everything in WordPress. Author feeds, category feeds, and tag feeds all come very in handy sometimes. There's even one for comments to a particular post. Assuming you've got your permalinks set up, this is how they are built up:

- `mydomain.com/author/USERNAME/feed/`
- `mydomain.com/category/SLUG/feed/`
- `mydomain.com/tag/SLUG/feed/`
- `mydomain.com/POST-PERMALINK/comments/feed/`

So if my username is "tdh" on notesblog.com, and I want to pull out all my posts via RSS, this would work: `notesblog.com/author/tdh/feed/`.

Build a Custom Feed URL

Sometimes you may want your feed to exclude a category, or consist of a couple of tags only, perhaps. This can be achieved by hacking the feed URL, which actually takes some parameters. Then, if you want to, you can run that feed through a service such as Feedburner, since the URLs tend to be pretty long and ugly.

For example, say you want to exclude the category with ID 47 from your custom feed. Then the URL would look like this:

```
http://mydomain.com/feed/?cat=-47
```

That would output the full RSS feed, but nothing in the category with ID 47. Notice the minus sign in front of the ID; it works here just as it does in most other cases.

How about a feed for a search query? Just as simple:

```
http://mydomain.com/feed/?s=keyword1+keyword2
```

Or maybe you want to just run category 39, and show the tag with the slug `ninja`? If so, then you'd do it like this:

```
http://mydomain.com/feed/?cat=39&tag=ninja
```

Basically, what you do is that you add parameters to the URL, and work from there. The following parameters are accepted:

Parameter	Description
author	Author ID
cat	Numeric ID
tag	Tag slug
keyword	Search keywords
year	The year (for example, 2009)
day	The date (for example, 15)
monthnum	The month by number (for example, 3 for March)
hour	The hour (for example, 19)
minute	The minute (for example, 45)
second	The second (for example, 13)
p	The post ID
paged	A specific page relating to the front page post listing

Basic SEO Implementations

Getting the most out of the search engines is a topic for a book itself. However, there are some things you can get right in your theme from the start. Also, be sure to check out the plugin lists later in the book for links and advice on good SEO plugins that make your WordPress site even more attractive to the search engines. The cold, harsh truth is that the best SEO optimization is manually edited on per-post and per-page basis, rather than automatically generated.

Here are some tips to consider when setting up your theme:

- **Validate!** Valid code is better. You can check it here: `validator.w3.org`.
- **Permalinks, obviously.** Permalinks change those ID-based, ugly URLs to more user-friendly as well as search-engine-friendly ones. The earlier keywords in your permalinks get picked up first, so you should really get the post and page title slug in there (not the ID), and possibly the category as well. Some claim that having date-based data in the permalinks helps the search engines as well, and that may very well be true if the site is updated often enough. The big bump, however, will be when you switch to permalinks, so make that a must in every setup.

- **Tags and keywords.** Tagging your posts not only helps describe the content for your readers, it is also an opportunity to tell the search engines more about them. You can use a plugin to populate the meta keywords field with your tags (not linked of course), or similar.

- **Generate a sitemap.** The most heralded solution for this is the Google XML Sitemap Generator plugin: `www.arnebrachhold.de/projects/wordpress-plugins/google-xml-sitemaps-generator/`.

- **The title tag.** Your title tag should include both the post name (first) and the site name (last). A divider between the two helps differentiate.

- **Headings.** On the front page, your blog's name should be in an h1 block. When viewing single posts or Pages, the title of the post or Page should be in the h1 block. On archive listings (search, categories, tags, and so on), I tend to set the listing title as h1, and have the post titles returned as h2.

- **Reconsider links.** Links are only good when they are relevant, so pushing that massive blogroll in the sidebar all the time may not be good. This is a bit fuzzy, however, so consider it wisely. Relevant links are always good.

- **Related posts are relevant links.** There are numerous related post plugins out there, and as long as they return relevant links to your posts, they are a good thing.

- **Breadcrumbs.** Breadcrumbs are links, usually on the top of the page, showing where the page is located, for example Home → Reviews → WordPress 2.8. They are not only helpful for the user, they also help the search engine read your page. You need to use a plugin for this functionality. This one is popular and easy enough to add: `yoast.com/wordpress/breadcrumbs/`.

- **Load time.** It is not only users that appreciate a fast-loading site, search engines do too, so clean up your code. You may even want to consider a caching plugin, although some of these may end up creating duplicate content so be sure you read up on it accordingly.

Naturally you'll want your theme to be as search-engine-friendly as possible, since a lot of traffic comes that way. That being said, the one thing that truly makes an impact on the visitors you do get is the load time, and we'll examine trimming the theme next.

Trimming WordPress on the Theme Side

All sites should be as fast-loading as possible, and that applies to WordPress-powered sites as well. You can do quite a lot on the theme side of things, but the question is how much you really want to do. If you take it to the extremes, you'll end up with one-line files that will be completely impossible to edit, which means you'll need a non-optimized workfile that you later optimize. This usually applies to stylesheets, which can be smashed together quite a lot, and hence you'll save a few bytes, but it also means that you won't be able to scan them easily when looking for something.

So with that in mind, what can you do to speed up your theme?

- **Clean out unnecessary code.** Most themes would do well with a going-over or two after they appear to be finished.

- **Minimize PHP usage.** Direct links to images in your theme directory, usually called with `bloginfo('template_directory')`, will save you several PHP calls. There are a lot of those in most themes, as there is automatic output of the site's name and things like that. If you expect large amounts of traffic, hardcode that into the theme instead.

- **Beware of plugin overload.** Plugins are great, but sometimes they aren't all that well designed. At the very least, they represent one or several more PHP queries and possibly database processing. You should consider each and every one of them carefully.

- **Outside services.** This is not strictly in your theme, but outside services such as chat widgets or Twitter badges take time to load and will impact the performance of the site in the eyes of your visitors.

- **Accelerate and cache PHP.** Your hosting solution of choice may offer PHP accelerators and caching for often-called functionality. Talk to your hosting provider for options, and then make sure that they are compatible with WordPress; all may not be.

- **WordPress caching.** There are caching plugins for WordPress that store static files rather than serving data from the database all the time. This can actually speed up a site, so it may be worth considering.

- **Tighten the files.** You can Google your way to both HTML and CSS compressors, which tighten your files but make them a whole lot harder to read. Be sure to check the output to ensure that the compressors' scripts haven't added something malicious. You can never be too sure.

In the end, tightening a WordPress theme is more or less the same as tightening any site. Good and tight code, preferably valid, will load faster than clunky and bloated code, so get it right from the start.

And if you're doing everything right but your WordPress site keeps chugging slowly, then maybe you've outgrown your host. After all, when all the PHP calls are minimized, the code is tight and valid, and you've got your accelerators and caching, then there's just not much more that you can do other than crank up the voltage to power your beast.

Some Final Words on Themes

The themes are not only the look and feel of a site these days, they are also simple plugins. You use themes to get everything to display where you want, and to break the normal flow of posts provided by the loop. Thanks to the template and conditional tags, there are a lot of things you can achieve, and by adding extra functionality in functions.php, by using action hooks, and by being crafty overall, you can build just about anything.

As I've hinted at in this chapter, cramming functions.php full isn't always such a great idea. A lot of things you do in that file can just as well be done by a plugin, and while that is unnecessary or even redundant at times, sometimes it truly is the best decision. After all, the whole idea with various skinning concepts in publishing systems is to separate as much design from the code as possible. When it comes to WordPress themes, it means that you'll have to break that rule a bit if you want to do crafty things.

A lot of those things can be plugins rather than code in the themes, which would fit better with the whole dividing design and code concept. So it makes sense that the next chapter deals with plugins.

DEVELOPING WORDPRESS PLUGINS

7

ANATOMY OF A WORDPRESS PLUGIN

It goes without saying that plugins are different from themes, but a lot of things concerning them share the same ground. If you simplify things, you could say that when you're adding functionality to your theme by adding code to the functions.php template file, you're actually writing a plugin.

But there is a huge difference. Themes are there to display the WordPress site, using the tools available. Plugins, on the other hand, are used when you need to extend the WordPress functionality with additional features. You should remember that, because bloating your theme's functions.php with features sometimes isn't the way to go.

In this chapter we'll look at plugins from a slightly different standpoint than we did with the themes chapters previously. The reason for this is simple: your plugin can do anything. It is basically a way for you to add whatever feature you want; compare that to doing funky stuff with a select few template tags, and you see the difference.

With plugins, it is not a matter of what you can do, it is more a question of why. So that's where we'll start.

Plugin Basics

A plugin's essentials don't differ too much from a theme's essentials. Instead of the necessary style.css stylesheet file with its theme-identifying top header, you have an aptly named PHP file with a similar header. Then you can expand by adding even more functionality outside of the main plugin PHP file if you want, just like you add template files to the child theme's style.css.

Start from the beginning: the main plugin file. There are just two things to observe here:

- The main plugin file needs to be a PHP file with a unique filename, or a unique folder name if your plugin consists of several files inside a folder.
- The PHP file needs an identifying top, just like a theme's style.css does, so that WordPress can recognize it as a plugin.

Giving your plugin a unique filename or folder name is very important, since plugins reside in wp-content/plugins/ and you wouldn't want any weird conflicts. Name it appropriately, and in such a way that there is no doubt which plugin it is should someone need to find it using FTP but only know it by the name it is displayed with from within the WordPress admin interface.

The identifying plugin header block will look familiar. The following is a dummy:

```php
<?php
/*
Plugin Name: My Smashing Plugin
Plugin URI: http://my-smashing-plugin-url.com
Description: This is what my Smashing Plugin actually does.
Version: 1.0
Author: Thord Daniel Hedengren
Author URI: http://tdhedengren.com
*/
?>
```

Actually, you don't need all that; only the plugin name line, the first one within the comment notations, is mandatory. The rest should be there, however, so that the user knows what the plugin is, where to get updates, version numbering, who made it, and so on.

You should include licensing information as well. This is the standard GPL licensing dummy that is recommended in the WordPress Codex:

```php
<?php
/*  Copyright YEAR  PLUGIN_AUTHOR_NAME  (e-mail : PLUGIN AUTHOR E-MAIL)

    This program is free software; you can redistribute it and/or modify
    it under the terms of the GNU General Public License as published by
```

```
     the Free Software Foundation; either version 2 of the License, or
     (at your option) any later version.

     This program is distributed in the hope that it will be useful,
     but WITHOUT ANY WARRANTY; without even the implied warranty of
     MERCHANTABILITY or FITNESS FOR A PARTICULAR PURPOSE.  See the
     GNU General Public License for more details.

     You should have received a copy of the GNU General Public License
     along with this program; if not, write to the Free Software
     Foundation, Inc., 51 Franklin St, Fifth Floor, Boston, MA  02110-1301   USA
*/
?>
```

Naturally, you'd want to change `YEAR` and `PLUGIN AUTHOR E-MAIL` to the correct information. You can also include the full license as a text file, aptly named license.txt of course. Obtain the license from `www.gnu.org/copyleft/gpl.html`.

And that's about it. All you need for WordPress to find the plugin is this, one single file with an identifying top. Dropping it in wp-content/plugins/ will result in it being listed in the Plugins section within WordPress. Activate it, and it will be available to you in your theme, and from WordPress's actions themselves.

This is where the fun part begins, because this is where you have to figure out what you need to do, and how you'll accomplish it.

Whether you're planning on writing the plugin you think will change the way you use WordPress, or just need some extra functionality for your latest project, you should go through the plugin checklist before getting started. It may just save you some time and headaches.

- Is there a plugin for this already? If there is, consider using that instead, or forking/hacking it if it nearly does what you want.
- Make sure you've got a unique name for your plugin. Don't just check the `wordpress.org` plugin directory, you should Google it to make sure.
- Decide on a unique prefix to all your functions, and stick to it. That way you're doing your part in eliminating any unnecessary conflicting functions due to similar naming structure.
- Do you want to internationalize your plugin? You really should; it works the same way as with themes and is pretty easy after all.
- Should this plugin have widget support? If it should, what kind of settings should it have?
- Do you need a settings page within the admin interface?
- What license should the plugin have? Remember, it has to be GPL-compatible to get hosted by the wordpress.org directory.
- Don't forget the final check. Is the header up to date? Is the version number correct? Do all the links work? Is every necessary file in the package? And last but not least, have you spell-checked your plugin?

Hooks and How to Use Them

Remember the action hooks from the previous chapter? They come in handy for plugins as well, not just for themes. Thanks to hooks, you can add your cool plugin functionality to the various parts of WordPress, like `wp_head()` or `wp_footer()`, which are both useful for a lot of things. The Web statistics example in the previous chapter, where you added a function in the theme's functions.php template file and then added it to the `wp_footer()` hook using `add_action()`, is very much the way of the plugin.

More often than not, you'll end up writing a function in your plugin, and then you'll add it to one of the hooks. This is how `add_action()` works:

```
add_action ('hook-name', 'function-name', X, Y );
```

The `'hook-name'` is of course the name of the hook you want to add the action to. What happens is that WordPress, when encountering that hook when running the code, will check to see if there are any added functions registered for that hook in particular. If there are, the function will run; if not, it won't. And the function is, of course, the one you've defined in `'function-name'`.

X and Y are optional integers. The first, X, is the priority argument (which defaults to 10), used to sort actions when there are several added to a specific action hook. The lower the number is, the earlier the function will be executed, so if you need to make sure that something happens before or after something else, this is where you control that.

Y, on the other hand, is the number of arguments your function can accept (defaulting to 1). If you need the function to handle more than one argument, you can set it by entering another number here.

Most of the time you won't see the priority or number of arguments in plugins, but sometimes they can come in handy. As they are optional, you can just leave them out when you don't need them.

To sum it up, this code snippet would cause the `'smashing-shortcode'` function to run when `wp_head()` is executed:

```
add_action ('wp_head', 'smashing-shortcode');
```

Filters work more or less the same way, but you use `add_filter()` rather than `add_action()`. The parameters are the same, and you pass them the way as well. The only difference is that you can't use the action hooks with `add_filter()`; you use the filter hooks instead. Other than that the two act in the same way.

Moving on, there are two types of hooks. *Action hooks* are triggered by specific events when a WordPress site is running, such as publishing a post, which would be the `publish_post()`

hook. *Filter hooks*, on the other hand, are functions that WordPress passes data through, so you'd use them to do stuff with the data. Useful filter hooks include the_excerpt(), the_title(), and so on. You ought to recognize them from the template tags.

Adding functions to a hook, whether it is on of the action or filter kind, is easy enough, but what about removing functionality? Sometimes you don't want an action or filter hook to run, and that means you need to make sure it gets removed. This is done with remove_action() and remove_filter() for action and filter hooks, respectively. The syntax is simple:

```
remove_action('action-hook','the-function')
```

And the same for remove_filter().

This is not just used to remove functionality you have added, you can also remove core functionality from within WordPress with these. Any action or filter function can be removed this way, from pinging to deleting attachments, so some plugins may actually consist only of limiting WordPress functionality, rather than extending it, all depending on what your goal is.

Creating Your Own Template Tags

Another way to access your plugin functionality is by creating your own template tags, much like bloginfo(), the_title(), and so on. This isn't hard at all, in fact just by creating a function in your plugin (or in functions.php for that matter), you can access that function by a simple little PHP snippet:

```
<?php function-name(); ?>
```

Not very complicated, right? It really isn't, but that doesn't mean that it is the best way to include plugin content, even though it is by far the easiest method. By doing this you don't need to add any hooks or anything, and the function will be executed when the plugin template tag is loaded, which means that you'll just put it where you want it within your theme files.

There is really just one thing you need to keep in mind before going down this route, and that is usability. Not everybody is comfortable with editing the theme files, and if you intend to release your plugin, or deliver it to a client, then it may not be a good idea to force template file hacking for usage.

Then again, maybe you'll be doing the deployment yourself, in which case it really doesn't matter. However, if the end user will have to fiddle with the plugin's position or perhaps will need to pass parameters to it, then it is probably a better idea to look at other solutions.

At other times, just adding functionality using template tags won't cut it, and you need to overwrite parts of the core WordPress functionality. That's when you turn to the pluggable functions.

The Pluggable Functions

Sometimes you may need to overwrite parts of the WordPress core functionality, but just removing a hook won't do it. That's when you turn to pluggable.php, located in wp-includes. Naturally, you won't hack it, because that would be a tedious thing to manage with updates, but rather you'll write a plugin that does the override.

Now this is dangerous stuff. First of all, you can only do an override once, so if two plugins do different overrides on the same pluggable function, the site will act up (at best) or break (at worst). This means that two plugins both relying on overriding the same pluggable function can't be installed at the same time, which is a serious drawback. Therefore, you should probably keep your pluggable function stuff to sites you are in complete control of.

Also, to avoid unnecessary errors, you may want to wrap any code pertaining to a plugin relying on these things in a check to see if the function exists:

```php
<?php if (!function_exists('function-name')); ?>
```

There are, naturally, times when the pluggable functions can come in handy. See the most up-to-date list of what functions you can get in this way in the Codex: codex.wordpress.org/ Pluggable_Functions.

And use with caution, obviously. Just writing the plugin in the correct way, which is covered next, isn't enough when you're nulling out parts of the WordPress core. Don't be surprised when things stop working or conflicts come out of nowhere when you dive into these things. After all, the WordPress functionality you're bypassing is there for a reason.

Must-have Functionality

Strictly speaking, the only thing your plugin really must have is a main PHP file containing the identifying top, and whatever code is needed to get the job done. However, in reality, you should probably take it a few steps further than that. After all, someone will have to work with your plugin, and so it should be as simple and accessible as possible. That means that you should go to great lengths to make the plugin blend in nicely with the WordPress admin interface.

The same goes for whatever parts of the plugin will show to end users. Some plugins add visual functionality, and that should work with as many themes as possible if you intend to release the plugin. Naturally, if you've developed a plugin for use with a particular project only, this won't be an issue. The same goes for localization support; there's no need for that if there won't be any language support other than the default one, is there?

Finally, I think every plugin should come with a license, and some sort of instructions as to how the plugin should be used. Readme files are nice and all, but better yet to build the instructions into the actual plugin since a lot of users are reluctant (or just too impatient) to read the attached readme files.

Plugin Settings

Sometimes you want to save things in the database. You've got the freedom of any PHP script here really, which means that you can add full tables and so on to the database should you want to. I won't cover that.

I will, however, tell you how to use the WordPress options database and store small snippets of data in it. This is the wp_options table in the database. Remember, don't store too much data in there. If your plugin is dealing with a lot of content, you should definitely consider other solutions.

To demonstrate usage, we'll turn to a really simple plugin called Footer Notes. What it does is add an admin page where the user can save some HTML code that is added at the end of posts (using a plugin-specific template tag). It also supports adding the HTML code at the end of post items in the RSS feed should the user want to. This manifests as a simple options page in the admin interface with two text boxes where the HTML code is pasted, and a Save button. That's it.

```php
<?php
/*
Plugin Name: Footer Notes
Plugin URI: http://notesblog.com/footer-notes/
Description: Footer Notes adds a simple code block to your posts and feeds.
Version: 0.1
Author: Thord Daniel Hedengren
Author URI: http://tdhedengren.com
*/

// add menu to admin --
if (is_admin()){
    add_action('admin_menu', 'nb_footernotes_menu');
    add_action('admin_init', 'nb_footernotes_register');
}

// whitelist options --
function nb_footernotes_register() {
    register_setting('nb_footernotes_optiongroup', 'nbfn_post');
    register_setting('nb_footernotes_optiongroup', 'nbfn_feed');
}

// admin menu page details --
function nb_footernotes_menu() {
    add_options_page('Footer Notes Settings', 'Footer Notes', 8, 'nb_footernotes', 'nb_footernotes_
  options');
}

// add actual menu page --
function nb_footernotes_options() { ?>
    <div class="wrap">
        <div id="icon-options-general" class="icon32"><br /></div>
```

```
        <h2>Footer Notes</h2>
        <p>This is the settings page for the <a href="http://notesblog.com/footer-notes/">Footer
    Notes</a> plugin. This plugin adds HTML code at the bottom of your posts and your feed items.
    Just add the HTML code you want for the two possible spots.</p>
        <p>Leave either of these <strong>completely empty</strong> if you do not want to return
    anything!</p>


        <form method="post" action="options.php">
        <?php settings_fields('nb_footernotes_optiongroup'); ?>


        <table class="form-table" style="margin-top: 20px; padding-bottom: 10px; border: 1px dotted
    #bbb; border-width:1px 0;">
            <tr valign="top">
                <th scope="row">
                    <h3 style="margin-top: 10px;">Code to be added after posts</h3>
                    <p>The code below will be added where you put the <code>nb_footernotes()
    </code> template tag in your theme, on a per-post basis. It needs to be within the loop.</p>
                </th>
            </tr>
            <tr>
                <td><textarea name="nbfn_post" style="width: 90%; height: 150px; padding:
    10px;"><?php echo get_option('nbfn_post'); ?></textarea></td>
            </tr><tr valign="top">
                <th scope="row">
                    <h3 style="margin-top: 10px;">Code to be added after feed items</h3>
                    <p>The code below will be added at the bottom of each item in your feeds.</p>
                </th>
            </tr><tr>
                <td><textarea name="nbfn_feed" style="width: 90%; height: 150px; padding:
    10px;"><?php echo get_option('nbfn_feed'); ?></textarea></td>
            </tr>
        </table>


        <p class="submit">
            <input type="submit" class="button-primary" value="Save Changes" />
        </p>


        </form>
    </div>
<?php }
// custom hook for the posts --
function nb_footernotes() {
    do_action('nb_footernotes');
}
// and now for the post output --
add_action('nb_footernotes', 'nb_footernotes_post_output');
function nb_footernotes_post_output() {
    echo get_option('nbfn_post');
}
// feed output time --
```

```
function nb_footernotes_rss() {
    echo get_option('nbfn_feed');
}
// feed filters --
add_filter('the_excerpt_rss', 'nb_footernotes_rss');
add_filter('the_content_rss', 'nb_footernotes_rss');
// that's it! -- FIN//
?>
```

The plugin also consists of a license.txt and a readme.txt, as well as an uninstall.php file for cleaning out the database. For now, though, focus on the actual plugin.

At the very top is the plugin file header, which is the actual plugin description. Then you're doing a check to see if it is the admin you're at, and adding the nb_footernotes_menu() function defined further down. You'll recall that this is the way to create an options page in the WordPress admin; if you don't remember how this was done, see the themes chapter for a more in-depth description.

The first code snippet that interests us at this time is this one:

```
// whitelist options --
function nb_footernotes_register() {
    register_setting('nb_footernotes_optiongroup', 'nbfn_post');
    register_setting('nb_footernotes_optiongroup', 'nbfn_feed');
}
```

What it does is register 'nbfn_post' and 'nbfn_feed', which are two pieces of options data that you want to save stuff to (into the database obviously), with the nb_footernotes_optiongroup. This one is within the form further down on the page:

```
<?php settings_fields('nb_footernotes_optiongroup'); ?>
```

This saves a lot of time, actually, and does away with a bunch of hidden input fields that you had to use in previous versions of WordPress. All you need to do is register everything using register_settings and add it to an option group, and then you use settings_fields() within the form to get it working.

The options page is pretty straightforward. Remember that the form tag should have action="options.php" and if you want the table to act in a typical WordPress manner you give it class="form-table". The submit button at the very end is a simple submit, and it will do the job well enough. You can, of course, style it otherwise if you want.

In this case you've got two text areas where the idea is to have the user put some HTML code. This is how the one for 'nbfn_post' looks:

```
<textarea name="nbfn_post" style="width: 90%; height: 150px; padding: 10px;"><?php echo
    get_option('nbfn_post'); ?></textarea>
```

The interesting part is `get_option('nbfn_post')`, which means that it both collects (and outputs thanks to `echo`) and saves to `'nbfn_post'` in the database. The same in a typical input field would have the `get_option()` part as the value rather than between the opening and closing tag. Like this:

```
<input type="text" name="nbfn_post" value="<?php echo get_option('nbfn_post'); ?>" />
```

Right, so that's it. Now to output the stuff you've saved. First, the HTML code meant to go with the post content. To give the user freedom I opted to create a plugin-specific template tag to add to the theme, rather than to just append it to `the_content()`. This is the custom template tag:

```
<?php nb_footernotes(); ?>
```

And this is what creates it (the first part) and loads it with the content from `'nbfn_post'`. That is where the HTML for its post is stored, remember? Echoing `get_option('nbfn_post')` will return the saved content:

```
// custom hook for the posts --
function nb_footernotes() {
    do_action('nb_footernotes');
}
// and now for the post output --
add_action('nb_footernotes', 'nb_footernotes_post_output');
function nb_footernotes_post_output() {
    echo get_option('nbfn_post');
}
```

As for the feed HTML code, you just want this added to the bottom of each post in the RSS feed, so use a filter to do that. But first you need to store the content from `'nbfn_feed'` in the `nb_footernotes_rss()` function so you can add it:

```
// feed output time --
function nb_footernotes_rss() {
    echo get_option('nbfn_feed');
}
// feed filters --
add_filter('the_excerpt_rss', 'nb_footernotes_rss');
add_filter('the_content_rss', 'nb_footernotes_rss');
```

Database Content and Uninstalling

Something to consider when creating a plugin that stores data to the database is what happens when someone doesn't want to use it anymore. Do you need uninstall functionality to clean up after yourself? You usually do if you have saved a bunch of things in the database, which shouldn't be sitting around full of unused data anyway, should it?

Of course not, so you need to remove it. There are a number of ways of removing unwanted functionality, the latest one being an uninstall.php file with your plugin. This would contain the uninstall code, which basically would be code to delete the database content you have added:

```
delete_option('my-data');
```

This would delete the `my-data` field in the `option` database table. Since a lot of plugins store some option data in that table, it can get cluttered, and that's never a good thing. Naturally, you'd add whatever you need to remove to the uninstall.php file. And also, this applies for uninstalls made through the WordPress admin interface.

Take a look at the uninstall.php file for the Footer Notes plugin mentioned in the previous section. It contains this:

```php
<?php
// for old versions --
if ( !defined('WP_UNINSTALL_PLUGIN') ) {
    exit();
}
// delete the option data --
delete_option('nbfn_post');
delete_option('nbfn_feed');
?>
```

The first part is a check to see if the uninstall feature is present, which it isn't in earlier versions of WordPress and hence the script will exit, not doing anything. That way, this file is backwards compatible. Then you just delete the option data stored in the database: `'nbfn_post'` and `'nbfn_feed'`, as you'll recall. This is done when deleting the plugin from within the WordPress admin interface, and hence the user gets a cleaned-up database.

Naturally, you can do the same thing without an uninstall.php file, but then you need to do a little more coding. The `register_uninstall_hook()` can be used to do the same thing, just check for it like you normally do. If you're contemplating using the hook approach, chances are you have your own uninstall thing happening on the plugin's page within the WordPress admin interface. Or maybe you just don't want your plugin to contain an uninstall.php file, and prefer to build the uninstall process into the plugin itself. There's nothing wrong with that, keeping it clean and tight.

The important thing is that you remember to add uninstall functionality should you have stored anything in the database. You may want to make it optional, however, to remove the data, since it may be useful later on. Also, it is probably a good idea to remove the data on deactivation, which is recommended for all plugins when doing manual WordPress upgrades.

Leaving the database the way you found it is all you need to think about, really. And it is common sense as well.

After Uninstalling

It is easy to forget that when a plugin is uninstalled, it may leave things lying around. Database data is one thing, and hopefully the uninstall at least gave the user a chance to clean up after the plugin, but there is one thing that is even more pressing: shortcodes.

What happens when a plugin relying on shortcodes gets uninstalled? The shortcode won't be parsed, hence it is output as regular text. Your [myshortcode] shortcode will end up printed just like that, in the middle of your post.

It won't look good.

So while the plugin may not be active, or even present anymore, you still need to maintain some sort of backwards compatibility to it. That means that you should offer some sort of solution for the user to make sure the posts aren't littered with un-parsed shortcode. One way would be to run a SQL query and simply remove all the shortcode automatically, but that may be a bit drastic, and what happens if something breaks during this process? It may destroy the database. Or, more likely, how do you know that there isn't a human error within the post that for some reason causes the remove shortcode query to cut too much?

How you choose to handle redundant shortcode depends on the kind of usage you have introduced in your plugin. One ugly fix would be to include a plugin that changes the shortcode from outputting whatever you had it doing in the first place to outputting nothing at all.

It goes without saying that you need to consider all these things in order to not put the user in a fix when uninstalling the plugin after some time of active usage.

Obviously, not all types of plugins will need this treatment. For example, plugins utilizing widgets will just stop displaying the widget when removed.

Adding Widget Support

A widget is one of those elements you can put in the widget area(s), dragging and dropping it from within the WordPress admin interface. The idea with widgets is to make it easy to customize the contents of a blog or site. WordPress ships with a few widgets, such as one for outputting RSS, one displaying the latest posts, listing the Pages, the categories, and so on. These widgets may not be enough, however, and when you create a plugin you may want to give the user the chance to run it from within a widget area. This is a lot more user-friendly than having to put the plugin PHP template tag in the theme's template files, so it may be a good idea to widgetize your plugin if it is doing something that would fit being displayed in a widget area.

The means to create widgets was greatly improved as of WordPress 2.8, with the release of a new widget API. Thanks to this, creating widgets for your plugins isn't even all that complicated anymore. What you do is extend the built-in widget class, called `WP_Widget`, give it some instructions, and then register it so it will show up:

```
class SmashingWidget extends WP_Widget {
    function SmashingWidget() {
        // The actual widget code goes here
    }
    function widget($args, $instance) {
        // Output the widget content
    }
    function update($new_instance, $old_instance) {
        // Process and save the widget options
    }
    function form($instance) {
        // Output the options form in admin
    }
}
register_widget('SmashingWidget');
```

In the example above, what you did was extend the `WP_Widget` class with your `SmashingWidget` widget. The first function, which is just `function SmashingWidget()`, is the actual widget with the functionality you want, so that's where the action is. The `widget()`, `update()`, and `form()` functions are necessary to get the widget to behave the way you want. Obviously, you wrap it up by registering the widget with `register_widget()`.

And no, there are no submit buttons or anything here. Both the cancel link and the submit button are built into the widget API, so you needn't worry about them when it is time to save whatever changes you'll let your users meddle with.

157

TRY IT OUT Creating a Widget

This section walks you through creating a simple widget. It'll just output some text, though you can have it do anything). This one will say hello to the visitor, and you'll also be able to rename the heading from within the admin interface.

1. Remember, all this is within a plugin file, which is PHP and has the plugin identifying header.

You start with the widget class:

```
class SmashingHello extends WP_Widget {
```

The widget is named `SmashingHello`, so you probably see what's coming.

2. Next you get the widget function:

```
function SmashingHello() {
    parent::WP_Widget(false, $name = 'Smashing Hello');
}
```

3. Remember, you need **widget()**, **update()**, and **form()** to make cool things happen. This is the next step, starting with **widget()**:

```
function widget($args, $instance) {
    extract( $args );
    ?>
            <?php echo $before_widget; ?>
                <?php echo $before_title
                    . $instance['title']
                    . $after_title; ?>
                Well hello there! Ain't that just Smashing?
            <?php echo $after_widget; ?>
    <?php
}
```

You take `widget()` and extract the arguments. Notice the `$before_widget`, `$after_widget`, `$before_tile`, and `$after_title settings`. These shouldn't be changed unless necessary, although you can if you really want to of course. They are controlled by the widget API and default theming, so they make things look good.

So what happens? You echo the `$before_widget` and then the `$before_title`, without telling them to do anything fancy, so they'll just pick up the default code. Then there's the `$instance` title, which is the title of the input field that you'll be making in the widget interface within admin, so that people can write whatever they want there. Then you're done with the title, getting to `$after_title`, and then there's your lovely text that the widget will display: "Well hello there! Ain't that just Smashing?" Not high prose, of course, and you can put just about anything here, a WordPress loop query or whatever. Finally, the widget is all over and you get the `$after_widget`.

Again, these `before` and `after` things are to make the widget behave the way the theme wants them to. This is something the theme designer can control, so if you want to keep your widget cross-compatible, you can stick to the defaults and worry about how it looks in the design. You know, as it should be.

4. Moving on, you need to make sure the widget is saved properly when updated.

```
function update($new_instance, $old_instance) {
    return $new_instance;
}
```

This is easy, since `update()` only takes `$new_instance` and `$old_instance`. Naturally, you want to return the `$new_instance`, which is whatever you changed. You may want to do some tag stripping with `strip_tags()` here if the kind of widget you're creating may run into some nasty HTML stuff. That's easy, just do something like this for an input field named 'music':

```
$instance['music'] = strip_tags( $new_instance['music'] );
```

See `strip_tags()` at work there? It makes sure no stray HTML code gets through. Very handy.

5. Now add some settings, or the one setting, really: changing the widget title:

```
function form($instance) {
    $title = esc_attr($instance['title']);
    ?>
        <p>
            <label for="<?php echo $this->get_field_id('title'); ?>">Title: <input class="widefat"
    id="<?php echo $this->get_field_id('title'); ?>" name="<?php echo $this->get_field_name('title');
    ?>" type="text" value="<?php echo $title; ?>" /></label>
        </p>
    <?php
}
```

The key here is `get_field_name()` and `get_field_id()`, they all handle what field does what. And then, when you've built your pretty little widget settings form, just save it (with the widget API automatically-created save button) and it does the trick.

6. Finally, you need to close the class curly bracket, and register the widget:

```
}

add_action('widgets_init', create_function('', 'return register_widget("SmashingHello");'));
```

Figure 7-1 depicts the widget.

There you have it, a widget where you can change the title and output some text. This can just as easily be something else, more or less anything thanks to the fact that widget output is just PHP spitting something out. After all, if you can echo some text, you can do anything.

Another thing to remember is that not all widgets need to take options at all. If you just want to drop an element in a widget area, with the ease it brings, then by all means just create the widget and forget about the settings. It is really all about what you need in terms of functionality.

Figure 7-1: The widget you just created, dropped in the sidebar widget area

Dashboard Widgets

As of WordPress 2.7, there's support for Dashboard widgets as well. That means you can add widgets to the admin area of WordPress, commonly referred to as the Dashboard. All those boxes you see on the front page of the Dashboard are in fact widgets, and you can add your own.

To create a Dashboard widget, you need to create a plugin. This one is a simple reminder to the users of a group blog to visit the internal pages, and hence it only outputs some text and some links. First you need to create the function that does this:

```
function dashboard_reminder() {
    echo '
        Hey you! Don\'t forget the internal pages for important stuff:<br />
        &larr; <a href="http://domain.com/internal/forum">Forum</a><br />
        &larr; <a href="http://domain.com/internal/documentation">Documentation</a><br />
    &larr; <a href="http://domain.com/internal/staff">Staff</a><br />
    OK THX BYE!
    ';
}
```

It's a simple function called `dashboard_reminder()` that echoes some HTML. This is what you want the widget to display. The next step is to add the Dashboard widget itself.

```
function dashboard_reminder_setup() {
    wp_add_dashboard_widget('dashboard_reminder_widget', 'Staff Reminder', 'dashboard_reminder');
}
```

The key here is `wp_add_dashboard_widget()`, to which you pass first an identifying ID of the widget (which is `'dashboard_reminder_widget'` in this case), and then the text label that should describe the widget, and finally the name of the function containing the Dashboard widget's content (obviously the `dashboard_reminder()` function).Worth knowing is that the Dashboard widget ID, which is the first parameter passed to `wp_add_dashboard_widget()`, is also the class the widget will get should you want some fancy CSS stylings.

Pause for a moment and look at the `wp_add_dashboard_widget()` function. The first parameter is the widget ID, the second the widget name that you want to display, and then there's the callback of the function containing the actual widget content. There's a fourth parameter as well, called `$control_callback`, and it passes a null value by default, and is optional. You can use that to give your widget settings by passing a function containing whatever settings you want to let the user fiddle with. None for this example, but it may be a good idea to keep in mind that you can pass a fourth parameter for more functionality in your Dashboard widget.

Returning to the example, you need to add the widget action to the `wp_dashboard_setup` hook, using `add_action()`:

```
add_action('wp_dashboard_setup', 'dashboard_reminder_setup');
```

There you have it, a Dashboard widget! (See Figure 7-2.) As of now there is no Dashboard widget order API so you widget will end up at the bottom in the Dashboard. The user can reorder widgets manually, of course, but you may want to force things to the top. For now, there are some hacks available online, such as the one described in the WordPress Codex (`codex.wordpress.org/ Dashboard_Widgets_API`) should you need to achieve this.

Now that you've gotten your hands a little dirty with plugins and widgets, it's time to discuss database usage. It is easy enough to store data in the options tables, but sometimes it is just not the right thing to do.

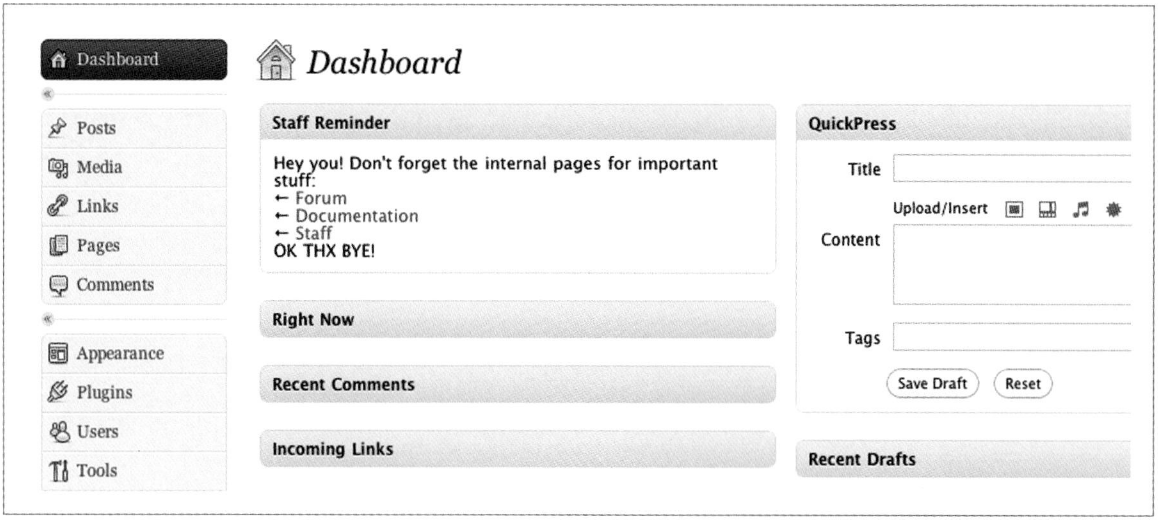

Figure 7-2: The Dashboard widget in all its glory

Things to Consider When Using the Database

The database is sometimes necessary to make your plugins function the way you want. From storing some simple options, to adding full tables with more data for the users to utilize, it is truly a tool that should be put to good use. Putting data in the database means you can query for it easily; it is just very convenient.

However, it comes at a price. A cluttered database isn't very nice to maintain, and you have to make sure the user can uninstall the data stored by the plugin. And if that's not enough, you need to decide where to save this data. Either you use the *options* table created by WordPress, a nice solution for smaller settings, or you create your own table within the database for the plugin only.

The latter solution is probably better if you need to store a lot of data, but it extends the database in such a way that it may create issues with other plugins doing database things, should you want to integrate with them in any way. It also means that there is a part outside WordPress that needs to be backed up, and should you want to move the install the Export/Import method won't cover the data.

So what's best? Data in options, or in its own table? It is entirely up to you depending on what you need to store. My personal guideline is that settings should go in options, and if it is actual content or larger amounts of data, I'd consider the external table option.

Just make sure you inform the user, and make sure that it is possible to clean up after uninstallation should it be necessary, and you'll be fine.

Backwards Compatibility

One thing to consider when developing plugins is whether or not you want or need backwards compatibility. There are new functions and hooks added to WordPress all the time, and if you rely on the new ones, previous versions not featuring them naturally can't run the plugin. That's why you should be careful when using new features because they may just not work in older versions of WordPress.

However, it is not just WordPress functionality that changes; the system requirements have seen some revamps too. As of writing, PHP 4 is still supported, while most PHP developers agree that PHP 5 is a lot better. The basic premise should be to support the hardware that WordPress runs on, but sometimes that's just not enough. You may need PHP 5, or want it enough to accept that hosts running PHP 4 will cause your plugin to not work, despite WordPress running just fine. When you walk down that route, be sure to output an error should someone try and run your plugin under PHP 4, when it really requires PHP 5. Technically, the same issue can apply to MySQL.

How far back you want to let your users go with your plugin is up to you. Since the addition of automatic updates, one can only hope that the updating frequency of the end users is higher than it was pre-auto updates, but a surprisingly large amount of blogs still run on old version of

WordPress, which is bad news for developers and for site owners. After all, there's a bunch of security issues and so on to take into account.

You may also want to consider whether your plugin is original WordPress only, or if you will support the multi-user version, called WordPress MU. Many, but not all, plugins will work in both, so you should consider that as well.

Plugins and WordPress MU

WordPress MU is short for WordPress Multi-User, which is what powers Automattic's hosted blog service, `wordpress.com`. It is used to power multiple blogs at once, and while it shares a lot of code with the stand-alone version of WordPress that this book is focused on, it may not play nicely with your plugin. That being said, most plugins (and themes for that matter) will work with WordPress MU. The only time you may run into issues is if you add tables to the database, and possibly play with the core tables.

WordPress MU can most easily be described as something of an umbrella that allows a super admin user (with its own blog, the WordPress MU front page) manage other blogs created underneath. On `wordpress.com` anyone can create a blog, but that isn't necessarily the way a WordPress MU install works; you can just as well run it to power multiple blogs (like a blog network, for example) and not let users register and/or create their own blogs.

As for the directory structure, you'll recognize the WordPress in WordPress MU. The only real difference is the blogs.dir directory, which contains all the created blogs' data, such as images and uploads and such. You won't be using that much, since WordPress MU has a central theme and plugin management part in the main wp-content, just like you're used to.

You can download WordPress MU from `mu.wordpress.org`. You'll find up-to-date documentation links there as well.

Developing Plugins for WordPress MU

The process of developing plugins for WordPress MU doesn't differ from that for traditional WordPress plugins. The same necessary identifying information is needed for WordPress MU to recognize the plugin as a plugin. The differences are in the database, and somewhat in the directory structure.

Your plugins can reside either in wp-content/plugins/, which you'll recognize, or in wp-plugin/mu-plugins/. The latter is something of an autorun for plugins; if you drop them there they won't show up on the Plugins page in the WordPress MU admin interface, and they'll be considered activated all the time. The only way to deactivate a plugin in mu-plugins is to delete it from the folder. They are known as site-wide plugins.

Actual plugin development is just as for stand-alone WordPress. You do, however, need to make sure you're not relying on creating additional database tables, because that won't be allowed. Editing core tables in the database will also present problems, but some changes are known to work so you'll have to try for yourself, or check out any of the hacked plugins out there. Other than doing database stuff, there really aren't all that many issues with WordPress MU. You may want to check out the WordPress MU functions to further open the doors to MU plugin development: codex.wordpress.org/WPMU_Functions.

Another thing to consider when creating plugins for WordPress MU is how they are intended to be used. Naturally this always applies, but since you can run WordPress MU in so many ways, open or closed, with plugins enabled for bloggers, just for admin, and so on, you may have to rethink the way the plugin works.

All in all, don't be daunted by WordPress MU when it comes to plugin development. It is basically the same, and will most likely actually be the same in the future. A merge is in the works, according to the WordPress developers, so the issues you're experiencing with MU plugins right now may actually work themselves out on their own.

Site-wide WordPress MU Plugins

Plugins placed in wp-content/mu-plugins/ are called site-wide plugins, and they are always activated per default. To uninstall or even make them inactive you need to remove them, which makes them a bit special. After all, not being able to turn off a feature may change the way things work.

As of WordPress MU 2.8, the option to activate plugins site-wide from within admin was added. This means that you can activate plugins located in wp-content/plugins/ to be active site-wide, just like the mu-plugins. This is of course a lot more user-friendly, so you should definitely consider managing site-wide plugin-powered features this way, rather than with mu-plugins. After all, since WordPress MU supports automatic updates, just like regular WordPress, the more that are available at a click from within the admin interface, the better.

So that's it, you're writing a plugin. Now you can share it with the world by releasing it in the official WordPress directory.

Good Practice for Releasing Plugins

Just like with themes, there is an official plugin directory on wordpress.org where you can host your plugins. You don't have to, of course, but it is through this that the users can get the automatic update to work, and keeping them up-to-date with your latest fixes is usually a good idea.

However, there are some terms that your plugins needs to fulfill to be hosted on wordpress.org:

- The plugins needs to be licensed under a GPL-compatible license.
- The plugin can't do anything illegal, nor be "morally offensive."
- The plugin needs to be hosted in the wordpress.org subversion repository.
- The plugin needs a valid readme file.

To get access, you need to be a wordpress.org user. Then, submit your plugin (wordpress.org/extend/plugins/add/) and wait for approval. This process can take some time, depending on workload of the people involved.

When approved, you'll get access to the subversion directory, to which you submit a zip archive containing the plugin, along with a valid readme file. Yes, valid; there is a readme validator that makes sure that all the data needed for the wordpress.org directory to list the plugin information is there: wordpress.org/extend/plugins/about/validator/.

You should read the Developer FAQ for the Plugin Directory before submitting a plugin to make sure you have the most up-to-date information on the matter. This will almost certainly speed up the approval process. You'll find it here: wordpress.org/extend/plugins/about/faq/.

The benefits of being hosted in the wordpress.org repository are not only the automatic update functionality from within the actual users' admin interfaces, but also the statistics it adds. You'll see how many people have downloaded the plugin, get ratings, and you can get comments on it. Not only that, wordpress.org is also the central point for WordPress, which means chances are people will find your plugin, as opposed to just hosting it on your own site and hoping people come across it. Add the new in-admin plugin search interface, and your plugin can be found from within any up-to-date WordPress system out there, and installed at a few clicks at that.

That is, if you're in the wordpress.org repository. So get in there!

This Is Really All You Need

Developing WordPress plugins differs quite a lot from creating WordPress themes. Sure, there are a lot of similarities but in the end what you're really doing is writing PHP scripts that tap into the WordPress functionality. That means that while just about anyone with a little scripting knowledge can bend WordPress themes to their will, the same just doesn't apply when it comes to plugins. You need to understand PHP, and you need to be wary when working with plugins since you can wreck a lot, especially if you're tinkering with the database.

That being said, if you know a little PHP then developing plugins can be the solution to building the site you want, so knock yourself out.

The next chapter discusses when to use a plugin, and when to rely on your theme's functions.php file.

8

PLUGINS AND FUNCTIONS.PHP

WordPress themes and plugins usually work pretty much by themselves, coming together only when it comes to implementing features. This is usually managed by having the correct widget areas available in the theme's template files, so that the user can drop the plugin's widget where it should be, or by actually putting plugin PHP code snippets into the theme. And sometimes the plugins will output or activate the functionality by use of the WordPress hooks, which in essence means that the theme only has to comply with WordPress to trigger the plugins. It is all pretty straightforward.

However, there is one case where themes and plugins collide, and that's when functions.php comes into play. The theme file can do more or less anything a plugin can, which means that it can be an optional solution for a publisher that normally would require a plugin. It also means that functions.php can clash with plugins, if used without caution.

This chapter discusses when to use what solution, and why.

When to Use a Plugin

In short, there is a good rule for when to use a plugin: everything that extends WordPress functionality should be a plugin.

This means that if you add something to WordPress that you wouldn't be able to do otherwise, you should do the actual addition with a plugin. What that addition of functionality actually is would of course depend on what needs you have, but anything from added data management to integration with third-party apps would qualify.

However, there's a big grey area here. A lot of plugins are actually mimicking WordPress and its loop, such as recent post listings and similar solutions that exist so that the user won't have to create a lot of custom loops within the theme. They do that for you, and they do it in a more user-friendly fashion, with options pages that set up the custom loop for you, and widgets that let you drop them wherever you like. Compare that to having to actually write the loop code and put it in your theme file to be output where you want to. That may not seem like a big deal to you and me, but for most users, it is a real hassle. The loop is, after all, a scary thing.

So what it boils down to isn't only if the plugin has any reason to exist according to the rule mentioned above, but also what needs the actual users have. That isn't to be forgotten, since a WordPress site isn't much use if the people maintaining it can't seem to understand how it works.

Custom fields are another example. They are great for a lot of things, as has been covered already and will be shown to an even greater extent later, but at the same time they aren't exactly easy to use, with a bulky interface and so on. A plugin can do the same thing, and in fact use custom fields, but with a sleeker interface. That is something to consider since it can potentially make updating the site easier.

When opting for the plugin solution over the functions.php option, or comparing the use of a plugin with a custom hack in the theme, you need to consider the following things:

- Is the plugin really needed?
- Does the plugin extend WordPress functionality in a way that is either too complicated or so stand-alone that it really isn't an option to try and do the same thing in the theme files?
- Does the plugin need to work outside of the chosen theme?

A positive answer to all these means that you should go ahead with your plugin. If you can't provide anything additional, you should really think things through again.

The Issue with Speed

Nobody likes a slow-loading site, no matter how flashy it is. How fast it needs to be, and how much patience the visitor will have, depends on the target audience and kind of content being served. After all, Flash intro pages are still fairly common, and they should really not exist unless there is an audience for them.

All those things aside, no site should be slower than it needs to be, and a sure way to bloat your WordPress site is to fill it to the brim with plugin-powered functionality. Think about it: most plugins needs to be initialized to work when the visitor encounters their functionality on the site, and that in turn can mean anything from running a PHP function (at the very least), to a full-sized loop with database queries. Say you have 10 plugins on a page, and each one initializes a loop and outputs relevant database content. That will not only take time, it will also put additional strain on the server, possibly making it move sluggishly.

The thing is, a lot of plugins are really the loop in disguise. If you're displaying posts, comments, tags, or anything that builds around that, you're really querying the database. It is just like putting all those custom loops in your theme and watching them spin.

Now, a decent server won't mind this, but a lot of visitors at the same time can bring it to its knees. Database queries are heavy stuff, so you should be wary of having too many of those on the same page without the hardware to back it up.

The same goes for other types of functionality, from simple PHP functions to inclusion of third-party content. True, the biggest issue with these things comes whenever you fetch something from outside the server, which means that you'll be relying not only on your own host's hardware, but also the speed that the content can be reached (in other words, the speed of the Internet), and how quickly the target server can serve you the content. That is why a bunch of widgets pulling data from various services online will slow down any site out there.

The lesson is to not use too many plugins that put a strain on the server. That way you'll keep site load times as low as possible.

When to Use functions.php

When, then, is it really a good idea to use functions.php? I have a rule for that too: only use functions.php when the added functionality is unique to your theme.

The reasoning around this is simple: functions.php is tied to one particular theme, which means that if you switch themes, your added functionality won't come along, forcing you to either recreate it in the new theme or abandon it altogether. This effectively disqualifies functions.php from any kind of use that controls output of content, since that would mean, when you're switching themes, the output would not occur or, at worst, it would render the site broken and full of errors.

Most of the things you do to extend your sites will be minor, and to be honest, a lot of it would probably be better off put in the actual theme template files, keeping the plugin count to a minimum. However, some things are such a big part of the actual site that they need to be added, and nine times out of ten you'll have chosen to add the particular functionality because you'll need it in the long run. And while you may think that you just created the perfect theme, sooner or later you'll end up switching to the next perfect theme, and that means that you'll have to tackle the loss of whatever you've added to functions.php.

True, you can just move the code from the old theme's functions.php file to the new one, but isn't that just an unnecessary hassle? These are things you need to decide upon.

The rule of just putting functionality in functions.php that is unique for the particular theme is a good one, I think. These things include layout settings (obsolete in a different theme) and theme option pages that would slightly change depending on how something/what is added and/or shown in the theme. Since putting that in a plugin would make the plugin obsolete when you switch themes, functions.php is a better choice.

So, plugins are for extending WordPress functionality, and functions.php is for things unique to the actual theme. That pretty much wraps it up.

Planning Your WordPress Site

Whenever you feel the need to extend the WordPress functionality on a project, you will have to figure out whether you can tweak the theme to pull off your ideas, or if you need to develop a plugin. More often than not, when stepping outside of the typical flow of content it is a mixture of both, and that's okay. The important thing is that there are solid ideas behind the choices being made. The obvious questions are:

- Do I need a plugin for feature X?
- Is it possible to extend feature X without replacing the solution?
- Will feature X work if/when the project gets a new theme?
- Will feature X perhaps become an issue when WordPress is updated?
- How will feature X integrate with the theme and other plugins/features?

The point is to establish a plan on how to build your WordPress site. This is true whether you just want to pimp your blog, publish an online newspaper, or do something completely different altogether with the platform. Naturally, the more extreme things you do, and the further you take WordPress beyond the blog, the more thought you'll need to pour into the project.

For examples of what can be done, just look at the solutions in the next part of the book.

IV

BEYOND THE BLOG

9

WORDPRESS AS A CMS

Using WordPress for things other than blogging is something that comes naturally to a lot of developers today, but not so much for the general public. That being said, larger publishing companies are already putting WordPress to good use for their editorial group blogs and others are powering opinion sections using the system.

This chapter tackles the various problems and decisions you need to make when you want to use WordPress as a more traditional CMS, powering non-blog sites with the system. It is not only possible, it is also a perfectly sane solution that saves time and money.

What Is a CMS?

CMS is short for content management system, which basically tells you that it is a way to manage content. It is what you use to write, edit, and publish your work online, assuming you're not hacking the files or database yourself. WordPress is a CMS, even though it originates from blog publishing only. By now you've gathered that WordPress is about way more than just blogs. Basically, you can do just about anything that involves managing written content, but also images, sound, and video. When I'm talking about WordPress with traditional publishers, I usually say that there is no newspaper or magazine site that I couldn't rebuild in WordPress. These are sites usually powered by expensive licensed systems, and while it was unlikely that anyone would make that claim a couple of years ago, today it is taken seriously.

So WordPress is a CMS and you should treat it as such. It is great to power blogs, but it has other uses as well.

Why WordPress?

While WordPress's CMS status is hard to debate (although some people still try), that in itself doesn't really say anything. There are enough bad CMS alternatives out there to go around, so it really isn't a proof of anything. Picking the right CMS is important, since it should excel at what you want it to do.

WordPress is your choice if you want a CMS that is:

- Open source and free
- Fast and easy to use
- Easily extendable
- Easy to design and develop plugins for
- Excellent with text
- Good enough with images

Basically, if your site is an editorial one, based on text and not thousands of images (although that will work too, as Matt Mullenweg of WordPress fame has shown on ma.tt), you'll be safe with choosing WordPress.

So when should you go a completely different route than WordPress? Some would say whenever you need community, but the release of BuddyPress for the multi-user version of WordPress, and the easy integration with bbPress, actually make this argument a pretty weak one. What some of the heavier CMSs have is of course a more modular structure, which means you can create pretty much anything you want, wherever you want. This usually at the expense of usability so you need to compare features and workflow before deciding on which route you should take.

Also, one of the most common criticisms against open source CMS alternatives overall is that commercial ones offer support as a part of the package. That's why it is considered worth something to pay for a CMS. Naturally, this is ridiculous; the money allocated to licensing could be spent on a consultant and/or developer when needed, and not just be the cause of a big hole in the coffers. The point is, any open source CMS, WordPress included, can be met with that criticism. The defense would of course be that you can take those licensing fees and build your adaptations, should you not find the solution being available already. And after that, it is all free.

WordPress is a great CMS option, especially if you're building an editorial site. Whether you think it is right for your project or not, you should always sit back and figure out what you actually need first. Then, find the ideal CMS and consider how you would use it for this particular project. More often than not, you'll revert to a CMS you know, which may or may not be a good idea.

Just remember: you can build just about anything with WordPress. All you have to do is figure out how, and that's why you bought this book, right?

Things to Consider When Using WordPress as a CMS

So you're considering using WordPress as a CMS for a project huh? Great, and probably a good choice too! However, there are several things to consider when planning, designing, and setting up the WordPress install. That's when this checklist comes in handy. You need to think of these things first to avoid running into unwanted surprises along the way.

The first questions:

- Do you need a CMS for this project? Sometimes hacking HTML is the way to go, after all.
- Is WordPress the correct CMS? It may be great, but sometimes other things would work better.

The WordPress admin interface:

- What additional functionality do you need for the admin interface?
- Should you use plugins to cut down on functionality? The admin interface can be pretty overwhelming to non-savvy users.
- If you're going to employ user archives, consider what usernames to give everyone involved.
- Should the menu(s) be editable from within admin? If yes, how will they be updated?
- Does it matter that the admin interface is branded WordPress? If yes, you need to give it some new style, and don't forget the login form.

Categories and tagging:

- What is your strategy with categories and tags?
- Which categories should there be, and do you need to do custom category coding and/or templates?
- How should tags be used, and how will you educate the users in the praxis you've chosen?

Pages and posts:

- Do you need custom fields?
- Do you need to create Page templates to achieve things on your site? If so, make sure you've got those Pages created from the start.
- How should Pages relate to each other? What should be a top-level Page, and what should be a sub-Page? Make sure you know the hierarchy, and how you will present the various sections.
- How will you present the posts? Do they need any specific treatment to fit in?
- What will be on the front page? A static page, latest news updates, or something else?

Other things:

- Figure out your permalink structure right away, and stick to it. You may need plugins to tune it the way you want.
- Do you need specific shortcode to speed up the publishing and avoid unnecessary HTML code in the posts?
- What features does WordPress not cover itself, and what plugins can you use to achieve those features? Also, how likely is it that this will cause you trouble with regard to upgrades in the future?
- Is there a good translation available, should you be working for a non-English speaker? There are plenty of language files for WordPress, but what about themes and plugins? Is there additional work there?

Don't Forget the Manual

To you and me WordPress may seem a breeze to use, and truly it is, today more than ever with WYSIWYG writing and the like. The problem is, not everyone sees it that way. In fact, people not as used to Web-based systems at all may find WordPress daunting, despite being perfectly at home in regular word processors and more or less well-designed software.

While the `wordpress.org` Web site and `the wordpress.tv` screencast-fest may be a good tool to point your users to, in the end you're probably better off creating a small how-to guide to describe how WordPress works. This is especially important if you're using WordPress as a CMS for a static Web site, hence not doing any of the blogging stuff really. If you point your users to the Codex then, they'll just be confused. Besides, the Codex is great, but it is not the most user-friendly creation online.

If you're a WordPress developer and/or designer, and you do a lot of WordPress sites, I advise you to put together a starter kit that describes the most common tasks of the day-to-day usage. This kit, which can be anything from a simple document to a printed booklet, should be easily updated as new versions of WordPress come along. It should also be constructed in such a manner that you can add to it whatever custom functionality is used for the client sites. Maybe you have a category for video that acts differently from the other ones, or perhaps there's the ever-present issue with custom fields and their usability. Add plugin usage, widgets, and possible settings that you've devised for your client, and you can save yourself a lot of questions if you deliver a simple getting started manual with your design.

Trimming WordPress to the Essentials

Usually, when doing work for clients or other people within your organization, you'll have to think a little bit differently than if you were going to be the primary user yourself. Remember: you're a savvy user, but that may not be the case for everybody else. That's why you need to trim WordPress to the essentials, and make sure that there aren't too many options to confuse the user.

The first and foremost trimming action you can perform is to limit the user privileges. As was discussed in the security section in Chapter 1, not all users need full admin accounts. Most of the time, the Editor account role will be enough, and sometimes you may want to go below that as well. Either way, for every step down the user level ladder you take, less options are displayed for the user, and that is a good thing in this case.

It goes without saying that you should make sure there are no unnecessary plugins activated, since these not only potentially slow things down, they also clutter the admin interface with option pages and things like that. So keep it clean.

Tweaking the Admin Interface

You can make the WordPress admin interface appear in tune with your needs by using one of the CMS plugins available. There are several, but WP-CMS Post Control (`wordpress.org/extend/plugins/wp-cms-post-control/`) will probably get the job done. With this plugin, you can hide unnecessary elements for your users, disable autosave (which can be a nuisance), control which image uploader should be used, and a bunch of other things. It can really make the WordPress interface a little easier on the eye of the scared and non-savvy new user. I especially like the message box option, which can contain information for the user on how to proceed, and links to more help.

There are also several plugins that let you hide parts of the admin interface. You may want to consider them if you will be responsible for running a site at your company, or for a client, for a long time. But beware if it is a one-time gig! As you know, new WordPress versions roll out all the time, and that means that plugins may stop working, or need to be upgraded. While that is easy enough in WordPress, it also means that you have to educate the client in how to do it if you're not responsible.

Still, to use WordPress as a CMS makes a lot more sense if you hide the stuff you don't need. The competition may not be doing it, but if you're using WordPress to power a semi-static corporate Web site, then it certainly sounds like a good idea to remove all the stuff the users don't need to see. Just make sure you've got the upgrades covered when they roll out.

Your Own Admin Theme

Did you know that you can create your own WordPress admin theme? Unfortunately, it isn't nearly as impressive as the traditional themes, but still, you can change the look and feel. and that may be important.

You can hack wp-admin.css in the wp-admin folder, which is where all the admin styling goes, but a much cleaner, not to mention upgrade-safe solution, is to create your own WordPress admin theme as a plugin. This really isn't all that complicated. What you want to do is to use the `admin_head()` action hook to attach your very own stylesheet, and then just override the stuff you don't like in wp-admin.css. You'll recognize this bit:

```php
<?php
/*
Plugin Name: Smashing Admin Theme
Plugin URI: http://tdhedengren.com/wordpress/smashing-admin-theme/
Description: This is the Smashing Admin Theme, disguised as a plugin. Activate to make your admin
    smashing!
Author: Thord Daniel Hedengren
Version: 1.0
Author URI: http://tdhedengren.com
*/

function smashing_admin() {
    $url = get_settings('siteurl');
    $url = $url . '/wp-content/plugins/smashing-admin/wp-admin.css';
    echo '<link rel="stylesheet" type="text/css" href="' . $url . '" />';
}

add_action('admin_head', 'smashing_admin');

?>
```

The first part is obviously the now familiar plugin header, which lets WordPress know that, hey, this is a plugin and I should show it off in the plugins page. I'm calling this admin theme the Smashing Admin Theme, so it makes sense that the function is called `smashing_admin()`.

You're going to put the plugin in its own folder, smashing-admin, which the users will drop in wp-content/plugins/, so first of all you load the `$url` variable with the siteurl value, using `get_settings()`. Then you update it by getting the siteurl value and add the path of your own wp-admin.css stylesheet, located within the smashing-admin plugin folder. Or /wp-content/plugins/smashing-admin/wp-admin.css to be precisely. Finally, you echo it.

To get this echoed stylesheet link into admin, you use `add_action()` to attach the `smashing_admin()` function to the `admin_head` action hook. And there you have it, one stylesheet loaded in admin. Now all you want to do is pick the original wp-admin.css to pieces by altering the stuff you like. Just edit the wp-admin.css stylesheet in your plugin folder.

You can just as easily add actual content to the top or bottom of the WordPress admin. Just use `add_action()` and attach it to `admin_head` or `admin_footer`, and you've got the control you need.

What about the login screen? You can get to it as well, but the easiest solution is to use one of the numerous plugins available. See the admin plugins list in Chapter 11 for more on this.

Unblogging WordPress

A lot of the time when using WordPress as a CMS to power simpler Web sites, most of the functionality is completely unnecessary. A company Web site built around static pages containing product information doesn't need comments or trackbacks, and the only fluid kind of content it may have would be a news or press clippings section. It just makes sense; some functionality just isn't needed, and neither is the blog lingo.

So when you need to build the kind of site that just doesn't need all the bling and the functionality, you obviously won't include this in your theme. The following are all things that should either be rephrased or removed in an entirely unbloggish site.

Template Files

Ideally you'd stick to just one, index.php, for all your listing and search needs, but you can chop this up into several templates if you want to. Naturally, comments.php is completely unnecessary. Page templates, on the other hand, are very useful, and you'll most likely end up having a static front page using one of these.

Also, remember to remove any `get_comments()` calls from the template files. Yes, you can just note that you won't accept comments in admin, but that means that you'd have to change the "Comments are closed" output in comments.php, which would look pretty bad. So better to just remove `get_comments()` from index.php, and any other template tags where it may be used.

Lingo

There's a lot of bloggish lingo within WordPress by default: words like "permalink," but also "categories" and "tags." The last two can be defined on a URL level in the permalink settings. Maybe you want to go with "news" instead of the default "category," and perhaps "view" or "topic" rather than the default "tag?" Actually, a good way to create a news section for a static corporate site is to use Pages for any serious content, like company information and product descriptions, whereas you'll use the one category, called News with the slug "news," for the news posts. That way, you can set up your permalinks so that `/news/` will be the category listings, or the News section in this case, and then you let all the posts (which of course are just news items) get the `/news/post-slug/` permalink by applying the `/%category%/%postname%/` permalink structure in the settings. Really handy, and no need to build a custom news section or anything.

This inevitably leads into what you can do with static Pages and how what used to be blog posts can fill the needs of a more traditional Web site.

Static Pages and News Content

I touched upon static Pages and categories as a news model previously. It is truly a great tool whenever you need to roll out a typical old-school Web site quickly. Maybe it is a product presentation, a corporate Web site, or something entirely different that just won't work with the blog format. That's when this setup is so useful.

Pages, as in WordPress Pages, were originally meant to be used for static content. The fact that you can create one Page template (recall that template files for Pages are individual) for each and every one of them should you want to means that they can really look like anything. You can break your design completely, since you don't even have to call the same header or footer file, you can have different markup, and you can exclude everything WordPress-related and display something entirely different instead, should you want to. It is a really powerful tool that can just as easily contain multiple loops or syndicated RSS content from other sites. Each Page template is a blank slate, and it is your primary weapon when using WordPress as a CMS; this is where you can make the site truly step away from the blog heritage that the system carries.

And don't get me started on the front page! Since you can set WordPress to display a static Page as a front page (under Settings in admin), and pick any other Page (keep it empty, mind you) for your post listings should you need that, you can really do anything. You can even put in one of those nasty Flash preloader thingies with autoplaying sound (but you really shouldn't). The point is that a Page template, along with the front page setting, is just as much a clean slate as a blank PHP or HTML file would be outside WordPress, but you have the benefits of the system right there should you need them!

On the other side of things, you've got the traditional blog posts. These need to belong to a category and each and every one of them will be more or less the same, visually. Sure, if you want to you can play around a lot with these too, but on a semi-static site Pages are a much better idea. Naturally, it is a whole different ball game if you're going to handle tons of content, but that's usually not what you're talking about when "WordPress as a CMS" gets mentioned.

Pages for static content, posts for newsy stuff. It makes sense when you think about it.

Finding the Perfect Setup

You're looking for the perfect setup with Pages for all those product descriptions, and posts for news, announcements, and press clippings. This is what I start with whenever I do a corporate Web site with WordPress as a CMS, which is basically any corporate Web site I'll do these days.

Assuming I've got the design worked out, here is the process I'll follow:

1. I decide what will be a Page and what will not. Usually, everything except news and announcements are Pages, so that is really easy. I create these Pages and make sure they get the right slug. This includes making sure that the basic permalink structure is there, which means I'll make sure the post and category URLs look good. Chances are I'll use a plugin to further control this, but it all depends on the needs of the site.

2. I start creating the Page templates. Chances are the company profile Page will have other design needs than the product Pages, so I'll want to put emphasis on different things, and construct any possible submenus and information boxes in ways that fit the style.

3. I create the categories needed, one for each newsy section. This is usually just one, called News or Announcements, but sometimes it is both, and even more at that. In some cases I really just want just one category—Announcements, for example—and then I opt for sorting within it using tags, one for News, one for Press Releases, one for Products, one for Announcements,

and so on. Naturally, I'll need to make sure the category listings as well as the single post view look good.

4. I tie it all together by creating a menu (usually hardcoded, since most sites like this will be pretty static in this department as well) which links to both the various Pages, and the categories involved.

That's it, the elements of a static simple Web site using WordPress as a CMS. You can take this concept as far as you like really, since it is WordPress and you can build upon it as much as you like.

Some Web sites obviously need more attention: the more advanced the site, the more tweaks and adaptations are needed to make it fit. Sometimes this means you'll have to write custom loops or use Page templates, and at other times you may want more flexibility without touching the code for every little update. That's when widgets come in, not only because a lot of cool features come as plugins that are widget-ready, but also because widgets offer drag-and-drop functionality that non-techy users will surely appreciate.

Putting Widgets to Good Use

Widgets and widget areas are your friends when rolling out WordPress as a CMS. It is perhaps not as important for the small and static company Web sites primarily discussed so far, but rather for the larger ones. Take a look around online; there are numerous sites that push out mixed function-ality, especially on their front pages, and display teaser images when it is suitable.

You can do this with widgets, and with the revamped widget API that WordPress 2.8 brought with it, this is now even easier to do. The most straightforward usage is to litter your site with widget areas wherever you may want to output something all of a sudden; just make sure that the area doesn't output anything by default should you want it to be invisible (as in not con-taining anything) whenever you haven't populated it with a widget. That being said, it is good to think your widget areas through, and put the areas where you need them, not where you think you may need them in two years time. After all, you will have redesigned the site by then anyway …

So you've got your widget areas in. Now, how to use them? Besides the obvious answer of drag-and-drop widgets on the Appearance → Themes page in WordPress admin, you'll need widgets that do what you need. The ones that ship with WordPress are simple and somewhat crude; the Pages widget (listing your Pages) won't even let you display just the Pages, it forces an h2 title out there, and this is a bad thing. You want control, so if you're moving down this route, be sure to look at other plugins that offer widget support. These days, a great many do, including ones that just list the Pages. (Seems I'm not the only one annoyed with that default h2 heading, after all.)

The most usable widget is by far the text widget. Why? Because it accepts HTML code, which means that putting text and images in it is a breeze. This is good, because if you want to show off that special promotion just below the menu in the header, you can just put the necessary HTML code in a text widget and drop it there for the duration of the campaign, and then just remove it, and the area will disappear. That is, if you kept it empty.

Making Widgets a Little More Dynamic

Why stop there? Why not just put empty widget areas where your various elements on the site could be? It will do the job, but you'll have to cram them in wherever they will fit, and this will have to take the rest of the design and content into account. You will have to do that either way, of course, but there is an alternative.

Replace parts of the content.

If you're running an magazine-ish site, you may sometimes get the opportunity to roll out big so-called roadblocks, ads that take over a lot more of the site than just common banners and leaderboards. These things usually run for a shorter amount of time, and you get paid a lot for them, compared to ads.

Or, take another approach: say you're an Apple blogger and you want to cover the Apple WWDC or MacWorld in a timely manner, making sure that your readers won't miss it. How? Plaster the site in promotional graphics of course!

Both these examples will work poorly (in most cases) if you just add stuff to widget areas positioned around the site's normal elements. They will, however, work perfectly well if you replace parts of the site's content, meaning any element really. This effect is pretty easy to get working, thanks to the fact that widget areas can come preloaded with content.

This is a widget area called Teaser, and it should come preloaded with the content you want in that particular spot on a day-to-day basis:

```
<?php if ( !function_exists('Teaser') || !dynamic_sidebar() ) : ?>
    [The normal content would go here. Links, headlines, whatever. . . ]
<?php endif; ?>
```

Just put it in there; it can be anything, really. A headline section, a poll, must-read lists, loops, links—you name it. Anything.

However, when you drop a widget in the Teaser widget area within the WordPress admin interface, the default content won't show; it will be replaced with the widget you dropped. So dropping a text widget with your big fat promo image for the Apple event, or your new e-book, or whatever, will replace the original content. When you remove the image from the Teaser widget area, the default content will return by default.

Pretty nifty, huh? And actually pretty simple to maintain as well; if something goes wrong, you can just remove the widget you put there, and you'll always revert to default.

Another great use of widgets is navigational menus, which make sure users can add menu items themselves without having to rely on the theme designer.

Managing Menus

Menus are important: they need to look good and be easy to maintain. When you're using Word-Press as a CMS, this is perhaps even more important. Thanks to WordPress widgets, you can make this a whole lot easier. Naturally, if you know the menu won't need updating anytime soon, you can just hardcode it into the theme, but that may be too definitive for a lot of cases.

In Notes Blog Core, there is a widget area called Submenu just under the header (see Figure 9-1). It is empty by default since not all people would want anything there, but should you populate it with an unordered list you'll get your menu. The widget area is defined in functions.php and the actual area is just like most widgets, but contains nothing: hence when not outputting anything, it should it be empty. It does, however, come with some extra flair that lets you apply some CSS to it when it does in fact contain data. This is how the Submenu widget area is defined in functions.php:

```
register_sidebar(array(
    'name' => 'Submenu',
    'id' => 'submenu',
    'before_widget' => '<div id="submenu-nav">',
    'after_widget' => '</div>',
    'before_title' => false,
    'after_title' => false
));
```

And this is what it looks like in header.php:

```
<div id="header">
    <h1><a href="<?php bloginfo('url'); ?>" title="<?php bloginfo('name'); ?>" name="top"><?php
  bloginfo('name'); ?></a> <span><?php bloginfo('description'); ?></span></h1>
</div>
<?php if ( !function_exists('dynamic_sidebar') || !dynamic_sidebar('Submenu') ) : ?><?php endif; ?>
```

Notes Blog THE FREE WORDPRESS THEME

Core   About the Project   Subscribe   Contact Information

Notes Blog Core and WordPress 2.8.2

There's a brand new release of WordPress available, being 2.8.2. It's a security release that you should upgrade to. Notes Blog *Core* users needn't worry, the theme works perfectly well with this release as well. Incidentally, this very site now runs 2.8.2.

Figure 9-1: The Notes Blog Core submenu in action on http://notesblog.com

The first part is the header title and the blog description, within the `div#header` element. The PHP snippet is the widget area, looking for the `'Submenu'` one.

Speaking of which, a menu like this should be an unordered list, and that applies to most menus, although perhaps not all. Why? Well, what is a menu if not a list of items? You're applying this kind of basic markup:

```
<ul>
    <li>[menu item]</li>
    <li>[menu item]</li>
    <li>[menu item]</li>
</ul>
```

The basic CSS (found in your stylesheet of course) will apply some instructions to the `ul` tag, and then float the list items to the right with proper spacing. Something like this:

```
div#submenu-nav
    {
    width:100%;
    float:left;
    border: 1px solid #444;
    border-width: 0 0 1px 1px;
    border-left: 1px dotted #e8e8e8;
    }
    div#submenu-nav ul {}
        div#submenu-nav ul li { list-style: none; float:left; padding: 8px;
                border: 1px dotted #e8e8e8; border-width: 0 1px 0 0; }
```

Naturally, you'll want to adapt this to your design.

So, how can you put this technique to good use? The easiest solution is using a text widget. Create a widget area where you want the menu, and just drop a text widget in there. Then, just put the HTML code for your menu in the text widget and you're good to go. You may in fact want to preload the area with the necessary markup for a default menu, usually an unlimited list and some list items.

This is the easy solution; it works well enough, and if you know HTML like the back of your hand it's a breeze to update. However, far from all users do that, so you may want to reconsider this option should you need a menu that changes on a regular basis. Still, it gets the job done and doesn't really require much altering or editing.

Another solution is to work Page listings with Widgets Reloaded. It is common that you only want to display the Pages when it comes to the main menu; the actual posts are usually used as news items and you don't want to litter your menu with categories and trivialities like that. That's when a widget area (yes, you're back to the Submenu one from Notes Blog Core) and the Page widget are tempting. After all, what it does is list the Pages correctly and lets you control the manner in which they'll appear (sort of). That sounds just about perfect when Pages are what you want to show off, right?

Wrong. The default Page widget has the poor taste of forcing a title, even when you leave that field empty in the widget. That means that you'll end up with an ugly Pages h2 heading at the top of your listing, which honestly looks like crap in a menu.

Luckily you can solve this by using a plugin, such as the ever popular Widgets Reloaded (`wordpress.org/extend/plugins/widgets-reloaded/`). Among other things, it lets you include Pages and decide what depth (usually one, showing only the top-level Pages) it should include. Also, when not giving the widget a title, it won't output one, which is great news.

That does it for most of the main elements of a design. Sometimes, however, you'll want to add visual enhancements to the actual content. You can do this by just writing HTML code, but if your users aren't so code-savvy it may be a better idea to create some custom shortcodes that translate to the HTML code needed. In the next section we'll do just that.

Custom Shortcodes

Shortcode is tagged code that you can input in your posts to get something else. The `[gallery]` tag is shortcode. You can create your own shortcode, which can come in handy when using Word-Press overall, but in particular when you're doing non-bloggish things with it.

You can add shortcode functionality through a plugin, or by using functions.php. In this next section, we'll do the latter.

TRY IT OUT Adding Shortcode with functions.php

1. Start by creating a simple shortcode tag that outputs some simple text, then you'll put it to more interesting use later.

2. First off, you need a function that does what you want, so let's write that, within the PHP tags of functions.php of course.

```
function text_example() {
    return 'Why, this text was just output using the shortcode tag you created! Smashing.';
}
```

3. Now you need to add **text_example()** to a shortcode. You do that with the **add_shortcode()** function:

```
add_shortcode('textftw', 'text_example');
```

This creates the `[textftw]` shortcode, and loads it with the contents of the `text_example()` function. So `[textftw]` in your blog post will output in your post, "Why, this text was just output using the shortcode tag you created! Smashing."

Simple enough. Now do something useful with it, like doing a shortcode for promoting your RSS feed.

4. Starting with the function, this time you'll use it to output some HTML code as well, which gives you control of how the promotion appears:

```
function rss_promotion() {
    return '<div class="rsspromot">Never miss a beat - <a href="http://notesblog.com/feed/">
  subscribe to the RSS feed!</a></div>';
}
```

5. Then you need to create the shortcode, and add the `rss_promotion()` function content to it:

```
add_shortcode('rsspromo', 'rss_promotion');
```

6. Now you've got the `[rsspromo]` shortcode that outputs the `div` container from the `rss_promotion()` function. All you have to do to wrap this up is to add some styling to the style.css stylesheet. Maybe something like this:

```
div.rsspromo {
    background: #eee;
    Border: 1px solid #bbb;
    color: #444;
    font-size: 16px;
    font-style: italic;
}
div.rsspromo a { font-weight:bold; font-style:normal; }
```

Or anything that fits your design. Now you can add an RSS promotion box anywhere you like, using the `[rsspromo]` shortcode. Another idea on the same topic would be to add e-mail subscription forms using the same technique, and why not load a function with your default ad code? That way you can easily change it should you get a better deal/click ratio somewhere else.

Spiffing up Text with Pullquotes

The next example features the pull quote functionality built into Notes Blog Core. It adds the `[pull]` shortcode, which takes one attribute: float. Here's the code in functions.php:

```
function pullquote( $atts, $content = null ) {
    extract(shortcode_atts(array(
        'float' => '$align',
    ), $atts));
    return '<blockquote class="pullquote ' . $float . '">' . $content . '</blockquote>';
}
add_shortcode('pull', 'pullquote');
```

Pretty much the same as the previous example, except that you're extracting the `shortcode_atts()` array, and the `$content = null` part which tells you that you need to close this shortcode. You'll also call that in your return statement to get the stuff in between the opening and closing shortcode tags. In other words, it is `[shortcode]$content[/shortcode]`, and whatever else you cram in there.

That is where the attributes come in, in this case just `float`. The idea is that when using the `[pull]` shortcode, the user sets `float` to either `alignleft` or `alignright`, like this: `[pull float="alignright"]My text[/pull]`. Seasoned theme designers know that both `alignleft` and `alignright` are standard classes for positioning used in WordPress, so your theme should have those already. You'll use them to position the pull quote.

In other words, you return the code, being a block quote with the class pull quote, and whatever value the user has given the `float` attribute, and output it. The use `[pull float="alignright"]My text[/pull]`, will output this in code:

```
<blockquote class="pullquote alignright">My text</blockquote>
```

Handy for people not wanting to hack the HTML code. Of course, if you want more attributes you can just add them to the array, and then include them where you wanted them.

Shortcode Tidbits

You may be wondering if nested shortcode works. It does, and you can put one shortcode tag inside another, just as long as you open and close them properly, just like HTML. For instance, this will work:

```
[shortcode-1]
    [shortcode-2]
    [/shortcode-2]
[/shortcode-1]
```

But the following would probably break and give you funky results:

```
[shortcode-1]
    [shortcode-2]
[/shortcode-1]
    [/shortcode-2]
```

However, for this snippet to work you have to allow shortcode within your shortcode by using `do_shortcode()`. So if you wanted to allow shortcode in the `[pull]` tag, from the previous example, you'd have to put `$content` within `do_shortcode()`, like this:

```
function pullquote( $atts, $content = null ) {
    extract(shortcode_atts(array(
        'float' => '$align',
    ), $atts));
    return '<blockquote class="pullquote ' . $float . '">' . do_shortcode($content) . '</blockquote>';
}
add_shortcode('pull', 'pullquote');
```

Otherwise, any shortcode placed between [pull] and [/pull] wouldn't be properly parsed.

Remember, shortcode only works within content, not in headers or even excerpts. It is tied to the the_content() template tag. However, you can make it work by using the do_shortcode() function and adding a filter. It may be a good idea to at least add shortcode support to widget areas, if you intend to do impressive stuff with them. After all, that text widget can be mighty handy if you want it to be.

The following code in your functions.php file will add shortcode support to the default text widget:

```
add_filter('widget_text', 'do_shortcode');
```

It applies the do_shortcode() function to the widget_text() function as a filter (with add_filter() obviously). Simple, just the way I like it!

The shortcode API is actually pretty extensive. You may want to read up in the WordPress Codex: codex.wordpress.org/Shortcode_API.

Using shortcodes is a great way to let the users add both features and functionality to their content. However, sometimes you need to go outside the obvious design elements (be they widgets or loop hacks) and the content itself, especially if the Web site in question needs to promote other services. Integration of non-WordPress content is tackled next.

Integrating Non-WordPress Content

Sometimes you need to get non-WordPress content into your WordPress site. This can be tricky, since not all publishing platforms play along nicely. At best, the content you need to expose within your WordPress site can either be exported in a widget-like fashion (not the plugin kind, the JavaScript sort), included in whole with PHP, or perhaps even displayed in an iframe if all else fails.

These days RSS feeds are a savior if you're looking at text content especially, but also when it comes to video and images. If the outside content is in fact material from the image service Flickr, for example, you can fetch the RSS feed either with a separate plugin (there are Flickr plugins along with RSS variants), or with the built-in WordPress functionality for displaying feeds.

This is the basic `fetch_RSS` code that can be used with WordPress. In this case, you're calling `notesblog.com/feed/` and displaying the last five posts from it in an unlimited list:

```php
<h2>Latest from Notes Blog</h2>
<?php // Get RSS Feed(s)
include_once(ABSPATH . WPINC . '/rss.php');
$rss = fetch_rss('http://notesblog.com/feed/');
$maxitems = 5;
$items = array_slice($rss->items, 0, $maxitems);
?>

<ul>
<?php if (empty($items)) echo '<li>Oops, nothing here!</li>';
else
foreach ( $items as $item ) : ?>
    <li><a href='<?php echo $item['link']; ?>' title='<?php echo $item['title']; ?>'>
    <?php echo $item['title']; ?>
    </a></li>
<?php endforeach; ?>
</ul>
```

So whenever you need to display content that is available in a RSS feed, this can be used, or any of the other available plugins of course.

Either way, when you've figured out how to display the content you want within your WordPress site, chances are you'll be creating a Page with its own template containing this code. It is the easiest way, and something I recommend before reverting to ExecPHP and similar plugins that let you put PHP code within posts and Pages, as they can really break things. Putting the code in the template files instead is my advice.

At other times, the solution may involve you making a plugin that acts as the middle ground. I've actually done this in the past, when I ran my own CMS and wanted to move to WordPress, but had this huge database of games along with a lot of data. Text and images were easy enough (says I, who just played the role of project manager at the time; my coder was less happy) to import into the WordPress databases, but flexible taxonomies and native tagging support didn't exist back then, so we had to be creative with the games database. The solution was to write a plugin that read that part and displayed it using shortcodes. A lot more hassle than just displaying something from an RSS feed, but sometimes you just can't get the content into WordPress itself without extending it further. So we did.

Finally, if all else fails, just fake it. Make the page look like your WordPress theme, but have it outside of the actual theme. I know, not as fun, but sometimes systems just clash, and while you can usually sort it out it may just not be worth the time.

Taking the CMS One Step Further

It is a common misconception that WordPress isn't a fitting choice when looking at CMS solutions for various projects. Obviously, it is not always the perfect choice—no publishing platform will ever be—but the ease with which you can roll out a site with WordPress is a strong factor in its favor. Add a simple user interface and great expandability thanks to plugins and themes, and you've got a fairly solid case right there.

Just to drive the point that WordPress is more than just a blogging platform even further home, the next chapter is dedicated to uncommon usage. This means that you'll build things that most people probably haven't even considered using WordPress for, and you'll do it quick and dirty as concepts in need of brushing up for launch, but still ready to go. When creating these site concepts in the next chapter, I put an emphasis on development speed. That means that these sites could be built in less than a day.

How's that for rolling out new projects the WordPress way?

10 UNCOMMON WORDPRESS USAGE

That WordPress can power blogs as well as other editorial sites should be fairly obvious by now. You can use it for static Web sites, newspaper or magazine-like sites, and just about anything where you are publishing text, images, or any kind of multimedia really.

But why stop there? WordPress can be used for projects even further from its bloggish roots, which this chapter will show. You can be build sites on top of WordPress that the developer's definitely didn't have in mind from the start. Hopefully these adaptations of the platform will help you see the full potential of the system.

The Job Board

The first special project we'll work on is a job board. You have probably seen this kind of site already, where people and companies can post job openings. You'll use WordPress posts for storing each job offer, and for sorting them into main categories. Tags will be used to pinpoint more precisely what the job is all about, and among other things you'll tag each post with the company that posts the opening, which may prove to be an interesting way to sort jobs by in the future.

So far, so good. It is really pretty close to what WordPress was made for, isn't it? Despite it not being a blog, I mean.

The problem comes when you want to let the parties offering jobs post their jobs themselves, so you won't have to. Granted, you can just give them a username each (and even open up the signup form), but not let them have publishing rights, but should they really be mucking about in the WordPress admin interface? I say no; that isn't a particularly clean nor user-friendly solution, since all they really want to do is to fill out a form detailing their job opening, send it in and then have it approved by the site staff.

And that's exactly what they'll do. You'll employ a plugin for this functionality, offering a specific page containing said job form.

In the end, what you'll get is a site where parties offering jobs can send them in through a form, so that they end up in WordPress as posts that the site staff will approve. Approved jobs (published posts in reality) will be sorted into categories (depending on the type of job), and be tagged appropriately. You'll take as much of this data from the job submission as possible, without hacking any plugins, so anything that will not go straight in easily will have to be added manually.

The whole idea is to build this job board in a quick and dirty way, launch it with WordPress, and then continue to build it after launch. Time to get started.

The Theme

The actual theme is less important for this project, since it will be so straightforward. The idea is to have a header featuring a horizontal menu, and then have the content in three columns.

1. **Jobs available.** This column will display jobs posted in the Job offerings category.
2. **Looking for work.** This column will display jobs posted in the Looking for work category.
3. **Other things.** The third column will show info text, search, promotions, tag clouds, and other things that should make using the site easier.

Finally, you'll wrap the whole thing up with a footer containing some basic information.

In terms of template files, you'll need a specific front page template (home.php), and of course a header (header.php) and a footer (footer.php) template, respectively. The home template will contain columns 1 and 2, but column 3 will in fact be the sidebar template (sidebar.php) so that you can call on it when people are viewing the actual job postings as well, which will be posts really, so you want a single post template (single.php) too. And, of course, a stylesheet (style.css); the theme can't very well work without it.

All listings, from category and tag listings, and things like that, can be managed from an index.php template, since it is the fallback template file for everything. You can even put the 404 error into index.php if you want to.

To get started as quickly as possible, you'll build this on Notes Blog Core, as a child theme. That's right, you won't even have to bother with the fundamental basics, just getting right into the fray. I did mention that's the beauty of child theming, right?

So what are you building? A simple job board theme that will display the latest job offerings available (Figure 10-1). It is more a concept than a finished product obviously, but should be enough to get you started.

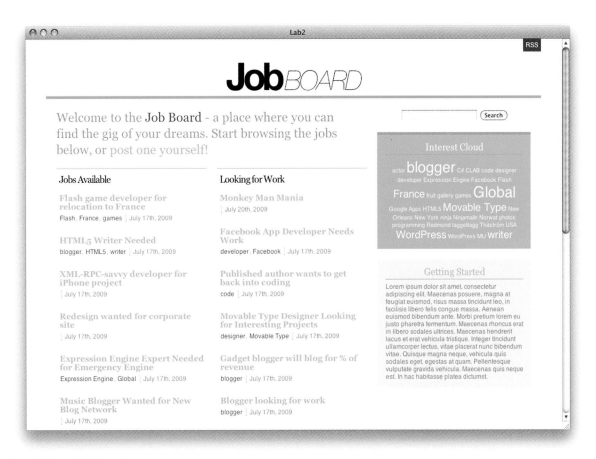

Figure 10-1: A simple Job Board theme

The Header and Footer Templates

The changes planned for the header file are actually all cosmetic, or managed by the Submenu widget area, so there is no need to create a new header.php file. The child theme's stylesheet (style.css) will cover this, and it resides in the wp-content/themes/ directory in a folder called notesblog-jobboard, alongside with notes-blog-core-theme, which is needed because it's your template.

As for the footer, you won't alter anything there besides some styles using style.css. The fact that Notes Blog Core's footer has four widget areas by default means you can show the latest jobs there using widgetized plugins, and add graphics (using the text widget for example) for promotions. In the future you may want a more customized footer, but this will do for now.

The Front Page

To make things easy, you'll create a home.php template file for the job board child theme. You're using div#content for your two job listing columns, and the third column will be the sidebar, easily managed with widgets and some CSS. There's no need for an additional sidebar.php template file in the child theme at all.

Start off in home.php, with a div.welcome class being the full width of the div#content container. Underneath are two div's, one floating left and the other right, with a custom 'homecol' class to control how these two columns look and feel, and specifically how wide they are. Each of the two column div's contain a loop using query_posts() to fetch just 10 posts from the relevant category. Remember, the left column is for the "Jobs Available" category, and the right is for the "Looking for Work" category, so I don't want them to mix on the front page.

That's it. This is what it looks like:

```php
<?php get_header(); ?>

    <div id="content" class="widecolumn">

        <div class="welcome">
            Welcome to the <span>Job Board</span> - a place where you can find the gig of your
    dreams. Start browsing the jobs below, or <a href="/post-a-job">post one yourself!</a>
        </div>

        <div class="column left homecol">
            <h1><a href="/category/jobs/" title="Jobs Available">Jobs Available</a></h1>
            <?php query_posts('category_name=jobs&showposts=10'); ?>
            <?php while (have_posts()) : the_post(); ?>
                <div id="post-<?php the_ID(); ?>" <?php post_class('homephp'); ?>>
                    <h2><a href="<?php the_permalink() ?>" rel="bookmark" title="<?php the_title();
    ?>"><?php the_title(); ?></a></h2>
                    <div class="postmeta">
                        <span class="tags"><?php the_tags(",', ',"); ?></span>
                        <span class="timestamp"><?php the_time(__('F jS, Y', 'notesblog')) ?></span>
```

```
                    </div>
                </div>
            <?php endwhile; ?>
            <div class="more"><a href="/category/jobs/">There's More &rarr;</a></div>
        </div>

        <div class="column right homecol">
            <h1><a href="/category/positions/" title="Looking for Work">Looking for Work</a></h1>
            <?php query_posts('category_name=positions&showposts=10'); ?>
            <?php while (have_posts()) : the_post(); ?>
                <div id="post-<?php the_ID(); ?>" <?php post_class('homephp'); ?>>
                    <h2><a href="<?php the_permalink() ?>" rel="bookmark" title="<?php the_title();
  ?>"><?php the_title(); ?></a></h2>
                    <div class="postmeta">
                        <span class="tags"><?php the_tags(",', ','); ?></span>
                        <span class="timestamp"><?php the_time(__('F jS, Y', 'notesblog')) ?></span>
                    </div>
                </div>
            <?php endwhile; ?>
            <div class="more"><a href="/category/positions/">There's More &rarr;</a></div>
        </div>

    </div>

<?php get_sidebar(); ?>
<?php get_footer(); ?>
```

Remember, home.php will only be used when someone visits the front page of the site. That means that the default index.php won't be used on the job board's front page, but it will be in any other instance where there is no template overriding it.

Single Post View

In single post view, job postings should probably be presented less like a blog post and more like an actual job offering. This isn't so different from traditional blog posts, but it is one other place where it is a good idea to unbloggify the lingo. In other words, do away with everything that smells of "blog" terminology, from comments (unless you want that sort of functionality) to permalinks and category labels. Make it a page just like everything else, and then spice it up, perhaps with some categories similar to the following:

- **Related jobs** are an obvious extension to any job posting. After all, you want people to use the site.

- **Most recent updates** in each particular category can also encourage the visitor to dig deeper into the site.

- **Tags** may sound a bit bloggish in themselves, so you may consider calling them something else. Either way, showing what tags the job offering has is a way to allow the visitor to find more of the same, should a particular tag be of interest to them.

- **Contact information** is, of course, crucial for any job listing, so it should be a required field in the job postings form. Make it stand out in the listing as well; a container sporting a different background tends to do the trick.

Consult Chapter 9 for more on how to make WordPress less of a blog platform, and more like a CMS.

Obviously I'm not including the job listings page here. After all, it is really just more of the same, so you can easily build it from just about any single.php template out there, or hack one yourself.

Listings and Other Results

Post listings, search results, and even the 404 error are managed by index.php by default in Notes Blog Core. This is good in this case, but you need some job boardification of both the search result page (because you want people to search for jobs) and the 404 error message.

Let's start with the various job post listings that may occur: category listings, tags, and so on. You don't want these to display the full ad (which is the same as your post content), but rather list things in a job boardesque kind of way, so that means that the archive.php template will do, and that it shouldn't contain the_content(). Do the listings as a table since that's the best way to display the content:

```php
<?php get_header(); ?>

    <div id="content" class="widecolumn">

    <?php
    if (is_category()) {
            echo '<h1 class="listhead"><strong>';
            single_cat_title();
            echo '</strong></h1>';
        } if (is_tag()) {
            echo '<h1 class="listhead"><strong>';
            single_tag_title();
            echo '</strong></h1>'; }
    ?>

        <table width="100%" class="joblistings">
            <thead><tr><td colspan="3">You found the current job listings:</td></tr></thead>
            <tbody>
                <?php
                    query_posts($query_string.'&posts_per_page=20');
                    while (have_posts()) : the_post(); ?>
                <tr>
                    <td class="timestamp"><?php the_time('M j, Y') ?></td>
                    <td id="post-<?php the_ID(); ?>" <?php post_class('joblisting'); ?>><h2
class="joblisted"><a href="<?php the_permalink() ?>" rel="bookmark" title="<?php the_title(); ?>
"><?php the_title(); ?></a></h2></td>
                    <td class="tags"><?php the_tags('Tags: ',', ',''); ?></td>
```

```
                    </tr>
                    <?php endwhile; ?>
                </tbody>
            </table>

        <div class="nav widecolumn">
            <div class="left"><?php next_posts_link('Older Jobs') ?></div>
            <div class="right"><?php previous_posts_link('More Recent Jobs') ?></div>
        </div>

    </div>

<?php get_sidebar(); ?>
<?php get_footer(); ?>
```

Remember, archive.php is one of the fallback template files for any kind of archive page, which is just about anything that isn't actual content, the front page, or the search results.

The search.php template is basically the same thing, you just need some searchy stuff, like proper wordings and so on. Just change the top message and make sure there's an error message that makes sense whenever someone searches for something that doesn't return a result.

Finally, the Stylesheet

The stylesheet starts off like any other theme would, but you'll find the `'template'` reference to Notes Blog Core's folder since that's your template. You're also starting off with a CSS import because the template's stylesheet will give you a good start. That is optional, however.

After that it is pretty smooth sailing. You'll need some ugly, forceful CSS overwrites to make sure that some elements really get the correct style, but that's about it. Nothing fancy.

```
/*
Theme Name: JobBoard (built on Notes Blog Core)
Theme URI: http://notesblog.com/core/jobboard/
Description: <a href="http://tdhedengren.com/">Made by TDH</a> and maintained at <a href="http://
   notesblog.com/">notesblog.com</a>. Requires WordPress 2.8 or higher.
Version: 1.0
Tags: two columns, fixed width, custom, widgets
Author: Thord Daniel Hedengren
Author URI: http://tdhedengren.com/
Template: notes-blog-core-theme

    Requires the Notes Blog Core Theme:
    http://notesblog.com/core/

*/


@import url('../notes-blog-core-theme/style.css');
```

The preceding code is the necessary theme header, note the notes-blog-core-theme template referenced, and the imported stylesheet from said theme. This is to make sure that WordPress understands what theme this child theme is relying on.

```
a:link, a:active, a:visited { color: #0cf; }
a:hover, div#header h1 a:hover, div.homecol h1 a:hover { color: #f90; }

div.welcome a:link, div.welcome a:active, div.welcome a:visited, div.homecol div.more a
    { color: #f90; }

body { background: #effffe; }

div.column { width: 290px; }

div#header { border-bottom-color: #0ad; } /* add bg img */
    div#header h1 { text-align:center; }        div#header h1 a { border: 0; }
        div#header h1 span { display:none; }
```
Next are some simple overrides for link colors and setting the background as well as the header
  details. Following this is some styling for the submenu, and giving the main part of the design
  residing in div#blog a white background. After that is the welcome text block, div.welcome.
  Nothing fancy.```div#submenu-nav { border:0; background: #0cf; }```
```
    div#submenu-nav div.textwidget {}
        div#submenu-nav div.textwidget p { padding: 10px; margin:0; text-align:center; font-size:
  14px; line-height: 14px; }
            div#submenu-nav div.textwidget p a { margin: 0 2px; text-decoration: none; color:
  #fff; font-weight: bold; padding: 10px 5px 20px 5px; }
            div#submenu-nav div.textwidget p a:hover { background: #0ad; }

div#blog { background: #fff; }

div.welcome { margin: 0 0 20px 0; padding: 0 20px; font-size: 24px; line-height: 30px; color:
  #888; }
    div.welcome a:hover { color: #000; }
    div.welcome span { color: #444; }
```

The job listing columns are next, residing in a table within the `div.homecol` element. Mostly small fixes here to make it look decent.

```
div.homecol { margin-left: 20px; margin-bottom: 20px; border: 1px solid #0cf; border-width: 1px
  0; }
    div.homecol h1 { font-size: 18px !important; line-height: 18px !important; padding: 10px 5px
  !important; }
        div.homecol h1 a { border: 0; }
    div.homecol div.more { width: 100%; text-align:right; padding-bottom: 10px; font-size: 11px;
  text-transform: uppercase; font-weight: bold; }

div.homephp { margin-bottom: 10px; padding: 0 5px 5px 5px; border: 1px solid #eee; border-width:
  0 0 1px 0; }
```

```
    div.homephp h2 { font-size: 16px !important; line-height: 16px !important; font-weight:bold
  !important; }
    div.homephp div.postmeta {}
        div.homephp div.postmeta span.timestamp { margin-left: 3px; padding-left: 6px; border:
  1px dotted #888; border-width: 0 0 0 1px; }
        div.homephp div.postmeta a { font-weight:normal; }

table.joblistings { float:left; margin:0; padding: 0 10px 20px 10px; border:0; }
    table.joblistings thead { margin: 0 10px 8px 10px; background: #f90; font-size: 14px;
  font-weight:bold; color: #fff; }
        table.joblistings thead tr td { padding: 5px; text-align:center; }
    table.joblistings tbody {}
        table.joblistings tbody tr { float:left; width:100%; padding: 8px 0; border: 1px dotted
  #888; border-width: 0 0 1px 0; }
            table.joblistings tbody tr td { font-size: 11px; }
            table.joblistings tbody tr td.timestamp { width: 80px; }
            table.joblistings tbody tr td.post { width: 330px; }
                h2.joblisted { margin-bottom:0 !important; font-size: 14px !important; line-
  height: 14px !important; font-weight:bold !important; }
            table.joblistings tbody tr td.tags { width: 190px; text-align:right; }
```

Following job listings columns are some navigational fixes (to add white space around the links, since the actual content now resides on a white block on a colored body background), and then the design fixes for the right column, being ul#sidebar. Then there's the footer and the copy text at the very end.

```
div.nav div.left { padding-left: 10px; }
div.nav div.right { padding-right: 10px; }

ul#sidebar {}
    ul#sidebar a:link, ul#sidebar a:active, ul#sidebar a:visited { color: #fff; }
    ul#sidebar h2.widgettitle { color: #fff; text-align:center; border-color: #d70 !important;
  text-transform: none !important; font-size: 18px !important; font-weight:normal; }
    ul#sidebar li.widget { background: #f90; color: #fbead9; padding: 12px 15px 15px 15px; bor-
  der: 5px solid #d70; border-width: 5px 0 0 0; }
    ul#sidebar li.widget_search { padding:0; border: 0; background: none; text-align:center; }
    ul#sidebar li.widget_tag_cloud { text-align: center; }
    ul#sidebar li.widget_text { background: #e8e8e8; border: 0px solid #b8b8b8; color: #777; }
        ul#sidebar li.widget_text h2.widgettitle { color: #f90; border-color: #b8b8b8; }

div#footer { border-bottom-color: #0ad; }

div#copy { background: none; }
```

Finally you've got some font overrides. I tend to put those at the end, by themselves. This makes it easier to play with various types of fonts for different elements without going hunting for the elements within the actual code.

```
/* FONTS */
body
    { font-family: Helvetica, Arial, sans-serif; }

div.welcome, h2.widgettitle
    { font-family: Adobe Garamond, Garamond, Georgia, Times New Roman, serif; }
```

There you have it, you've constructed the basics of a job board! Next, you should get it some user-submitted content, or at least the functionality the board needs to receive the content.

Receiving the Jobs

There are numerous ways to receive the actual content for the job listings. The easiest way would be to just have people e-mail listings to you, and you'd then put them in yourself, but that's tedious work. Better to use a plugin and have the advertisers put the data straight into a draft post that the administrators can approve.

We'll be using a plugin to do this, TDO Mini Forms, in fact (`wordpress.org/extend/plugins/tdo-mini-forms/`). It is by no means the only option available, but it seems simple enough while offering cool options for more advanced features in the future.

Anyway, the only thing you're interested in at this time is a plugin that lets users, which in this case are the people either advertising for a job, or the people looking for one, to post content into WordPress that is stored in draft form in categories. So you want to build a form where you can send in the following data:

- Type of job ad (user will choose from the two categories, either Jobs Available or Looking for Work)
- Listing submitter (the post submitter will have to give a name and an e-mail, and optionally a Web page URL)
- Job post title (the intended title)
- Post text (the job post's content)
- Contact information (otherwise a job listing wouldn't do much good, now would it?)

That's it, although you may consider spam protection as well. The TDO Mini Forms plugin can handle this easily enough, but you may want to build or use other solutions.

When using TDO Mini Forms to build this solution, you can specify that the posts be saved as drafts and append the advertiser information to the post content so you won't have to create a WordPress user account for everyone posting an ad. You can do that, though, and force advertisers to register first to access the actual "post a job" page. If you do, they will use the user info from WordPress instead, and there's support for that in TDO Mini Forms. If you force advertisers to register, you can easily create archives for all their posted job offerings, for example, which can be handy. It also means that you can mark some advertisers as reliable and hence bypass the administrative approval stage, publishing their ads automatically.

You can do it any way you like. The important thing is that you can get advertisers and people looking for work to post content directly into WordPress (as drafts) so you can manage the job listings easily enough.

Further Development

So where to go from here? After all, at this stage the WordPress-powered job board is fully functional, but there's certainly room for improvement. The first thing one may come to think of is how to charge for job listings, and how to control how long they are visible. After all, a lot of job boards out there are charging for use, and you may want that, so attaching PayPal or a similar payment service is a natural next step. Controlling how long a post is displayed can be done by running a script that automatically changes the post status from "published" to "draft," but it is probably better to just add a code snippet at the top of the post that either outputs a "this job listing is outdated" message, or even hides the job information or redirects the visitor. This can be easily done with PHP and a little use of conditional tags, for example.

Other natural enhancements would involve more control when an advertiser submits a job listing. This may include image attachments, tagging, not to mention geographical localization. That last part can either be maintained by a custom taxonomy, or using custom fields. That way, it can easily be queried and listed for location-based job offerings.

Sticky posts can be used to make some jobs featured, for those generous advertisers that want more exposure. You can just style the sticky posts accordingly (larger fonts, stronger colors, borders, or whatever) and let them jump to the top of the post display, which may not be so much fun in the job board example design presented here since it is based on just links in lists. Another solution would be to have a separate loop that queries just posts marked as sticky, and displays them independently. That would mean that you had full control over them, naturally.

There is no doubt that it is possible to take the job board quite a few steps further. The whole idea with this example is to show you that WordPress can be used to power such a site. Now it is up to you, or someone else, to make it grand and a killer site. Good luck!

And with that, the next section moves on to another non-bloggish concept. From job board to knowledge base. The step isn't as big as you may expect.

WordPress as an FAQ-like Knowledge Base

Companies that want their very own FAQ-like knowledge base can put WordPress to good use. The concept is really quite simple, revolving around user-submitted posts as well as tagging and/or categories. Thanks to commenting there can be a conversation around an issue that a user submits, and when it is resolved the administrator can move it to the knowledge base part of the site.

Here are the key features:

- User-submitted issues using a plugin; each issue is in fact a post.
- Two main categories: The FAQ and the Knowledge Base.
- Tagging of posts (which are the issues, remember) to make keyword searching easier.
- A custom tagging taxonomy for the Knowledge Base.

The site usage flow would be as follows:

1. A user submits an issue using a form on the site. The issue is saved as a post, marked as drafts, by using a plugin.
2. An administrator publishes the issue in the FAQ category.
3. The issue can now be commented on. If an administrator answers, their comments will be high-lighted, but it is possible to let anyone answer should you want that. If you turn off user comments you'll need to attach some way for the original submitter of the issue to ask for follow-ups without having to resubmit a new issue each time.
4. When the issue is resolved, an administrator adds the post to the Knowledge Base category.
5. All posts in the Knowledge Base category get proper tagging in the Knowledge Base Tagging custom taxonomy. This means that you can output a tag cloud (or whatever) based only on tags from within the Knowledge Base.

The point of the custom Knowledge Base Tagging taxonomy is so the users browse issues that are resolved, hence possibly already including solutions to whatever problem it is that they need to solve. It works alongside the standard tagging feature, which also includes FAQ posts and hence un-resolved issues. This can also come in handy.

Finally, there's also category browsing, which means that it is really easy to create these two sections of the site.

Adding the Functionality

The actual design of this theme will be simple enough, so I'll stick to the important parts. You can build it on top of just about any theme you like. I'll keep the examples below general though.

First of all, you need to build your new taxonomy. You can read more about that in Chapter 6; this is the code you'll be using in you functions.php file for the child theme:

```
add_action( 'init', 'kbase', 0 );

function kbase() {
    register_taxonomy( 'knowledge_base', 'post', array( 'hierarchical' => false, 'label' => 'Knowledge
  Base Tags', 'query_var' => true, 'rewrite' => true ) );
}
```

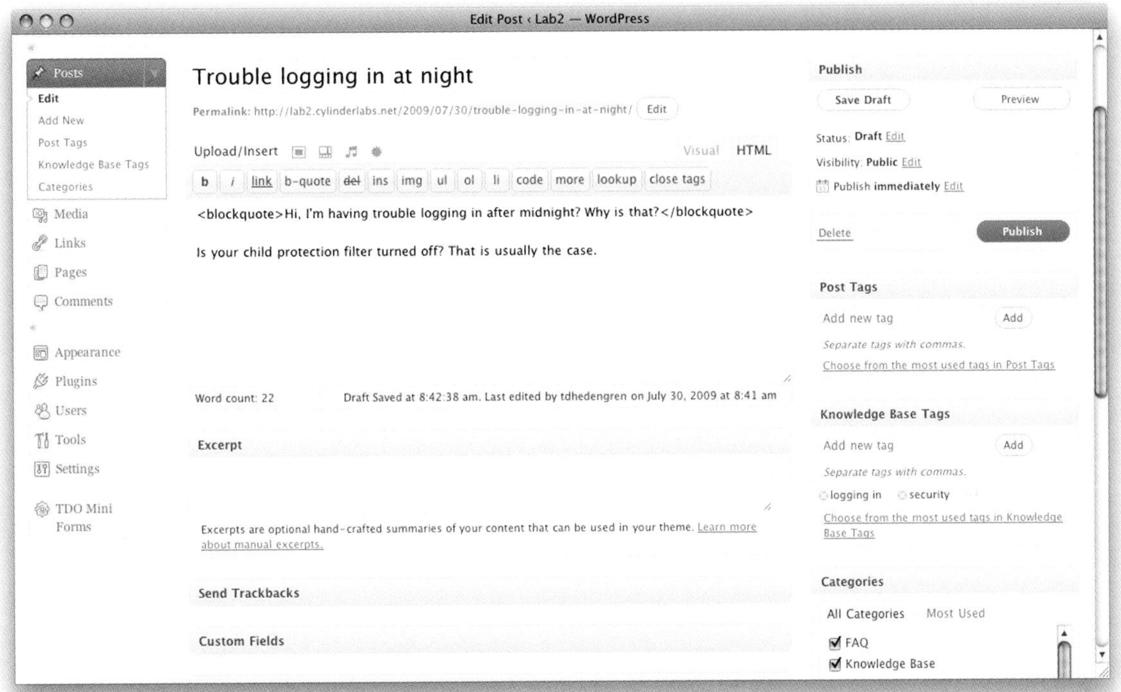

Figure 10-2: Knowledge Base tagging

That's it. Now you'll get another tag field in the WordPress admin interface to tag away on any post you like (Figure 10-2). Naturally, you'll just do this on posts marked with "Knowledge Base" status, as described previously.

With the taxonomy set up, the next step is to start receiving issues. This was discussed in more detail in the job board example previously, so refer to that for various solutions. The TDO Mini Forms plugin will work perfectly well for receiving issues, so you can use that, or something else. You'll most likely want to create a home.php template for featuring the most recent submissions, additions to the Knowledge Base (which would be just showing the latest posts in that particular category), and also either to promote or offer the submit issue form. Personally, I'd add a huge search box as well as a tag cloud showing the hottest tags from the Knowledge Base taxonomy. The latter is done by passing the taxonomy name to `wp_tag_cloud()`, like this:

```php
<?php wp_tag_cloud('taxonomy=knowledge_base'); ?>
```

The taxonomy parameter is new in WordPress 2.8, and you obviously pass the name to it, not the label. Style the tag cloud accordingly and you'll have a series of keywords belonging only to the Knowledge Base taxonomy, which in turn means that it is only issues that have been resolved that appear.

That's about it, really. By adding the submission part, along with the taxonomy, the rest is just about displaying the latest posts from each respective category, and trying to get the users to actually search for an issue before submitting it again.

Further Enhancements

While it is easy to get a FAQ/Knowledge Base site rolling on top of WordPress, there's also a ton of possible ways to make it better. The first thing you'd want to make sure is that the users understand that they should search and browse the site before submitting an issue, otherwise you'll end up with loads of them on your hands, most probably with a great deal of duplication. You want your visitors to search, and that means pushing for that functionality. Unfortunately, if WordPress is failing in one area, it is search, so you may want to consider using an external service like Google Custom Search Engine (google.com/cse) or a similar variant that can be easily embedded in your site and add function.

Here are some other ideas on enhancements to this setup:

- **Registration and editing.** Let people register and hence they can edit their own questions, get an author archive, and so on. You may even want to force it to make spamming a bit harder.
- **Grading.** Let the users grade your answers, in the comments when the post is in FAQ mode, and the actual resolution of the issue when it has moved to the Knowledge Base. In the latter case, you would obviously need a plugin that offers grading of the post rather than the comments.
- **Related issues.** Expose other issues automatically by using a related posts plugin. That way the user may find an answer.
- **Further enhance search.** With the use of JavaScript you can make it easier for users to find the answer to common issues. You know the type of search fields, the ones that ask you if you meant XYZ when you typed XPT . . .
- **Tweak the front page.** The better you can expose the issues, the faster the users will find them, and since that's what it's all about, you should tweak the front page as much as you possibly can.
- **Subscriptions and alerts.** Offer ways to subscribe to updates and resolved issues. There are several ways to manage this, and since WordPress has an RSS feed for just about anything, I'm sure the answer is there. Make sure your users know and understand that, so they can subscribe to things that interest them.

The knowledge base concept is another way you can use WordPress for a non-bloggy site. Naturally, there are a ton of other things you can do with the system. One of these is using WordPress to power an online store.

WordPress and E-Commerce

It goes without saying that WordPress can be used to sell stuff. In its simplest form you'll run a blog or traditional site with WordPress as the backend, and use your reach to sell products. You can add *affiliate links*, which basically means that whenever you link to Amazon using your affiliate URL and someone buys something, you'll get a provision. In fact, if you bought this book by following a link from any of my sites, I made a little extra. Thanks!

However, when most of us are thinking e-commerce we've got bigger things than affiliate links in mind. Shopping carts, digital distribution, payment received via PayPal accounts, that sort of thing.

You can have all this for sure, and in Chapter 11 there's even a bunch of ideas that can make such things easier to implement, from simple integrations to full shopping carts.

Running a Web Shop on WordPress

You may be wondering if you can run a Web shop on WordPress. In short, the answer is yes; you *could* if you wanted to, and if you didn't have too many products.

The long version: probably not, but don't let that stop you since there's really no reason why it shouldn't work perfectly well if you're prepared to extend WordPress with plugins, work with custom fields, and then figure out how to connect your shopping cart with PayPal and other payment solutions.

Kind of disheartening isn't it? Relax, it's not as bad as it sounds: there are plugins out there that do most of the work for you. Thing is, compared to the other e-commerce systems out there the available plugins are kind of bleak. There used to be a time when open source e-commerce meant tables and no SEO, ugly links and bulky admins. That was then, this is now, and with that in mind it is hard to truly recommend WordPress for e-commerce other than for hobby businesses or if you're selling a small number of products.

That being said, there's nothing that's stopping you from attaching any of the various shopping cart scripts out there right into your theme. Most will probably work with minor hassle, and that would only leave you with the discomfort of figuring out how to charge for your merchandise. Luckily companies like PayPal (and many others, I should add) have made that easy, so you can certainly monetize your blog or WordPress-powered site with a shop selling your goods if you want to.

Just make sure you know what you're getting yourself into. This is sales, after all, and not the content business anymore.

Selling Digital Products

Digital merchandise such as e-books are a completely different matter altogether. Absolutely nothing is stopping you from implementing a payment solution for a digital file, and when paid, you serve the file. In fact, it has almost nothing at all to do with WordPress since it is all about verifying that you got paid, and then directing the customer to the file in question. Adding that sort of solution to your blog is really easy if you rely on a third-party service (which will take a chunk of your processed money at the very least) to both manage payment and delivery of the files, such as E-junkie (www.e-junkie.com), for example. It's just a matter of setting up a link, and then your provider will handle the rest; much like an affiliate program, but with the benefit of you getting a larger chunk of the money, it being your product and all.

You can do the same on your own as well with the necessary plugins or scripts. However, it is really hard to sidestep the fact that you need to actually charge for your products, which means handling payments. You can, theoretically, handle payments yourself as well. I advise against it, if for nothing else but the fact that people feel more secure when they recognize the party handling their money. Better to have someone else worrying about that stuff, but again, it is entirely up to you.

Digital products fit any site perfectly. While WordPress may be no Magento when it comes to e-commerce, it is perfectly well suited for selling e-books, MP3s, design files, or whatever you want to make money on.

Building for E-Commerce

So you've decided to use WordPress as a basis to sell products—big or small, a lot or a few, doesn't matter. Now you need to figure out how you can set it up to make it as powerful as possible, and easy to manage at that.

There are really two premises here. Either you expect a lot of products, which means there would be a point to having a post per product and relying on categories, or you expect to have a smaller amount, which points to the use of Pages. If you think you'll have a steady stream of new products on, say, a weekly basis then it sounds to me like using posts would be best, but if you won't be adding new products more than a couple of times per year, you can probably do just as well with Pages. Remember, there's no real reason why you shouldn't have numerous Pages in a WordPress install, it's more a matter of what you can do with them and how you can output that.

Posts do have the advantage of being easily put into categories and then tagged, and you can even add custom taxonomies to add separate tag sets and such to them. Pages, on the other hand, offer Page templates, which give you extra control, and you can tackle the lack of categories with hierarchical Pages. Which way you go is up to you and how you want to manage your products; these days both have support for your premiere weapon of choice: custom fields.

There are hundreds of ways to set up an e-commerce site using WordPress. The easiest way is probably to dedicate a post or Page to a product, add a buy link, and then charge your customers. If you use a plugin you'll end up getting these decisions made for you, which can be a good thing, especially since any decent e-commerce plugin would have a shopping cart and a checkout sequence, and possibly even a payment scheme sorted out.

However, when it comes to product presentation the whole thing is in your hands. That means that you'll want to style image galleries properly and add product shots as custom fields so you can display them in nice listings.

I think that is the key for most WordPress-powered Web shops: putting custom fields to good use. You'll want at least one product shot saved in a custom field because you can call on it in listings, but you may also want a larger one to use in presentations, or perhaps one of those oversized product headers that are all the buzz on promo Web sites nowadays.

Here's a quick recap:

- Should products be in posts or in Pages?
- Do I need categories or tags? Then it's posts!

- Do I need custom control on a per-product basis? Then it's probably Pages!
- What custom fields do I need? Figure it out!

The Portfolio Site

Powering a portfolio site with WordPress is a great idea. Since a good portfolio—whether it features Web design work, print designs, photography, or anything else that is best presented with images or video—should be constantly updated, you can build it around WordPress to make it easy to maintain.

Figure 10-3: tdhedengren.com as of late Summer 2009

Most portfolio sites have three main functions that you just can't leave out:

- **It should feature the designer's work.** Mere links will usually not cut it, you need to highlight your best work and display it the way you designed it and intended it to be used.
- **It should sell the designer.** This really means two things. First, that it shows off your services so that people know what you're offering. Second, it needs to portray a reassuring image of who you are and how you are to work with.
- **It should offer an easy means of contact.** The whole point of the portfolio is to get more gigs, that's why one does it (unless you just want to brag, in which case this is just a bonus). Naturally, it should therefore be made easy to get in touch with you.

Most portfolios benefit from having a blog complementing them, since that brings traffic. You don't need that, and I didn't want it on my portfolio either, since I'm writing in other places as well, but if you're the blogging kind then by all means add it. Just make sure that people visiting your site for your portfolio get what they want.

Designing a Portfolio

I redesigned my portfolio in summer 2009 using WordPress thinking of the three things mentioned previously. The whole idea was to make it easy to update, offer the content smartly, and present the services provided as a designer, developer, and writer. I wanted to make use of big images and put my design work in the center, featuring big graphical blocks. However, I also wanted to make sure that any new writing gigs got some exposure when they came up, so that was something to consider as well. There isn't always a graphic chunk to show off, and that means that I couldn't build it entirely around that.

I left my blog out of my portfolio this time, since it can get a bit crowded. Most of the time I advise against this, but for this particular project it made sense to move the blog away from the portfolio.

My WordPress setup for this project was simple. First of all, I created a category for each type of project I wanted to be able to show off. I began with Design and Writing, but I also decided to add a category for Announcements. You never know. The reason for using categories is that I can easily use conditional tags to check whether something belongs to a specific category or not, and act accordingly.

Each project I wanted to display was a post in one of these categories, never several at once. I also tagged the posts for more sorting, especially with client names and types of gigs, things that may be interesting to query for in the future. The decisions I implemented in my own portfolio will be the basis of the following discussion and examples.

The Design Category

Posts in the Design category will be image-based, featuring a big fat image and some text on the front page. When the visitor clicks the image, they end up on the actual post, which contains more images, perhaps a gallery of elements you're particularly proud of, and as much text as you want.

This means that you don't want to show the post heading on the front page, at least not at the very top. You want the image, and text on the image. The solution for this is using custom fields, where you just store the URL to the background image in a custom field, and then query it on listings pages. You can check for what category each post is in listings, hence you're able to output it differently.

An alternative solution would be to put whatever you wanted to display in listings in the excerpt field, and then use `the_excerpt()` to output things. However that would mean that you would either have to settle for a linked image only, or that you would have had to hack a lot of HTML code for each post. The whole point is to make updating simple and quick, and you would probably much rather just upload the image and paste the URL in a custom field. Besides, the solution we're going for lets you output a heading in plain text, and that's a good thing for search engines in particular.

The single post view will use the `post_class()` styles to make smaller adjustments to the presentation of the projects.

The Writing Category

Posts in the Writing category will be text-based, since it makes sense. We'll output the post title in listings, and then use `the_excerpt()` to describe the gig in question. Using large fonts, you can achieve the visual style you're after and make it stand out. You could control the font size and basically all the stylings using the classes that `post_class()` puts on the containing `div`, but since you want to use `the_excerpt()` in this case, you need to have the conditional check for what category the post is in.

Single post view specials for Writing gigs will be controlled with the `post_class()` styles, just like with the Design category.

The Announcement Category

This is the default category and the code for this one is the loop you want to fall back on. In other words, if a post is in neither the Design nor the Writing category, this is the code to be used.

In short, it's a pretty basic loop. Since you want to be able to publish full announcements in your update stream, as well as longer ones with a read more link, we'll use `the_content()` rather than `the_excerpt()`. Other than that, there's nothing fancy here.

Single post view will be similar to the other two categories, but naturally you can add some custom styling to show that it is an announcement. There should be no doubt left in anyone's mind that `post_class()` is anything but a great tool, especially when it comes to sites like this.

Services and Contact Pages

These are simple. Just create a page.php template and make it general enough to work with pages that portray your services, as well as contact and other possible information pages. It is easy enough to add some custom styling or even a completely different behavior if you want to, thanks to the Page template features.

The Code

Here is the listings code for the front page, showing off how the various category checks are handled, as well as outputting the background image stored as a custom field for Design posts:

```php
<?php get_header(); ?>
    <div id="content" class="widecolumn">

        <p class="welcome">Welcome text goes here.</p>

        <?php query_posts($query_string.'&posts_per_page=10&cat=562,4,15'); while (have_posts()) :
    the_post(); ?>

            <div id="post-<?php the_ID(); ?>" <?php post_class(); ?>>
                <?php if (in_category('4')) { ?>
                    <?php
                        $design_background = get_post_meta($post->ID, 'design_background', $single =
    true); // check if there's a background
                        $design_background_height = get_post_meta($post->ID, 'design_background_
    height', $single = true); // check if there's a set height
                    ?>
                    <div class="design-background" style="background: #bbb url(<?php if($design_
    background !== '') { echo $design_background; } else { echo bloginfo('stylesheet_directoy') . '/
    design-listing-bg.gif'; } ?>) repeat; height: <?php if($design_background_height !== '') { echo
    $design_background_height; } else { echo '300'; } ?>px;">
                        <h2><a href="<?php the_permalink() ?>" rel="bookmark" title="<?php
    the_title(); ?>"><?php the_title(); ?></a></h2>
                    </div>
                <?php } elseif (in_category('15')) { ?>
                    <h2><a href="<?php the_permalink() ?>" rel="bookmark" title="<?php the_title(); ?>
    "><?php the_title(); ?></a></h2>
                    <div class="entry">
                        <?php the_excerpt(); ?>
                    </div>
                <?php } else { ?>
                    <div class="entry">
                        <h2><a href="<?php the_permalink() ?>" rel="bookmark" title="<?php the_
    title(); ?>"><?php the_title(); ?></a></h2>
                        <?php the_content(); ?>
                    </div>
                <?php } ?>
            </div>

        <?php endwhile; ?>

        <div class="nav widecolumn">
            <div class="left"><?php next_posts_link(__('Read previous entries', 'notesblog')) ?>
    </div>
            <div class="right"><?php previous_posts_link(__('Read more recent entries', 'notes-
    blog')) ?></div>
```

```
            </div>
    </div>

<?php get_sidebar(); ?>
<?php get_footer(); ?>
```

Obviously there is a limit on the loop before it runs, using `query_posts()`. This is because you have other categories as well, old stuff, and you don't want that to show on the front page. Most of these things can be handled by conditional tags, but since you'll probably be doing some more front page only stuff in the future, and you're basing this on the Notes Blog Core theme (no surprise there, huh?), you'll have opted for a home.php instead.

This particular loop first checks if the post is in the category with ID 4 (which is the Design category), then it checks for ID 15 (that's Writing), and if none of those fit it has a default output as well (that's everything else). Depending on which one of these three returns as `true`, the post will be handled differently.

The background image solution is the most interesting here, so take a closer look:

```
<?php
    $design_background = get_post_meta($post->ID, 'design_background', $single = true); // check
  if there's a background
    $design_background_height = get_post_meta($post->ID, 'design_background_height', $single =
  true); // check if there's a set height
?>
<div class="design-background" style="background: url(<?php if($design_background !== '') { echo
  $design_background; } else { echo bloginfo('stylesheet_directoy') . '/design-listing-bg.gif'; }
  ?>) repeat; height: <?php if($design_background_height !== '') { echo $design_background_height;
  } else { echo '300'; } ?>px;">
    <h2><a href="<?php the_permalink() ?>" rel="bookmark" title="<?php the_title(); ?>"><?php
  the_title(); ?></a></h2>
</div>
```

This one starts with checking for data in the two custom fields we're using, `'design_background'` and `'design_background_height'`. Then you move on to the actual code output, which starts with the `div.design-background` container, which then gets a hardcoded style containing either the URL to the background image that is stored in the `'design_background'` custom field, or a default one should that one be empty. The same goes with the hardcoded height that comes after, if there's something in `'design_background_height'` that will go in there, but if not it will default to 300 pixels. This is obviously so that the background image can have different heights, which may come in handy.

All in all, there's an index.php for listings as well as search and 404s. You don't need any of the other listings templates because you want things to look the same no matter what, except for some small outputs that show the visitor whereabouts he or she is on the site.

Neither the single.php nor the page.php does anything weird or fancy, so I'll save us some trees and leave those out.

Pretty simple huh? You can grab this Notes Blog Core child theme from `notesblog.com` for free, to build your own portfolio upon.

WordPress and One-page Designs

Is there any point in using WordPress for one-page portfolios? These are becoming quite popular these days and sometimes you can actually fit everything in one page. But why rely on WordPress for something that needs minimal attention and updates by nature?

The main reason is expandability. You may end up wanting to add things to your portfolio, like sub-pages or a search capability, or perhaps even commenting features or other things that WordPress does well. That will be a lot easier if you built the original site on the platform, since you can do so much from the admin interface.

Another thought is to use WordPress as an archive. What you do is set a Page to be your front page, and just not link to (or possibly even have) anything else on your site. However, when you're bored with your one-page portfolio and want to spice it up, you just create a new site and set that one as your front page, leaving you with your previous one archived in the WordPress database. That would mean that you can, if you want to, link to it, show it to clients, or just look at it yourself with a little bit of nostalgia. Granted, there is nothing that stops you from renaming static files rather than using WordPress, but it is something. And if you ever want to show off all your iterations over the years, you can do it easily enough.

There comes a time for every platform when it is just redundant. This may very well be the case for WordPress here. That being said, I recently built a one-page site on WordPress, just because I think that the client may want more in the future, and it will save me some trouble then.

The next section moves from a fairly straightforward portfolio to something completely different. The links site is a completely different sort of project, one not at all focused on selling your services or highlighting your particular qualities.

Building a Links Site

A links site can be a lot of things, so the examples in this section will perhaps be a bit more generic than the previous ones. The idea is to use posts as link items, making them sortable using both categories and tags. However, you're not just going to put a link in the post field, but rather use the title field as the actual link title, and then store the target URL in a custom field. Then you can utilize the excerpt of the content field to display descriptions, details, or whatever may fit your project.

But you need to start at the beginning. These are your premises:

- Every blog post is a link in your link database.
- You'll use the title field to save the link title (for example, Google).
- You'll store the destination URL in a custom field called 'URL' (for example www.google.com).

- You'll categorize your links in any number of categories (for example, Search Engines or Web mail).
- You'll tag your links with appropriate tags (for example, free, USA, or fonts).
- You'll use `the_excerpt()` rather than `the_content()` for link descriptions, mostly to keep your doors open for the future.

Now we can get started. First of all you'll want to store the URL in a custom field. This is easily done, just create a new custom field on the Write post screen in the WordPress admin interface and name it 'URL'. The idea is to put the URL in the value field for each post, and then link the title with it.

Right, now you need to alter your loop a bit. For a project like this you'll probably want to design a new theme that fits the bill, but the default theme is used as an example here.

This is the code you'll use inside the loop, found in index.php:

```
<div <?php post_class() ?> id="post-<?php the_ID(); ?>">
    <?php $CustomField = get_post_custom_values('URL'); if (isset($CustomField[0])) { ?>
        <h2><a href="<?php echo get_post_meta($post->ID, URL, true); ?>" rel="bookmark"
 title="<?php the_title_attribute(); ?>"><?php the_title(); ?></a></h2>
        <div class="entry">
            <?php the_excerpt(); ?>
        </div>
        <p class="postmetadata">Filed in <?php the_category(', ') ?> <?php the_tags('and tagged ', ',
 ', '); ?> <small><?php the_time('F jS, Y') ?></small></p>
    <?php } else { ?>
        <h2><del><?php the_title(); ?></del></h2>
        <div class="entry">
            <p>Sorry, this link is broken. Please tell an administrator!</p>
        </div>
        <p class="postmetadata">It's broken: <?php edit_post_link('Fix it!', '', ' | '); ?> Filed
 in <?php the_category(', ') ?> <?php the_tags('and tagged ', ', ', '); ?> <small><?php the_time('F
 jS, Y') ?></small></p>
    <?php } ?>
</div>
```

Yes, I know, it's an ugly hack, but the concept is simple enough. Anyway, you need to make sure that there is a URL submitted in the 'URL' custom field. That's what this line is there for:

```
<?php $CustomField = get_post_custom_values('URL'); if (isset($CustomField[0])) { ?>
```

If it returns `true`, it'll output the code you want, which contains the linked title and everything. Next is the actual link title heading, linked to the source obviously. That was the whole point after all.

```
<h2><a href="<?php echo get_post_meta($post->ID, URL, true); ?>" rel="bookmark" title="<?php
 the_title_attribute(); ?>"><?php the_title(); ?></a></h2>
```

Obviously you're echoing the contents of the 'URL' custom field, which hopefully is a valid URL (there's no check for that, only if there's something stored in there). The get_post_meta() function first asks for the post ID, then the name of the custom field (which is 'URL'), and then whether to return the content as a string or array (we want the former, hence the true value). And by echoing it, you get it in your little link, and there you go, one linked post title for you. The loop continues, and you do it all over again.

That is, unless you forget to add a URL to the custom field. Then the check mentioned above will skip to the else clause, which just outputs a struck-through post title and a message telling anyone that cares that the URL is broken. There's also an edit link added for good measure; you may want that in the successful results as well.

The rest is pretty basic, with the_excerpt() outputting whatever you put in the excerpt field (or the actual content should you have done this wrong), as well as categories, tags, and a date.

That's all there is to it, the basis of using WordPress as a links manager. Sure, you can refine it a bit, but mostly it is cosmetic stuff that you can tackle in your theme.

Some Thoughts about Usage

How can you put this to good use, and why should you use WordPress to power what at first looks like a simple links directory? Starting with the last question, the ease of WordPress management as well as the various feeds and sorting capabilities make the platform an excellent choice for this. Add the capability to let users submit their own links using plugins or by having them register, and you've got a solid basis to start from. You can even let other sites include the latest links from a certain category or tag using RSS feeds, although you'd probably want to alter the feed output so that the titles in such cases also lead to the destinations specified in the 'URL' custom fields.

With regard to what to do with this, well, there are obviously tons of opportunities. Niche link sites are popular, but you can take it up a notch with plugins. Why not let people vote or comment on the links, for example? That way you can spark user-contributed material and in turn put it to good use with top link lists and similar. For a closed group this can be a great way to share resources and stories online, and if nothing else it is a nice enough option for all those link directory scripts out there. After all, few platforms offer the ease of WordPress, and with the ever-present option of building new features into the site with the ease of theming and addition of plugins, there is no telling where you may end up taking a site like this.

Or you can just use it to share and save links you like, categorizing them and tagging for good measure. That's what delicious.com does, after all, so you can certainly put it to good use yourself.

Mixing Links Posts with Traditional Content

Maybe you want to mix this sort of linked title with your traditional content. You know, the kind of site where the post title leads to the actual post, and not elsewhere? Right, you're with me. Good.

So what you're looking at, then, is something of a linking aside. In fact, this is really easy to pull off. We'll just reuse the code and let the custom fields content check do all the work. Again, we'll use the index.php in the default WordPress theme as an example on how to pull this off:

```
<div <?php post_class() ?> id="post-<?php the_ID(); ?>">
    <?php $CustomField = get_post_custom_values('URL');
    if (isset($CustomField[0])) { ?>
        <div class="linkage">
            <h2><a href="<?php echo get_post_meta($post->ID, URL, true); ?>" rel="bookmark"
    title="<?php the_title_attribute(); ?>"><?php the_title(); ?></a></h2>
            <div class="entry">
                <?php the_excerpt(); ?>
            </div>
        </div>
    <?php } else { ?>
        <h2><a href="<?php the_permalink() ?>" rel="bookmark" title="Permanent Link to <?php the_
    title_attribute(); ?>"><?php the_title(); ?></a></h2>
        <small><?php the_time('F jS, Y') ?> by <?php the_author() ?></small>
        <div class="entry">
            <?php the_content('Read the rest of this entry &raquo;'); ?>
        </div>
        <p class="postmetadata"><?php the_tags('Tags: ', ', ', '<br />'); ?> Posted in <?php the_
    category(', ') ?> | <?php edit_post_link('Edit', '', ' | '); ?>  <?php comments_popup_link
    ('No Comments &#187;', '1 Comment &#187;', '% Comments &#187;'); ?></p>
    <?php } ?>
</div>
```

There are some minor changes compared to the code used in the original example. That's because you want to actually output the posts with linked titles when there is no custom field value in 'URL', but when there is you do it the way you did before. Minus some categories and stuff, and with the div .linkage added to make it easier to style (although you can use the post_class() styles for most of it).

This code will make every post with content in the 'URL' custom field have a title linked to that URL, rather than the post itself. It is simple enough to add to any theme.

So, obviously you can make a links-driven site using WordPress. How about doing a gallery? Of course.

The Gallery

Images and WordPress are a breeze these days—for most types of site, at least. The new media functionality, with the [gallery] shortcode and everything, makes it easy to add sets of photos. However, what do you do if you're the kind of user who wants to publish hundreds, maybe thousands of photos in the long run, and you want to have a traditional photo gallery on your site? There are photo sharing sites, of course, but sometimes you just want to roll things your way, on your own site. So what to do?

Figure 10-4: The Gallery model

Naturally, this is quite possible to do using WordPress. We'll rely on posts and categories to create a photo gallery. First of all, name the photo gallery category Gallery, which makes sense after all. You can have several categories getting the same treatment of course, but we'll stick to one in this example.

Moving on, the idea is to have each post as a photoset on its own. So your birthday bash and all the photos you snapped while blowing out candles and opening gifts would go in one post, for example, with a proper title and even tagging. Tags are great for sorting, so you can use those any way you like. If you don't want to mix photo gallery posts with regular posts, but still use tagging, you need to create a custom taxonomy for photo tagging. That way you won't get a mix of posts in the various tag archives.

So how would, or rather could, it work? Figure 10-4 is a simple concept sketch for how the posts relate to the Gallery category.

So you've got a Gallery category and each post is a photoset. You can go about the actual content handling any way you like. The simplest way would be to just upload the images to the post and include them as a thumbnail gallery, using the [gallery] shortcode. However, if you want to you can add a description as well, perhaps as the excerpt, and then use that for browsing, feed subscriptions, and also by outputting it under the_content() in the theme file. Or you can just write it under the actual photo gallery; it is fine either way.

The important thing with the posts is that they always have images attached to them when in the Gallery category. When you upload images through the media manager in WordPress when writing or editing a particular post, it will get attached to that post. You need that connection both for the [gallery] shortcode and for thumbnail display on the category archive page, the Gallery section in this case.

One more thing before you get to the code. You should make sure that your Media settings are suitable for your design and the Gallery section setup. Consult Chapter 14 for more on this matter, which incidentally also tackles things like styling the [gallery] shortcode and more.

The Category Template

So you've got out posts as photo sets, each containing at least one (but most likely more) images, and you're displaying them using the [gallery] shortcode. Now to create the Gallery section of

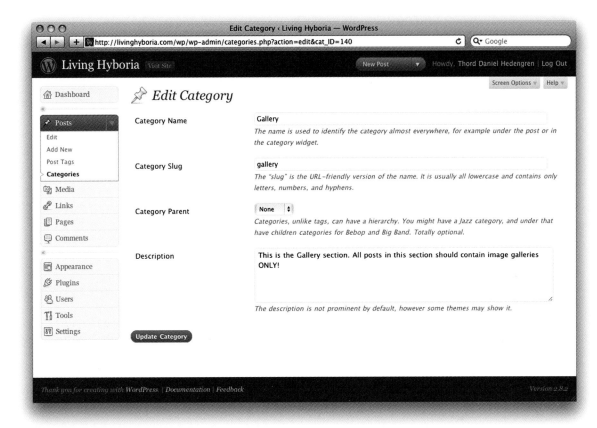

Figure 10-5: How to find the Category ID

the site using a category template file. You can tackle this in several ways, but the easiest way would be to find out the ID of the Gallery category by analyzing the URL field when editing it in the WordPress interface (Figure 10-5).

In this example we'll assume that the Gallery category ID is 140, so your category template file will be named category-140.php.

Now, in a Gallery section you'll want to display a thumbnail illustrating each photo set (which are the posts, remember?), and there are really two ways to go about this. For control, you can just pick one of the thumbnails and set it as a custom field, showing that when listing the photo sets. However, that is another thing you'd have to fiddle with, so instead just pick one of the attached photos and use as an illustrative thumbnail that leads into the photo set.

How you want to show off your photo sets is up to you. The code that follows is the most basic solution, just taking a traditional loop and changing how the post is displayed. Further on in this chapter we'll do some cooler stuff. Again, you may want to consult Chapter 14 for some thoughts on basic image setup before you start styling away.

```php
<?php get_header(); ?>

    <div id="content" class="widecolumn">

    <h1 class="listhead">Welcome to the <strong>Gallery</strong></h1>

    <?php if (have_posts()) : while (have_posts()) : the_post(); ?>

            <!-- Thumbnail listing -->
            <div style="padding-left:5px;">
            <?php
                $args = array(
                    'numberposts' => 1,
                    'post_type' => 'attachment',
                    'status' => 'publish',
                    'post_mime_type' => 'image',
                    'post_parent' => $post->ID
                );
                $images = &get_children($args);
                foreach ( (array) $images as $attachment_id => $attachment ) { ?>
                <div id="post-<?php the_ID(); ?>" <?php post_class('gallerypost'); ?>>
                    <a href="<?php the_permalink() ?>" rel="bookmark" title="<?php the_title(); ?>">
                        <?php echo wp_get_attachment_image($attachment_id, 'thumbnail', ''); ?>    </a>
                </div>
            <?php } ?>
            </div>
            <!-- /ends -->

        <?php endwhile; ?>

            <div class="nav widecolumn">
                <div class="left"><?php next_posts_link('Previous image sets') ?></div>
                <div class="right"><?php previous_posts_link('More recent image sets') ?></div>
            </div>

    <?php else : endif; ?>

    </div>

<?php get_sidebar(); ?>
<?php get_footer(); ?>
```

What's happening here is that you rely on `get_children()` to dig out the attachments from the posts. Since the loop gives you a bunch of posts in the first place, you can rely on that for what category you're in, for example. This is the interesting part:

```php
<?php
    $args = array(
        'numberposts' => 1,
```

```php
        'post_type' => 'attachment',
        'status' => 'publish',
        'post_mime_type' => 'image',
        'post_parent' => $post->ID
    );
    $images = &get_children($args);
    foreach ( (array) $images as $attachment_id => $attachment ) { ?>
    <div id="post-<?php the_ID(); ?>" <?php post_class('gallerypost'); ?>>
        <a href="<?php the_permalink() ?>" rel="bookmark" title="<?php the_title(); ?>">
                <?php echo wp_get_attachment_image($attachment_id, 'thumbnail', ''); ?>
        </a>
    </div>
<?php } ?>
```

The arguments passed to `get_children()` tell it to just get one image per loop, this being the `'numberposts'` value, since you don't want to output all attachments on a per-post basis, but only show one image, and a thumbnail at that. You just want attachments, you want them to be published, you're forcing them to be images via the `'post_mime_type'` because videos won't fit here for example, and finally you want the actual post to be the parent. All this is stored in `$args` via the array.

All this is loaded into `get_children()` and then associated with `$images`, which you use in the array in the `foreach` below. That one will only run once in this case, since you just want one image per attachment to associated with the actual post.

It's all downhill from there, with a `div` passing a special class through `post_class()` to make the styling a little easier. The `wp_get_attachment_image()` echoes the image belonging to the attachment ID you got from the `foreach` above, and then outputs the thumbnail version. The last parameter that isn't passed is for outputting media icons, which you don't want. So what you get is the thumbnail, linked to the post (see Figure 10-6).

You need some styling to make this look half decent. This is what I've used on the Living Hyboria site (`livinghyboria.com`) from which I took this code snippet:

```css
div.gallerypost { float:left; margin: 0 0 10px 10px; padding: 10px; background: #e8e8e8; }
    div.gallerypost:hover { background: #800; }
    div.gallerypost img.attachment-thumbnail { width: 120px; height: 120px; }
```

Remember that you may want to change the number of posts displayed if you're just outputting a bunch of thumbnails. Your default 10 posts per page will probably look a little bleak, so you may be better off going with something like 40, using `query_posts()` just before the loop:

```php
<?php
    query_posts($query_string . '&posts_per_page=40');
    if (have_posts()) : while (have_posts()) : the_post();
?>
```

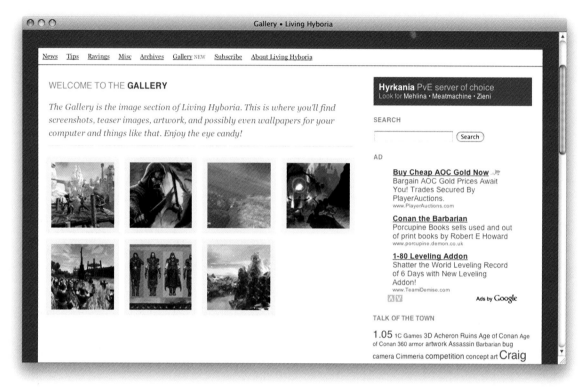

Figure 10-6: Thumbnail view

Say you want to add a short description to each photo set (again, that's a post) and list the whole thing with the thumbnail to the left, and the description to the right. The example below makes the thumbnail clickable, as well as the title, which is shown above the description. The code even includes the tags, since I like tagging. The code resides in the same template as the previous example, so the altered code within the loop is shown here:

```
<div id="post-<?php the_ID(); ?>" <?php post_class('gallerylisting'); ?>>
<?php
    $args = array(
        'numberposts' => 1,
        'post_type' => 'attachment',
        'status' => 'publish',
        'post_mime_type' => 'image',
        'post_parent' => $post->ID
    );
    $images = &get_children($args);
    foreach ( (array) $images as $attachment_id => $attachment ) { ?>
        <div class="gallerylisting-thumb">
            <a href="<?php the_permalink() ?>" rel="bookmark" title="<?php the_title(); ?>">
                <?php echo wp_get_attachment_image($attachment_id, 'thumbnail', ''); ?>
```

```
            </a>
        </div>
        <div class="gallerylisting-desc">
            <h2><a href="<?php the_permalink() ?>" rel="bookmark" title="<?php the_title(); ?>
    "><?php the_title(); ?></a></h2>
            <?php the_excerpt(); ?>
            <div class="postmeta"><span class="tags"><?php the_tags('Tagged with ',', ','); ?>
    </span></div>
        </div>
<?php } ?>
</div>
```

In this code, you're outputting the thumbnail in the same way as you did before. You're also getting the_title() and linking it, and the description is fetched using the_excerpt(), which means that you can offer that to people subscribing to a Gallery RSS feed, for example. This solution, illustrated in Figure 10-7, gives a better overview than just spitting out a thumbnail in a grid on a per-photoset basis.

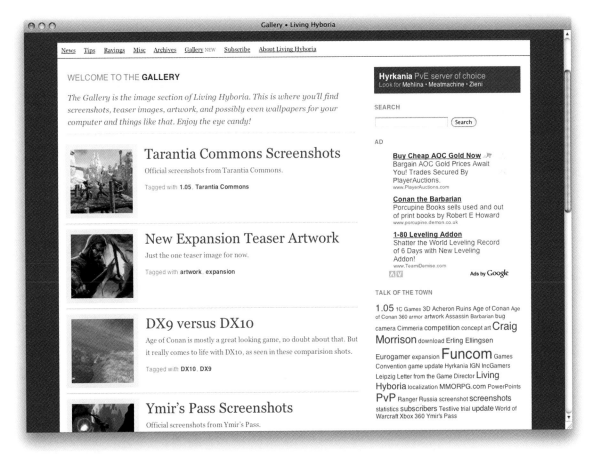

Figure 10-7: Simple thumbnail and description listing

About the Photosets

Each post is a photoset in this setup, containing all the images displayed in thumbnail gallery view using the [gallery] shortcode. Since images uploaded to a particular post are treated as attachments, that means you can browse to the attachment page (if you choose to link from the [gallery] shortcode output that way) and see the individual image, with a permalink and all.

You will probably have to style the single post view to properly fit your photosets. There are several ways to do this, and perhaps the post_class() output will be enough. If you want to output, say, the_excerpt() under the gallery you would have to add that, of course. This can easily be done by adding a conditional tag that checks if it is that particular category, and if it returns true it will output the_excerpt(), otherwise it won't.

```php
<?php if (is_category('gallery')) {
    the_excerpt();
} ?>
```

You can also add a template file for attachments (attachment.php, or image.php if you want to dig down deep) and style that accordingly. That would make it a lot easier to add back and forth links, as well as a link back to the original photoset. This is elaborated in Chapter 14, so consult that for more on working with actual images.

Another thing to consider is whether or not each image should offer the commenting functionality. Since each attachment is really a post with a different classification, this works. It also means that numerous plugins will work, including grading plugins, so why not let people add a grade to your images? There are a lot of possibilities here.

One of those possibilities is to bypass the attachment page entirely, by using an alternate way of displaying images. This usually means a lightbox effect. That too is discussed in Chapter 14, so turn there, and to Chapter 11 for plugins that help you implement the display technique.

No matter how you decide to display the photosets and the actual photos, you're probably wise to style them a little bit differently than any ordinary posts you may have. It is always a good thing when the visitor knows where they are on a site.

Other Uses

The preceding examples focused on adding a gallery section to just about any site that publishes a lot of images. It can be your personal blog just as well as a newspaper site covering an event; galleries have their place whenever there are a lot of images involved. Since WordPress supports including galleries across posts as well, with a tiny little addition to the [gallery] shortcode, it really isn't a big deal to first create a photoset post in the Gallery category, and then include that particular gallery using the [gallery] shortcode and the post identifier. All you need to do is pass the post ID to the [gallery] shortcode, like this: [gallery id="952"]. That would output a thumbnail gallery just as if you passed [gallery] on the post with the particular ID.

There is absolutely nothing that stops a site from expanding on the gallery functionality, involving more categories and, as mentioned at the start in this section, custom taxonomies for more sorting options. In fact, adding a separate taxonomy for tagging photos can be a really good idea if you're not too keen on mixing regular content results with photos. Chapter 6 tells you all you need to know about creating your own taxonomies.

Finally, there's the possibility that the galleries you publish are in fact the main content of your site. There is certainly no shortage of design galleries out there, featuring great CSS-based designs, or WordPress themes (or whatever, really), for example. You can build that kind of site on these premises, and even add a voting element thanks to the numerous available plugins. Since attachments are posts, just about anything you can do with a post can be accessed when viewing an image in attachment view. Naturally, it won't work as well when using lightbox overlays and such.

If you were to build an image gallery you'd probably bypass the whole custom code part for a specific category and rather make it the default way to output posts. A blog/news part of such a site would be the anomaly, so that would get the custom treatment rather than the other way around. You can categorize or tag any way you like, and put the_excerpt() to good use just as you did in the description example among the gallery template file code snippets. It would, in fact, be really easy to take this concept to the front page.

You Can Build Anything You Want

Well, maybe not anything, but just about—even WordPress has limits. WordPress is an extremely versatile platform and most content-based sites online will work perfectly well with minimal customization work to the system. Thanks to the flexibility of themes and the extensibility offered by plugins you can really do just about anything with WordPress. The whole idea with this chapter is to get you thinking along those lines. Whenever I start thinking about a new project, be it a personal site or something for a client, I turn and twist the concept in my head to figure out how to make it happen in as short a time as possible. More often than not, WordPress is the solution to achieving this.

This chapter has hopefully got you thinking about what you can do with WordPress and a bit of creativity. From here on we'll look at things to further expand your WordPress site, with plugins, design tricks, and other things that will help you reach your goals.

While you may not be able to build everything with WordPress, you'll find that most of your ideas are realizable with this lovely platform.

11

ESSENTIAL WORDPRESS PLUGINS

The amount of plugins available for the Word-Press platform is staggering; there is just no way to try them all, or even to keep up with all the changes that go on. That being said, naturally some plugins stand above the rest, not necessarily because they are the best at what they do, although they certainly are competing for that title, but because they have reached the users, been thoroughly tested, and fill a need.

This chapter is dedicated to just a smattering of the marvelous plugins that are available. Even though the plugins covered here may seem like a lot, they represent only a drop in the ocean compared to what's actually out there. Along with using the information in this chapter you'll have to look around, and keep up with updates as well, to make sure you've got the best there is. Or rather, to make sure that you've got what you need. That's what it's all about, isn't it?

Oh, and before you get to it, sometimes you'll get warnings when trying out a plugin, being told that the plugin has only been tested up to this or that version of WordPress, and you have a newer one. That doesn't necessarily mean anything at all, other than that the plugin hasn't been tested with your particular version and/or the plugin author hasn't updated the plugin files. So don't be put off just because a plugin isn't tested with your version yet; set up a test blog and give it a go for yourself. Most plugins will work across versions, after all.

Finally, do keep in mind that plugins are always changing, just as WordPress is. That means that what is working great today may not in the future. Most often that is not the case, but you never know; so please keep this in mind when playing with these plugins.

Content-focused Plugins

It's all about the content; you want people to find it, get hooked, and then spend an afternoon enjoying your sites. Wikipedia does it with links, and so can you. It's just a matter of making them interesting enough, and making it easy to dig into the archives. These plugins will help visitors get caught up in your content.

WP Greet Box (`wordpress.org/extend/plugins/wp-greet-box/`): Whenever you get a new visitor from a social bookmarking site, it may be a good idea to introduce yourself, or rather your site, to this person. That's what WP Greet Box does: it checks the referring URL and then outputs a message to the visitor. It can be something like, "Hi, welcome, please subscribe!" or something more tailored, like, "Welcome Digg visitor. Did you know I wrote a book on Digg? Get it here!" Very useful.

Yet Another Related Posts Plugin (`wordpress.org/extend/plugins/yet-another-related-posts-plugin/`): The "Yet Another" part of this plugin's name is not only a flirt with code lovers out there, the amount of related posts plugins is staggering, and that makes it hard to find the gold nuggets in amongst the rubbish. In my opinion, this is a strong contender for the throne of related posts plugins, because it offers so many options and serves relevant links as well. In part this is thanks to the relevance threshold limits you can set, which means that a site with a lot of content can be harsher on what is deemed as related content, for example. Other features include related posts in RSS feeds, support for Pages, caching, and also a template system that could really do with being easier to use, but still offers nice customization options if you want to take things a step further.

Popularity Contest (`wordpress.org/extend/plugins/popularity-contest/`): Do you know what is popular on your site? If not, this plugin is the solution, and even if you do it is a great way to promote the stuff visitors obviously like to others by outputting popular post lists using the plugin's widgets. Settings on how to weigh different things can make the plugin work even better.

Showing the most popular content on a site, especially if it is weighing in the time element (so that too old and outdated stuff doesn't suddenly pop up), is a great way to lead visitors through the site.

WP-PostRatings (`wordpress.org/extend/plugins/wp-postratings/`): WP-PostRatings is an excellent plugin for rating posts. There are several different grade images included, and you can choose where you want to output it by using the [ratings] shortcode, or by adding the plugin's template tags to your theme. It also lets you get the highest and lowest rated posts, sorting by time or overall, as well as category and so on. It is, in short, a pretty versatile ratings plugin all in all.

GD Star Rating (`wordpress.org/extend/plugins/gd-star-rating/`): Another ratings plugin is GD Star Rating, which stands out with its support for several kinds of rating per post (stars and thumbs up/down for example), as well as ratings for comments. It also features one of the flashier settings pages I've seen and a bunch of advanced settings. Well worth a look if you need ratings functionality.

PollDaddy (`wordpress.org/extend/plugins/polldaddy/`): It should come as no surprise that the PollDaddy plugin fully integrates the hosted poll and service manager into WordPress, with the option of creating polls without having to leave the admin interface. Automattic owns Poll-Daddy, which is why it's so integrated, and that's at least one reason to consider this service as well since it has the backing infrastructure needed. If you want to get rid of all the PollDaddy links in your polls, however, you'll have to buy a pro account, so if that's an issue you may want to consider one of the native poll plugins instead.

WP-Polls (`wordpress.org/extend/plugins/wp-polls/`): WP-Polls is a flexible poll plugin with archive support. You can either add it to your theme templates or use the widget to get the poll where you want it. It may take a while to set it up to fit your design, but it is a good alternative to the hosted PollDaddy solution.

Media Plugins

Media most often means images when it comes to WordPress sites, and that's the case on the plugin side of things as well. It's not so strange when you think about it. After all, if you want to spread a video you put it on YouTube, right? That way it gets exposure and you won't have to worry about bandwidth costs for your HD masterpiece.

NextGEN Gallery (`wordpress.org/extend/plugins/nextgen-gallery/`): NextGEN Gallery is a really cool gallery plugin that supports, well, a ton of things. You can have sortable albums, watermark your uploads, tweak the look with CSS, show a slideshow in the sidebar and localize it, it supports zip file uploads, and not to mention it lets your visitors browse your galleries in a smooth and user-friendly way. The admin interface is sleek, and you can easily get the short-code needed to display the gallery, much like you would with the normal gallery shortcode. This is, all said, one complete plugin.

The only caveat is that this plugin doesn't extend the normal image upload functionality, but rather works on its own. Images are stored in gallery folders residing in wp-content/gallery/ and while that is all fine and dandy, it means that WordPress can't find them in the Media Library. Also, when deactivating NextGEN Gallery, you'll end up with a lot of shortcodes not being parsed anymore, hence not outputting the images, and since you can't get to the images from WordPress that can be a problem should the plugin be discontinued. Worth thinking about, consequently. Still, though, a very cool and well-made plugin!

Lightbox Gallery (`wordpress.org/extend/plugins/lightbox-gallery/`): Lightbox Gallery adds the popular overlay lightbox effect to your gallery images, as well as making it possible to open any image by adding the `rel="lightbox"` tag to the link. You can do the same by implementing any of the available scripts out there, but this does it for you. Be aware that there are some hardcoded links in this plugin at the moment, so if you have moved your WordPress install to a subfolder but run the actual site in the root folder you may run into broken navigational images and so on. Hopefully this will be remedied in the future, otherwise perhaps go with another option.

Shutter Reloaded (`wordpress.org/extend/plugins/shutter-reloaded/`): If you want to keep your lightbox overlay effects light then Shutter Reloaded is worth checking out. It checks for any link leading to an image file, and then gives it the lightbox treatment. Granted, it's not as flashy as many of the other options out there, but still cool enough.

Podcasting (`wordpress.org/extend/plugins/podcasting/`): There was a time when podcasting with WordPress was synonymous with the PodPress plugin. Unfortunately it isn't really maintained anymore, which makes it even sweeter that there's a migration tool for PodPress users so that they can move to the Podcasting plugin. This plugin offers iTunes support and you can have both audio and video podcasts.

Short and sweet media plugins:

- fsThickboxAnnouncement (`wordpress.org/extend/plugins/fsthickboxan-nouncement/`) uses the Thickbox lightbox variant to overlay an announcement.
- jQuery Lightbox (`wordpress.org/extend/plugins/jquery-lightbox-balupton-edition/`) lets you add a lightbox-like overlay effect using jQuery and the `rel="lightbox"` to links leading to images.
- PhotoQ Photoblog Plugin (`wordpress.org/extend/plugins/photoq-photoblog-plugin/`) is another image plugin that keeps the images in its own structure, much like Next-GEN Gallery.
- AutoThumb (`maff.ailoo.net/2008/07/wordpress-plugin-autothumb-phpthumb/`) uses `phpThumb` to give you more control over the images, looking only at the sizes and filters you add to the image source.

- Featured Content Gallery (`wordpress.org/extend/plugins/featured-content-gallery/`) adds an image carousel meant to be used to promote featured content on a front page.

Administrative Plugins

By far the biggest section in this plugin compilation is the one for administrative plugins. That's probably because they range from backup solutions to statistics tools and WordPress admin fixes, as well as CMS-like functionality.

No Self-Pings (`wordpress.org/extend/plugins/no-self-ping/`): If you're tired of seeing your own pings ending up on your own posts just because you're linking internally, then this is a must-have plugin. In fact, it should be in every WordPress install out there in my opinion. If you want to crosslink internally, other than by the actual link in your post or Page, use a related posts plugin.

WP No Category Base (`wordpress.org/extend/plugins/wp-no-category-base/`): WP Category Base gets rid of the default "category" in permalinks. You can customize it to say other things in the permalinks settings, like 'topics' or 'products', but you can't do away with it altogether. This plugin fixes that, making `domain.com/category/my-category` become `domain.com/my-category` instead.

WP-DB-Backup (`wordpress.org/extend/plugins/wp-db-backup/`): You can never have too many backup solutions. This one uses the built-in WordPress pseudo-cron to e-mail you backups of the database or stores them on the server for you in case something goes wrong. No matter what other backup solutions you may be running already, I encourage you to add this one as well. Remember, it just backs up the database, and only the default tables and any ones you tell it to. Your uploaded files, plugins and themes will need a different backup solution. Hopefully this plugin will be shipped with WordPress in the future, as I'm sure it would help a lot of people.

Maintenance Mode (`wordpress.org/extend/plugins/maintenance-mode/`): A simple plugin that locks down your blog, displaying a message saying that the site is undergoing maintenance to every visitor except logged-in administrators.

Shockingly Big IE6 Warning (`wordpress.org/extend/plugins/shockingly-big-ie6-warning/`): Microsoft's Internet Explorer 6 is a scourge, and the only reason to run is if your operating system is forcing you to. That would be Windows 2000, among others, but the thing is there's nothing that stops users on these systems from installing any of the other Web browsers out there, it is just the newer versions of Internet Explorer that don't work. With this plugin you can educate your visitors to that fact, and make the Web a better place. Also, it will surely mean a better experience of your site for the user as well.

Branded Admin (`kerrywebster.com/design/branded-admin-for-wordpress-27-released`): Branded Admin lets you customize the header and footer of the WordPress admin interface to better fit your brand. You may want to use the Branded Login plugin (`kerrywebster.com/design/branded-login-screen-for-wordpress-27/`) as well for even more customization.

Sidebar Login (`wordpress.org/extend/plugins/sidebar-login/`): If you want a login form in the sidebar (or any other widgetized area) but don't want to hack the theme, then Sidebar Login is for you, doing just that, with no particular settings or anything. Sometimes it is that simple.

Theme My Login (`wordpress.org/extend/plugins/theme-my-login/`): The Theme My Login plugin replaces the traditional login page (wp-login.php) with a page in your theme instead. In other words, you get the login page integrated and therefore styleable, which can be a good idea if you want to give your users a login. You can also control where they'll end up after login, and add a login form to any widgetized area. Pretty useful thing, that.

Contact Form 7 (`wordpress.org/extend/plugins/contact-form-7/`): There are numerous contact form plugins out there. One of the better ones is Contact Form 7, which can manage multiple forms and offers customization options. The plugin is also fully localized, so you can get it in your own language, which is always nice. While there are spam protection measures built into this form, it may be good to know that it works perfectly well with the Really Simple CAPTCHA plugin (`wordpress.org/extend/plugins/really-simple-captcha/`) mentioned elsewhere.

TDO Mini Forms (`wordpress.org/extend/plugins/tdo-mini-forms/`): This is a cool little plugin that lets you build your own forms for submission of content, which then end up in the WordPress database. You can use it to get user reviews or anything, really, and you can choose to trust some users to post directly, while others may have to be approved (which means that the posts they submit will be in draft status by default). The forms are highly customizable, and you can even have the users submit custom field values, or submit files. There's also both simple questions and CAPTCHA as well as IP banning to help fight spammers flooding you with nonsense.

This plugin was featured in Chapter 10, when we looked at non-bloggish sites relying on user content.

Google Analyticator (`wordpress.org/extend/plugins/google-analyticator/`): Google Analyticator makes it easy to get Google Analytics (`google.com/analytics/`) running on your blog without having to hack the theme's template files. It even offers some stats in the admin interface, which is nice for those of you not addicted to checking the Analytics page ten times a day.

Google Analytics for WordPress (`wordpress.org/extend/plugins/google-analytics-for-wordpress/`): Another plugin for adding Google Analytics to your WordPress site without editing the theme files. Simple enough, with exclusions to make your statistics tracking more accurate.

WordPress.com Stats (`wordpress.org/extend/plugins/stats/`): If you're used to the statistics served within the WordPress admin interface on `wordpress.com`, you'll love WordPress.com Stats. It's the same, but for your stand-alone WordPress install. Nice and simple, but not offering as much information as Google Analytics or any of the other "real" Web statistics options out there. Needs a (free) `wordpress.com` API key to work.

Broken Link Checker (`wordpress.org/extend/plugins/broken-link-checker/`): This nifty little tool keeps track of your links. When installed, it will browse through your blogroll, Pages and posts, looking for links that are broken. Then it lets you do stuff with them. Very handy, but I'm not sure I'd trust it to be running all the time. It does recheck every 72 hours by default, but you can have it check manually as well.

WP e-Commerce (`wordpress.org/extend/plugins/wp-e-commerce/`): If you want to turn your WordPress site into a Web shop, or perhaps just enhance it to sell some merchandise, then WP e-Commerce will most likely be your first stop. The learning curve is a bit steep, but with some tweaking, both design-wise and settings-wise, you can get it to work the way you like. There is a lot of advanced functionality here, such as cross promotions, categorized products, and more. And if you want more you can always pay for the extensions, although the plugin will stand well enough on its own.

WordPress Simple PayPal Shopping Cart (`tipsandtricks-hq.com/wordpress-simple-paypal-shopping-cart-plugin-768`): A less advanced solution to sell stuff using a WordPress site is to implement the WordPress Simple PayPal Shopping Cart. Naturally, it connects to PayPal (only), and features a shopping cart for easy managing of products for buyers. You can add Add to Cart (or whatever text or image you want) anywhere you want by describing the product details in a shortcode fashion. That means that everything around the product, such as descriptions and images, will need to be managed manually.

The actual shopping cart can be added in a text widget, or anywhere you like really, which makes this plugin really flexible and easy to get working with just about any WordPress-powered site. Too bad it is PayPal only, but if you're fine with that you really should check this one out.

Redirection (`wordpress.org/extend/plugins/redirection/`): Redirection lets you set up redirects from your blog, so that `domain.com/smashing-company/` does a "301 moved" redirect to `smashing-company.com` instead, or whatever it is you need to do.

Pretty Link (`wordpress.org/extend/plugins/pretty-link/`): If you want to shorten your URLs for use on Twitter, or just hide your affiliate links (that's naughty!), then Pretty Link is something to look into. Especially if you intend to roll things on Twitter and have a short domain name, because it even has the option to attach a "Pretty Bar", in a manner similar to what Digg and others are doing. Pretty Link is your own URL shortener with options, basically.

Pods (`wordpress.org/extend/plugins/pods/`): Pods is a plugin aiming to make WordPress even more of a CMS. The developers call it a CMS framework, and that's not too far from the truth. You can create content types, data structures, set up relationships and so on. Building a site relying on Pods is sure to give you a lot of freedom. The only problem is it may be a bit daunting to get started with, especially if you're used to the straightforwardness of WordPress itself. Worth a look if you need WordPress to be more CMS-like, though.

WPlite (`wordpress.org/extend/plugins/wplite/`): To some, even WordPress may feel big and scary, especially if the only thing they need to do is publish a news post every month or so. That's when WPlite comes in handy, because it lets you hide parts of the admin interface from different kinds of users, hence making WordPress look less of a beast. This can come in handy when doing static sites for companies in particular, so keep it in mind if you're working with that sort of thing.

WordPress Download Monitor (`wordpress.org/extend/plugins/download-monitor/`): If you're interested in how many times a certain file has been downloaded, say a WordPress theme you've released or an e-book you're giving away, then you can monitor it with the WordPress Download Monitor plugin. It offers upload of files (but you don't need to use that, you can just input the file URL), localization, categories, and easy addition of the downloads to posts and Pages. And statistics of course; that was the important part, after all.

WP-Custom (`wordpress.org/extend/plugins/wp-custom/`): Custom fields may be great, but they are not the most user-friendly elements one can imagine having to educate clients to use. Or your fellow group bloggers for that matter, which is why WP-Custom is so great. It is basically a custom fields creator, but it outputs boxes that makes sense, no keys or values or anything, just a label and an input field.

Advertising Manager (`wordpress.org/extend/plugins/advertising-manager/`): Advertising Manager helps you with managing your ads, not to mention including them in your posts. The system recognizes and supports several ad networks, including the limitations they bring (the maximum three Adsense ad units per page comes to mind). There are also widgets so that you can place your ads in any widgetized area, which should be enough to get a lot of users to try this one out. It is a bit clunky at first, but honestly, compared to the fully-fledged ad managers out there this one's a breeze to use!

FeedWordPress (`wordpress.org/extend/plugins/feedwordpress/`): FeedWordPress lets you syndicate feeds into your WordPress database and publish them as posts. At first glance that sounds like the RSS scraper's dream, which it is of course, but it can also fulfill other purposes. Among other things it can power a "planet" Web site, which exists to pull together relevant content and then expose it to the visitors.

The plugin can be used for a lot of things; theoretically you can transform your WordPress install into a lifestreaming monster by sorting posts into appropriate categories and such.

Just so you're clear, scraping other people's content is bad mojo. Don't do it; write your own or obtain permission.

Members Only (`wordpress.org/extend/plugins/members-only/`): Members Only restricts viewing to registered users only; everyone else will be asked to login. When logged in you can redirect the user anywhere you like, so this works perfectly well with the P2 theme (`wordpress.org/extend/themes/p2`) if you need internal collaboration running on WordPress. There is even a setting for private RSS feeds.

A mixed bag of administrative plugins:

- Woopra Analytics Plugin (`wordpress.org/extend/plugins/woopra/`) is perfect for Woopra users, just as the Google Analytics ones are for Analytics users.
- Random Redirect (`wordpress.org/extend/plugins/random-redirect/`) creates a link that will send the user to a random post on your site.
- Post Editor Buttons (`wordpress.org/extend/plugins/post-editor-buttons/`) is a cool little plugin that lets you add your own buttons to the HTML part of the write post editor.
- TinyMCE Advanced (`wordpress.org/extend/plugins/tinymce-advanced/`) adds more features to the visual editor in WordPress.
- Viper's Video Quicktags (`wordpress.org/extend/plugins/vipers-video-quicktags/`) makes it easier to add videos from a number of sites, as well as to upload your own.

231

- Flutter (`wordpress.org/extend/plugins/fresh-page/`) is a CMS plugin that lets you create custom write panels as well as adding image functionality.
- More Fields (`wordpress.org/extend/plugins/more-fields/`) lets you add any number of fields and customize the Write/edit pages within the admin interface.
- Private WP 2 (`wordpress.org/extend/plugins/private-wp-2/`) limits your blog to logged-in users only, redirecting the ones not logged in to the login form.

Spam and Comment Management Plugins

Battling spam is important, and managing the comments in itself is important too. The following plugins will hopefully help.

Akismet (`wordpress.org/extend/plugins/akismet/`): Akismet is joined at the hip with WordPress and is one of those plugins that tackles the ever-present issue of comment spam. To use it you'll need an API key from `wordpress.com`, which means you'll have to be a user there. There are also some commercial licenses available, see `akismet.com` for more. You may also want to complement it with other spam-stopping plugins, or at least try out a few others if you find that a lot of spam is getting through.

WP-SpamFree Anti-Spam (`wordpress.org/extend/plugins/wp-spamfree/`): WP-SpamFree Anti-Spam differs from both Akismet at TypePad AntiSpam because it doesn't rely on a central service but rather battles the spam bots with a mix of JavaScript and cookies. It may sound like a trivial solution to this problem, but a lot of sites swear by it and it does seem to filter out a lot of spam, especially the trackback kind, that other plugins are missing. There's also a contact form included in the plugin, as a bonus, with spam protection of course.

If you're spending a lot of time fiddling with spam of any kind, you may want to give this plugin a go. It works perfectly well alongside Akismet for example, so there's really no reason not to give it a try if you need some help combating the spambots.

TypePad AntiSpam (`antispam.typepad.com`): TypePad AntiSpam is Six Apart's answer to the Akismet plugin, and it works in a similar way. Just like with Akismet it works against a server that logs and analyzes all spam, including the comments you mark as spam, and hence it "learns" all the time. Both the plugin and the necessary API key for your TypePad profile are free, so should Akismet fail for you, then this is worth a shot.

Really Simple CAPTCHA (`wordpress.org/extend/plugins/really-simple-captcha/`): CAPTCHA is one of those annoying "fill out what it says in the box to prove that you are human" things, and while you can argue that they aren't really user-friendly, sometimes you need to adopt desperate measures to stop spammers and other exploiters. This plugin really isn't about just slapping a CAPTCHA on your comments, for example, but rather it is meant to be utilized when you need a really simple CAPTCHA check. Works well enough in most cases.

Get Recent Comments (`wordpress.org/extend/plugins/get-recent-comments/`): The recent comments widget that ships with WordPress isn't exactly exciting, and besides it tends to fill up with trackbacks anyway. The Get Recent Comments Plugin is an excellent replacement, with adjustable layout, Gravatar support, cached output, order options, no internal pingbacks, and a lot more. If you're going to display the most recent comments, then this is an excellent solution.

IntenseDebate Comments (`wordpress.org/extend/plugins/intensedebate/`):
There are two hosted comments solutions that are competing for serving your reader's opinions, and IntenseDebate (`www.intensedebate.com`) is the one owned by Automattic. If you want to use IntenseDebate, this is your tool.

Disqus Comment System (`wordpress.org/extend/plugins/disqus-comment-system/`): The leading hosted comment service is Disqus (`disqus.com`) and naturally it is easy enough to get it running on your WordPress site using a plugin. If you're running Disqus you may also be interested in the (unofficial) Disqus Widget plugin (`wordpress.org/extend/plugins/disqus-widget/`), which shows off statistics for your Disqus comments.

CommentLuv (`wordpress.org/extend/plugins/commentluv/`): CommentLuv is a plugin that checks the applied URL for an RSS feed, and shows the latest update with the commenter's comment. It also connects to the ComLuv Web site (`comluv.com`) for more features such as link tracking. Luckily, the whole thing is pretty customizable because the default solution isn't very pretty, including bug buttons and such.

BackType Connect (`wordpress.org/extend/plugins/backtype-connect/`): The BackType Connect plugin checks the social Web for talk that is related to your blog posts, and publishes it as comments on your post. So if your mammoth article garnered a lot a buzz on Twitter, this will show up on your post as well. Pretty cool, but it can also be really messy when mixing both traditional comments and comments from, in particular, microblogging systems due to the 140 character limit. Use with care and make sure that your readership is savvy enough to understand what's going on.

233

Social Networking Plugins

The social Web is a concept, and you've got a ton of profiles to the left and right. Each social bookmarking tool has its own submit link, and while you can just add them all to your theme (which we'll get to later in the book), you can also rely on a plugin. It's all connected these days, after all. So why not add a little bit of the social Web to your site? Show off your Twitter and let your visitors submit your content to Digg. You can do most of that directly in your theme with some custom code (usually found on the various social networking sites' tools pages), but if you want to take a shortcut or add some extra social Web flair, then these plugins may help.

Lifestream (`wordpress.org/extend/plugins/lifestream/`): The Lifestream plugin easily adds lifestreaming features to your WordPress site. Just install it and set up what online accounts and RSS feeds it should fetch data from, and then you can include it using a shortcode on a Page, for example. You can also customize each element thanks to CSS classes being added, and there is built-in support for several of the largest social media properties out there, although just about anything with an RSS feed will work. And, of course, it is ready for localization as well as being constantly updated, which makes it an interesting option for those of you wanting to lifestream from within WordPress.

Twitter Tools (`wordpress.org/extend/plugins/twitter-tools/`): Twitter Tools connects your WordPress blog with Twitter, and lets you send tweets from the blog to your account. A simple enough settings page makes this a breeze to set up, and you can even control how the tweets you've sent should be tagged and handled on your own site. This means that you can have an asides category and send everything posted in it to Twitter, or the other way around.

Tweetable (`wordpress.org/extend/plugins/tweetable/`): Tweetable is a really cool plugin that lets you tweet from your WordPress admin, among other things. It auto-posts to Twitter as well, with optional Google Analytics campaign tags if you're curious about the stats, and there's even a widget to display your latest tweets and a TweetMeme (`www.tweetmeme.com`) feature. A must to try for any Twitter junkie using WordPress.

ShareThis (`wordpress.org/extend/plugins/share-this/`): Sending posts to social bookmarking sites is popular, and adding this functionality to each and every post on a site, well, that's a reasonable effect of this. ShareThis is more than just a plugin, it is a service that hosts your submit form, which means that you can get stats and everything if you sign up for an account.

The only thing to keep in mind here is that any third-party element will rely on that party's ability to serve the data. In other words, if the ShareThis server is slow or even unavailable, then so is some or all of your sharing functionality.

Add to Any: Share/Bookmark/E-mail Button (`wordpress.org/extend/plugins/add-to-any/`): This plugin integrates the hosted `AddToAny.com` sharing button. You may also want to look at the Subscribe button as well, if you like this service: `wordpress.org/extend/plugins/add-to-any-subscribe/`.

More social stuff:

- Wickett Twitter Widget (`wordpress.org/extend/plugins/wickett-twitter-widget/`) is a simple widget that shows your tweets.
- Twitter for WordPress (`wordpress.org/extend/plugins/twitter-for-wordpress/`) is another widget used to show off your tweets.
- Sociable (`wordpress.org/extend/plugins/sociable/`) is a popular social bookmarking plugin that adds links to your site.

Subscription and Mobile Plugins

The classification on this one may seem a bit weird at first, but think about it. Most smartphones have had RSS support for quite some time, and a few high end "regular" mobile phones as well. The natural next step is we will start to consume more and more content through mobile devices.

Align RSS Images (`wordpress.org/extend/plugins/align-rss-images/`): Images floating to the left and right on your site may be pretty to look at right there, but for RSS subscribers that same image will be in the midst of everything. You can just skip floating images, but that's a shame. Better to use Align RSS Images to parse the WordPress default align code (being `alignleft` and `alignright`) and swap for HTML equivalents to make things look good. No settings needed, just install and forget about it.

RSS Footer (`wordpress.org/extend/plugins/rss-footer/`): RSS Footer adds a line at the beginning or at the end of every item in your RSS feed. This means that you can insert a copyright notice to make things harder on the scrapers, or promote your site or other products to readers that prefer the feed to the original site. Very handy and easily customized.

Disable RSS (`wordpress.org/extend/plugins/disable-rss/`): This plugin does just one thing and one thing only: it disables the RSS feeds from a WordPress install. This can come in handy in static sites where RSS doesn't fulfill any purpose whatsoever.

Subscribe2 (`wordpress.org/extend/plugins/subscribe2/`): Subscribe2 is a really powerful plugin. It lets your users subscribe to your updates and hence get notifications via e-mail as per the settings you have. Perhaps you want to send a digest on a per-post basis, daily, or weekly. You can also send an e-mail to registered users, much like a traditional newsletter, if you will. The settings are easy enough to manage, as are the e-mail templates, so you can get started early on. As always, when it comes to sending e-mails, all hosts may not play nicely, so you should pay attention and do some tests to make sure that everything is being sent the way it was supposed to. Also, there is always the risk of being branded as a spammer in the eyes of ISPs, so use with caution.

MobilePress (`wordpress.org/extend/plugins/mobilepress/`): MobilePress is a cool plugin that serves a mobile theme rather than your regular one when the user is visiting from a mobile device, such as an iPhone for example. You can tell the plugin in which cases to serve the mobile theme and when not to, and there's even a theme interface similar to the standard one in WordPress so that you can create a mobile theme that fits your brand. An excellent choice for anyone expecting visitors from a mobile phone, which is just about anyone these days, right?

More mobile plugins:

- WordPress Mobile Edition (`wordpress.org/extend/plugins/wordpress-mobile-edition/`) is another plugin that gives your site a mobile interface when the visitor is using a mobile device.
- WordPress Mobile Pack (`wordpress.org/extend/plugins/wordpress-mobile-pack/`) is yet another solution for mobile visitors.

SEO and Search Plugins

What's good SEO and what's bad is hard to tell, except for the basics of course, which are pretty much agreed upon. The whole idea is to help people find content, and that's what this is all about.

All in One SEO Pack (`wordpress.org/extend/plugins/all-in-one-seo-pack/`): This plugin adds more settings for your posts so that they'll be better optimized for search engines. A lot of people swear by it, and there's no doubt that it will help, even if you just leave it doing its thing automatically. To really push it though, you should fine-tune each post all the time.

Google XML Sitemaps (`wordpress.org/extend/plugins/google-sitemap-generator/`): Google XML Sitemaps will create a compliant XML sitemap for your WordPress install, and then update it whenever you publish something new, or edit something old. This will help search engines crawl your content, which is a good thing. The plugin will even attempt to tell them that your sitemap is updated.

Better Search (`wordpress.org/extend/plugins/better-search/`): The built-in search functionality in WordPress is lacking, to say the least, which is why many users turn to plugins or Google Custom Search Engine (`google.com/cse/`). Better Search tries to change things by tuning the search, as well as adding popular searches and heatmaps. Since it automatically replaces the built-in search, it is easy enough to give a go.

Search Unleashed (`wordpress.org/extend/plugins/search-unleashed/`): Search Unleashed adds a bunch of settings and options for WordPress search functionality, such as keyword highlighting and extendable search engines. It also highlights incoming traffic search queries from sites like Google, so if someone searches for "Apples" on Google and visits your site as a result, Search Unleashed will highlight "Apples." The plugin is localized and you can even give priority to various parts of posts and Pages, as well as getting all those shortcodes properly searched should you rely on that. And best of all, no database changes! Give it a go, this is one of the better search plugins out there.

HeadSpace2 SEO (`wordpress.org/extend/plugins/headspace2/`): One of the more user-friendly SEO plugins out there is called HeadSpace2 SEO. It features great setup pages, and does more than just tweak the metadata and descriptions. You can, for example, have it manage your Google Analytics settings, which is nice. Whether this is a better choice than any of the other SEO options out there or not probably depends on what you want to achieve and how you go about it, but it is certainly the most user-friendly one.

Robots Meta (`wordpress.org/extend/plugins/robots-meta/`): Having a robots.txt for the search engines to crawl is a good thing, and Robots Meta helps you set one up by giving you simple settings for categories and other types of archives. Handy for SEO knowledgeable people, for sure.

Global Translator (`wordpress.org/extend/plugins/global-translator/`): Global Translator adds flags to your site using a widget, and then the user can get the site translated into their language. That is, if you enabled it and the translation engine used (Google Translate, Babelfish, and so on) supports it. Caching and permalinks for better SEO are among the features.

And then some more:

- Search Everything (`wordpress.org/extend/plugins/search-everything/`) is another search plugin with keyword highlighting and heavily expanded search parameters.
- GD Press Tools (`wordpress.org/extend/plugins/gd-press-tools/`) is not for the faint of heart. The plugin adds a lot of customizing to everything from meta tags to custom fields and cron, so use with caution.
- Breadcrumb Trail (`wordpress.org/extend/plugins/breadcrumb-trail/`) is a breadcrumb script that lets you insert a breadcrumb link by adding the plugin's template tag. Similar to Yoast Breadcrumbs (`wordpress.org/extend/plugins/breadcrumbs/`).

Code and Output Plugins

There are literally thousands of plugins to choose from in this category, and while a lot of them overlap, and quite a few fulfill almost no purpose whatsoever, there are some that don't fit in anywhere in the preceding sections but are still worth mentioning. Most of those are related to custom code, or are just small quirky things that can spice up a site by outputting the content differently. In other words, this is quite a mix.

SyntaxHighlighter Evolved (`wordpress.org/extend/plugins/syntaxhighlighter/`):
If you ever need to post chunks of programming code in your posts and on your Pages, from simple HTML to massive chunks of PHP, you know that the built-in parsing will get you in trouble. Sure, there are pastebins and the like, but why not solve this problem by adding the SyntaxHighlighter Evolved plugin, which not only takes care of your precious code, but also highlights it accordingly? It is styleable as well, so you can make the code boxes fit your content. Very neat. There are a bunch of other plugins that do similar things, but this one always performs.

Blog Time (`coffee2code.com/wp-plugins/blog-time/`): Blog Time outputs the time of the server in timestamp mode, either via a widget or the custom `blog_time()` template tag. It's not a clock, it's just the timestamp, which can be pretty handy sometimes.

WP-Cumulus (`wordpress.org/extend/plugins/wp-cumulus/`): Tired of your slack 2D tag cloud? Get one in 3D with WP-Cumulus and its rotating Flash rendition of the tag cloud. Flashy and fun, if nothing else, but I wouldn't recommend using it as the main navigation tool.

wp-Typography (`wordpress.org/extend/plugins/wp-typography/`): The wp-Typography plugin will improve your typography, obviously, which means that it will fix things such as not line-breaking unit values, give you prettier quote marks, dashes, and things like that.

Widget Logic (`wordpress.org/extend/plugins/widget-logic/`): This plugin is as simple as it is brilliant. It adds one tiny little field to every widget, and that field takes conditional tags. That means that you can add checks like `is_single()` to any widget, which makes the site really simple to make dynamic.

WP Super Cache (`wordpress.org/extend/plugins/wp-super-cache/`): This is the must-have plugin for any WordPress site experiencing a lot of traffic, but not wanting to go all haywire with the hardware. It lets you set up caching of your site, which means that it will serve static files rather than query the database all the time. If you plan on hitting the frontpage on Digg with your techblog and are on a share-hosting account, WP Super Cache will keep you online. It's a must-have, and better maintained than its predecessor, WP-Cache . The only caveat with WP Super Cache is that it will cache dynamic output as well, which means that your most recent comments may not actually *be* the most recent ones anymore. You can handle that by controlling what should and shouldn't be cached, but just be wary of it.

Query Posts (`wordpress.org/extend/plugins/query-posts/`): Query Posts is a really cool widget that lets you build your very own WordPress loop in the sidebar, without even having to know any PHP! It can be a very handy way to get custom output in the sidebar, or any other widgetized area really. It integrates nicely with the Get the Image plugin (`wordpress.org/extend/plugins/get-the-image/`), which lets you grab an image from the post's content, a custom field, or even an attachment.

Short and sweet:

- WP-DBManager (`wordpress.org/extend/plugins/wp-dbmanager/`) helps to keep your database up to speed, with repairs as well as backing up.

- Exec-PHP (`wordpress.org/extend/plugins/exec-php/`) lets you execute PHP code in posts, Pages, and text widgets. Make sure you don't let anyone who doesn't know what they're doing loose with this!

- WP-PageNavi (`wordpress.org/extend/plugins/wp-pagenavi/`) enhances the page navigation feature. Several styling settings are present, but you need to add the plugin's template tag to your theme files for it to work.

Do You Need a Plugin?

It's easy to get carried away with plugins and additional functionality overall when working with WordPress. There is just so much you can add, so many possibilities, and with the plugin install a mere click away now that you can do it from your admin interface, it's even harder to resist.

But resist you should, and hopefully you shall.

For every feature and every plugin you add, you'll bloat your install some more. It's not just the puny files sitting in the plugins folder, no; the problem is what they do to your database, and the amount of accesses and extra queries performed when you use them.

Plugins will slow down your site.

The lesson is, to ask yourself if the plugin is really necessary. Do I need this? Do my visitors need it? Do they want it, but don't really need it, and if that's the case, do I want to give it to them? What am I giving up by giving space and power to this feature? Can I use that spot for better purposes?

Don't get me wrong, plugins are nice. Some of the coolest WordPress sites just wouldn't be possible without plugins, and the extensive nature of the platform is one of the reasons it is so powerful and widely used. The fact that there's a whole chapter just talking about what plugins you should look closer at, and teasing you with what you can do with them, certainly counts for something!

Just don't go overboard, that's all I'm saying. Keep it as simple and as clean as you possibly can, and you'll be just fine.

V

WORDPRESS TOOLBOX

12 DESIGN TRICKERY

This chapter is all about making your Word-Press theme more interesting, and giving it that extra functionality that makes it pop. Yes, I know, that's a buzzword, but there are some techniques that are just too useful not to get into. Some are directly tied to WordPress and the kind of data you can get out of it, while others are more of adaptations of other techniques and solutions that can come in handy for your projects.

In other words, get ready for some design trickery, spinning tags and creating great menus. We'll also dive into how to properly work with JavaScript, getting ads into the loop, and customizing the login form.

Tag-based Design

In almost every case, a WordPress site should be built around categories and Pages. The former gives individual control of post listings and can be queried by conditional tags such as `in_category()`, which means that you can make them all behave differently. This in turn means that a category archive can easily become a section on a site in a most natural way, and posts belonging to that category can get adequate styling if you want them to. At the very least, this can be a specific set of colors for the category, or perhaps an icon or other kind of graphic, but if you take it further it could be a completely different style of content presentation.

Tags, on the other hand, are less fixed and generally work best if used to only describe individual posts. That means that they may seem redundant for more static (or other less Web 2.0-bloggish) sites. However, you can still put them to good use should you want to.

Tags offer three primary ways of achieving special interactions. The first one is the most obvious: the ability to control the tag archive pages. You may remember that tag.php in your theme can control the display of tags, but you can also use tag-X.php where X is the slug of the particular tag. That means it differs a bit from category-Y.php where Y is the category ID and not the slug. It means that you can actually have your very own properly styled post listing by tag, just like you can with categories. In theory this can mean that your tag archives can become sections on your site in the same way as categories.

The second way to control the content based on tags is the conditional tag `is_tag()`. It works more or less just like `is_category()` and you just pass the tag slug to identify a specific tag, like this:

```php
<?php is_tag('pirates'); ?>
```

Naturally, you need some conditions as well. This kind of usage usually covers it when it comes to categories, since most well planned WordPress theme designs are built around using as few categories as possible. Tags, however, are different so you may want to check for several tags at the same time using an array:

```php
<?php is_tag(array('pirates', 'ninjas', 'mushrooms')); ?>
```

That will return true whenever the tags `pirates`, `ninjas`, or `mushrooms` are used.

The final way to put tagging to good use is utilizing the fact that `post_class()` returns every tag as a class to post div. That means that you can have a lot of potential classes for more in-depth styling.

This, for example, is a post with the ID 129, which you can tell from the `id="post-129"`, as well as the fact that it even has the class `post-129`:

```
<div id="post-129" class="post-129 post hentry category-news tag-pirates tag-ninjas tag-mushrooms">
    <!- The actual post stuff would come here ->
</div>
```

Then you're getting a bunch of automatic classes, and finally you get one class per category and one class per tag. In this case, the category used has the slug `news`, so `post_class()` adds the `category-news` class. The same goes for the tags: you've got your `pirates`, `ninjas`, and `mushrooms` tags on the post, and they get added with the prefix `tag-` so that you can see them for what they are. Hence you get `tag-pirates`, `tag-ninjas`, and `tag-mushrooms`.

The brilliance of this is that it lets you get even tighter control of your content. If you want to give some posts more emphasis than others, but don't want to tie them to a particular category, then a suitable tag is an excellent solution. Common usage would be featured posts, or perhaps sponsor dittos. Say you want to push out a "Thanks to our sponsors" message among the content, but don't want the readers to mistake it as an actual post. Then you'd just tag it with something appropriate like `sponsor`, and add some CSS to your stylesheet making every post with the class `tag-sponsor` look different. An idea for that would be a different font, color, background, border, or image to show that it is something that is outside the regular content.

Just like with categories, you can build your sites around tags. My philosophy is that you should be really, really, really careful with adding categories; save them for the main sections. Then you can make things happen on a more per-post basis using tags and CSS styling in particular.

The Alternative: Custom Fields

Say you don't want to use tag-based design, for some reason. Perhaps you want to push out ads in your content as sponsored posts, and style them differently so that you don't risk fooling the readers, but don't want an ads-only tag to show up in tag clouds. Naturally, you can just exclude that particular tag from the tag clouds, like this:

```
<?php wp_tag_cloud('exclude=sponsor'); ?>
```

The excluded tag being `sponsor`, of course.

However, maybe this particular solution just won't do it for you, and you really don't want to use tags in that particular way because of other ways you use them, but want the same type of result. And a category isn't an option either, since you want to control which section of the site the ad posts show up in. That's when you turn to custom fields. In the example below we'll create one called `Poststyle`, which means that we'll just add it once, on any post, and then save a value for it. In this case, we'll go with `ad` to keep things apart. If you don't remember how custom fields work, revisit Chapter 4 for more.

Right, so you put the class you want in the value for the key `Poststyle`. You can easily get that by checking for the `Poststyle` key on a per-post basis and echoing it. Remember, that last `true` parameter is to make sure that just one value is echoed should more be added. That won't do in this case; you just want the one value that you'll use as a style for the particular post. This in turn means that when you give `Poststyle` the value `ad`, you want that added as a class so that you can style it accordingly. It also means that you can do even more stuff by adding other classes, but that's a different story.

The code to echo this is as follows:

```
<?php $specialstyle = get_post_meta($post->ID, 'Poststyle', true); echo $specialstyle; ?>
```

So how do you add that to the list of classes output by `post_class()`? This is the code for outputting the ID and classes for the post div:

```
<div id="post-<?php the_ID(); ?>" <?php post_class(); ?>>
```

Naturally, you can just add it to the ID, like this:

```
<div id="post-<?php the_ID(); ?> <?php $specialstyle = get_post_meta($post->ID, 'Poststyle', true);
   echo $specialstyle; ?>" <?php post_class(); ?>>
```

That would add #ad to the post should you give `Poststyle` the value `ad`, but it isn't all that pretty doing it in the ID after all. Let's get it into the `post_class()` template tag instead.

The good thing is that `post_class()` can take parameters, meaning that if you want to add a class—`turtles`, for example—you can do so like this:

```
<?php post_class('turtles'); ?>
```

That would make `post_class()` add `turtles` to the CSS classes output, which is what you want to do, but you want to squeeze your custom field value for `Poststyle` in there instead. This means you have to pass the PHP code above to `post_class()`, which luckily is pretty straightforward. However, you can't use it straight out, so you need to alter it a bit. This is the code you want to use:

```
<?php $specialstyle = get_post_meta($post->ID, 'Poststyle', true); ?>
```

The echo part is removed, since `post_class()` will return what you pass to it. And adding it is actually as easy as just removing the PHP declarations from the code above, and putting it within `post_class()`:

```
<div id="post-<?php the_ID(); ?>" <?php post_class( $specialstyle = get_post_meta($post->ID,
   'Poststyle', true) ); ?>>
```

This will add the value of the `Poststyle` custom field as a class to the post div, just like the `turtles` parameter did.

Controlling how posts appear, either by using tags or custom fields, is a great way to add more visual appeal to your site, as well as to highlight important content. Making the various elements in a design stand out on their own is important, assuming they fit together in the end. In the next section we'll move on and work with another important part of any design: the menu.

Improving the Menu

The menu is one of the most important parts of a design. It needs to be useful to the visitor by making it easy to dig deeper into a site, but at the same time it shouldn't contain too much content since that would make it both cluttered and hard to use. However, while usefulness is important, design is also an issue. The menu is one of the key elements of any design, since it is something so prominent for the user. That's why there are so many visual approaches applied to menus to make them more interesting, for better or worse because a lot of them tend to forget about the fact that a menu is supposed to be something the visitor can turn to at all times, and not just another flashy part of a cool design.

That being said, a useful and intuitive menu (Figure 12-1) can also be a spiffy looking one, and trying out different approaches to how the menu is used is always a good idea. Just as long as the main functionality—easy navigation—isn't lost, that is.

The kind of menu you opt for when using WordPress depends a lot on what kind of site you're working on. Some WordPress sites are built around Pages (static sites in particular), which is a scenario covered later in this chapter, while others are more free-flowing and really could do just with a tag cloud and a search field. In the middle you've got the most common usage (categories for sections) and Pages for static information (the boring "about" stuff), and tagging is just a way of describing the post's content better. Whichever it is, your site will have different menu needs, and you'll have to tackle different issues since it's not so easy to get everything together

Notes Blog THE FREE WORDPRESS THEME

Core   About the Project   Subscribe   Contact Information

Notes Blog Core and WordPress 2.8.2

There's a brand new release of WordPress available, being 2.8.2. It's a security release that you should upgrade to. Notes Blog *Core* users needn't worry, the theme works perfectly well with this release as well. Incidentally, this very site now runs 2.8.2.

Figure 12-1: A simple menu

seamlessly and entirely automatically. Hardcoding the menu is sometimes the only viable solution when you need Pages and categories to work well together in a horizontal menu, for example.

As if that weren't enough, you still need to decide how the menu should look, what orientation it should have, and if it needs additional bling to make it interesting. But that's a different story.

Proper Use of WordPress Pages

A lot of WordPress sites are built around Pages, which means that a natural menu would be one containing just that. You can of course put in the links to the relevant Pages manually in your WordPress theme's template files, but that would mean that you would have to hack the files every time a new section (which is actually just an added Page) is created.

Better to use `wp_page_menu()` then, a nifty little template tag where Page listing meets the needs of a menu. It fits the bill better than `wp_list_pages()`, another template tag that lists Pages, because of the `sort_column` parameter. This is another way of sorting in which order the Pages should be displayed, controlled by the user from the Write/Edit Page section in the Word-Press admin interface. You can give any Page a sort order value, and by doing this you can control which Page will be displayed when, if you're using `wp_page_menu()`, that is.

To use this, you need to pass the `sort_column` parameter:

```php
<?php wp_page_menu('sort_column=menu_order'); ?>
```

Naturally, `menu_order` is the parameter for your own Page sorting order. You can also sort by title (`post_title`), date published (`post_date`), date modified (`post_modified`), and so on. Really, the sorting options given by `sort_column` with `wp_page_menu()` make this a much better choice than `wp_list_pages()`, although a lot of things work the same way with both template tags.

Another useful little parameter that `wp_page_menu()` brings is `show_home`. By passing either true (as in show a Home link, by passing a 1 to the parameter) or false (no Home link, pass a 0; this is default) to `show_home` you'll get a link to your front page, shown as Home by default. Luckily you can change that to Start or Front or whatever you want by passing a text string to `show_home` instead.

You should really consider using `wp_page_menu()` if you want to build a Page-based menu for your WordPress site. Naturally, it can exclude Pages and change styles and so on, just like `wp_list_pages()`, so do check it out properly: `codex.wordpress.org/Template_Tags/wp_page_menu`.

Unfortunately there isn't a good way of combining Pages and categories in a menu that is output automatically. If you want to do things that way, I still think a text widget containing HTML code is the best solution.

Sliding Doors

The sliding doors CSS technique is a simple yet effective way of using graphics as the background in a horizontal menu, without having to set a fixed width. Without delving too deep into this—is a ton of things are written about it online, after all—the concept is most easily explained in images.

But first, this is the basis of your menu:

```
<ul id="navigation">
    <li><a href="menu-item-1">First Item</a></li>
    <li><a href="menu-item-2">Second Menu Item</a></li>
    <li><a href="menu-item-3">Third One</a></li>
    <li><a href="menu-item-4">Number Four</a></li>
    <li><a href="menu-item-5">Fifth!</a></li>
</ul>
```

Basically it's the typical output from most of the WordPress template tags that list categories and Pages, an unlimited list that is the proper usage for menus whenever remotely possible. What is a menu if not a list, after all?

Figure 12-2: A button background image with rounded corners

Say you want to use a button with rounded corners (Figure 12-2) for your menu items; that's pretty and modern, right? Right. Problem is, just applying it to the background of each menu item would require the actual menu item to be of a fixed width, and since you don't want to create a graphic for each of them but rather have the menu item text rendered by the browser with all the freedom that provides, it means that you have to be creative.

The solution is to chop up the image into three parts.

First you've got the left-hand side, being the rounded corners on that side. Second, there's everything that goes in between, which will be the background of your menu link. And the final part is the right-hand side's rounded corners. (See Figure 12-3.)

Figure 12-3: How to chop a button

What you want to do is to put the middle part in as the background of the link, and since I'm lazy and won't dwell on this subject too long we'll go for a one-colored middle. Then you want the left side's rounded corners to go to the left of the link, and the right side's rounded corners to the right, leaving the colored background to fill out the gap between. (See Figure 12-4.)

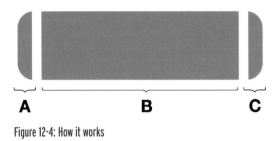

A　　　**B**　　　**C**

Figure 12-4: How it works

So how would you do this in HTML then? Easy, just add a span inside each link, like this:

```
<ul id="navigation">
    <li><a href="menu-item-1"><span>First Item</span></a></li>
    <li><a href="menu-item-2"><span>Second Menu Item</span></a></li>
    <li><a href="menu-item-3"><span>Third One</span></a></li>
    <li><a href="menu-item-4"><span>Number Four</span></a></li>
    <li><a href="menu-item-5"><span>Fifth!</span></a></li>
</ul>
```

And then you'd just add the images in the proper way using CSS. The link would get the left-hand side's rounded corners fixed to the left, and then it would fill out with the color of choice, and then you'd apply the right-hand side corners to the span but fixed to the right. What you get in effect is a button that can have any width you want, since the actual link background is a filler after the left-hand side's corners are displayed.

Or, to make it even clearer, here's some dummy CSS that you'd want to alter before usage, but it still explains how it works.

```
ul#navigation li {
    float:left;
    padding: 5px;
    list-style:none;
}
ul#navigation a:link, ul#navigation a:visited {
    display:block;
}
ul#navigation a:hover, ul#navigation a:active {
    background: #888 url(corners-left.gif) no-repeat left;
    float:left;
}
```

```
ul#navigation a span {
    float:left;
    display:block;
}
ul#navigation a:hover span {
    float:left;
    display:block;
    background: url(corners-right.jpg) no-repeat right;
}
```

So how would you make this work with `wp_page_menu()`, the template tag for proper output of menus? Easy, just add the necessary span HTML with the help of the `link_before` and `link_after` parameters, like this:

```
<?php wp_page_menu('link_before=<span>&link_after=</span>'); ?>
```

This would add the necessary span tag to each link in the menu, hence enabling sliding door usage.

But what about `wp_list_categories()` for the sites where you need your menu to list the categories rather than the Pages? That's a bit trickier, but if you run the whole `wp_list_categories()` through PHP, using `preg_replace` (PHP manual entry: `se2.php.net/preg_replace`), you can alter the output of `wp_list_categories()`. This code is a bit more technical; what it does is that it searches for some expressions (in this case the `li` and `a` tags) and then adds an opening and closing span tag around each link. On the WordPress side of things, it is important to pass a `false` (that is, zero) to the `echo` parameter to make sure that the `wp_list_categories()` tag doesn't output the content (that's what you do with the echo before `preg_replace()`, after all), and it is probably a good idea to pass nothing to the `title_li` parameter, hence not getting a heading for the category list, as well as pass 1 to `depth` to make sure you only get top-level categories.

Here's the code:

```
<?php echo preg_replace('@\<li([^>]*)>\<a([^>]*)>(.*?)\<\/a>@i', '<li$1><a$2><span>$3</span></a>',
    wp_list_categories('title_li=&echo=0&depth=1')); ?>
```

There is a third solution as well: use the built-in links manager and create a links category for the menu only, then output only that category with `wp_list_bookmarks()`. This works because of the existence of the `link_before` and `link_after` parameters, just like with `wp_page_menu()`.

For clarity's sake, here's `wp_list_bookmarks()` in action, showing only the links category Menu, which has the ID of 15. Naturally, you'd also add the necessary span code, and remove the heading:

```
<?php wp_list_bookmarks('category=15&title_li&link_before=<span>&link_after=</span>'); ?>
```

The next section contains some thoughts on how to use `wp_list_bookmarks()` for menus.

Using Links for the Menu

As mentioned in the sliding doors example, using `wp_list_bookmarks()` and the WordPress links manager can be a possible alternative for managing menus. It gives a certain freedom since adding and removing links is easy enough from within the WordPress admin interface, but there are drawbacks as well.

First of all, if you build your menu around links using the links manager, you need to make sure that anywhere you're outputting links the traditional way, as in links for link exchanges or linking friends and companies, you to exclude the menu links. After all, it wouldn't look in the least bit good if there was a Front Page or an About Us link in the middle of your corporate partner listings, so that needs to be covered. (See Figure 12-5.)

Luckily, solving this problem isn't such a big deal. With `wp_list_bookmarks()` you can choose to exclude a bookmark category as well as just display the one you want. That means that

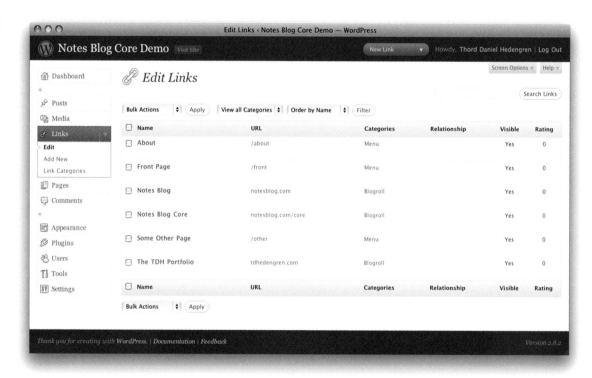

Figure 12-5: The WordPress links manager

you can just create a bookmarks category called Menu or something like that, and then choose to call just that one using the `category` parameter and the bookmarks category ID. It goes the other way around with the `exclude_category` parameter, which lets you skip a certain links category, and that one should of course be your menu category wherever you need regular link or blogroll functionality.

Naturally, you can control things on a per-bookmark basis as well, but that would mean ongoing fine-tuning to the `wp_list_bookmarks()` code, and every instance of it at that, so you're far better off putting all your menu links in their own category and handling things that way.

Another drawback is the limited sorting options that `wp_list_bookmarks()` offers by default. You can change the order of things using PHP, but that would mean that you'll be back to hard-coding things all the time, and then you may as well put the whole menu in there without messing around with WordPress template tags at all. So sorting is an issue, one that you may be able to sidestep with clever link titles and such. You may be able to sort it out by ordering by description, for example.

Finally, if you have a fairly advanced menu and you want to control the order of things, you may consider using several bookmark categories. Perhaps your problems would solve themselves if you could group links in various categories? Since you can control the output fairly well with the `wp_list_bookmarks()` parameters, it may in fact be that this is a solution.

Using the links manager may not be the conventional method to control your menu, but sometimes you need to control things outside of the code. Naturally, writing a plugin that totally adapts to your design and the needs it brings may be an even simpler solution than this, but certainly a lot more time consuming and complicated to actually do.

You can read more about `wp_list_bookmarks()` and the various settings it offers in the Codex: `codex.wordpress.org/Template_Tags/wp_list_bookmarks`.

Now we'll take a sharp turn, from spicing up first how the posts are displayed and then the menu to adding ads within the loop. Ads are elements too, and they need to be treated with care so that they do what they are supposed to—deliver some sort of message—but not at the expense of clashing with the overall concept of the design.

Placing Ads Within the Loop

A common question I get is how to insert ads—particularly Google AdSense ads—within the loop. Usually, bloggers want to run an ad after the first, second, or third post, and then continue with the loop as if nothing happened.

One way of doing this is to split the loop in two, first querying for a couple of posts (say two), and then displaying the ad. After that there's a second loop with a post offset corresponding to the amount of posts queried in the first loop; hence it looks like one big thing.

A better way, perhaps, is to just count the number of posts and then output the ad when a certain number has been reached. This is done with PHP of course, and by adding to a variable every time the loop runs, which it does for each post that is to be output.

In the first example you'll display an ad after the first post. Here's the common way of displaying an ad after the first post, stripped of all the post output code:

```
<?php if (have_posts()) : ?>
<?php $postcount = 0; ?>
<?php while (have_posts()) : the_post(); ?>
<?php $postcount++; ?>
    <?php if ($postcount < 2) : ?>
        <!- Post output ->
        <!- Ad code goes here ->
    <?php else : ?>
        <!- Post output ->
    <?php endif; ?>
<?php endwhile; ?>
<?php endif; ?>
```

What you have here is a basic loop, with some counting added to the mix. No doubt you recognize the first if (have_posts() line, but the one below that is new. What you do is give $postcount the value 0, which you'll add +1 to for every time the loop loops. This is done in the while (have_posts()) : the_post() line, as you know, which means that the first thing you'll do after that is add +1 to the $postcount value, and you do that with ++, which means just that, add +1.

After that it is pretty straightforward. If the $postcount value is < 2 (that is to say, it is less than 2, which means it is 1), you'll output the post and the ad code, and if not you'll move on to the else post output, which is your standard one.

This is how this code would look if you applied it to the default WordPress theme, focusing only on the actual loop part:

```
<?php if (have_posts()) : ?>
<?php $count = 0; ?>

    <?php while (have_posts()) : the_post(); ?>
    <?php $count++; ?>

        <div <?php post_class() ?> id="post-<?php the_ID(); ?>">
            <h2><a href="<?php the_permalink() ?>" rel="bookmark" title="Permanent Link to <?php
    the_title_attribute(); ?>"><?php the_title(); ?></a></h2>
```

```
        <small><?php the_time('F jS, Y') ?> <!-- by <?php the_author() ?> --></small>

        <div class="entry">
            <?php the_content('Read the rest of this entry &raquo;'); ?>
        </div>
        <p class="postmetadata"><?php the_tags('Tags: ', ', ', '<br />'); ?> Posted in
  <?php the_category(', ') ?> | <?php edit_post_link('Edit', '', ' | '); ?> <?php comments_popup_
  link('No Comments &#187;', '1 Comment &#187;', '% Comments &#187;'); ?></p>

        <?php if ($count < 2) : ?>
            <!— Paste ad code here —>
        <?php else : ?>
            <!— This would output if there was no ad code —>
        <?php endif; ?>
    </div>

    <?php endwhile; ?>
<?php else : ?>
<?php endif; ?>
```

Obviously you can check these thing in other ways, display things differently and so on. You just want to either display or not display an ad after the first post.

What if you want to insert the ad after the first two posts then? In that case, just change the if query for the $postcount value from 2 to 3 instead, which would mean that the ad output would happen on posts 1 and 2 in the loop.

```
<?php if ($postcount < 3) : ?>
```

Beware of the Ad Rules

Inserting ads between posts may sound like a great idea. After all, it is pretty unobtrusive and hence it isn't bound to annoy people greatly. It can, of course, but it is a lot better than putting ads in the actual content, which you also can do with some nifty hackery.

However, while it may seem like a great idea to spread out the ads between the posts, you need to observe the rules of the ad network you're using. Google AdSense, widely used, has a limit on how many ads per page you can show, and if you break that limit you're bound to get in trouble, and perhaps have your account suspended. Bad news for most people, but even worse for people earning a living from ad revenue.

So while I encourage you to spread out your ads across the site (it is, after all, a lot nicer than having them concentrated to the top of the page) I also feel obliged to remind you to check the ad network's rules for any limitations that there may be.

And be careful! Automatic outputs like this one can be dangerous stuff, and a mistake somewhere may land you with a lot of ads all over the place. Neither you nor your readers, nor the ad network, will like that, I'm sure.

Another thing you should be careful with is using 404 page not found error outputs with ads. Sure, you can display ads on these pages, but they won't perform well if they are contextual by nature, and I doubt advertisers paying for ad views would appreciate being on an error page. With that said, the next section discusses making proper 404 error pages.

404s That Help

Creating useful 404 error pages is important. These are the pages that will show whenever someone reaches a page within your site that doesn't exist, and although you may have everything covered at your end, people linking to you may not, so you need these. The theme template file to manage the 404 page not found errors is aptly named 404.php, and you can do just about anything you want with it because it is served from WordPress.

This section won't go into detail on how to build your own 404.php template file (that has been covered in Chapter 4 already), and since you can do just about anything you can do with, say, a Page template, the possibilities are somewhat staggering. I will, however, tell you what I think a good 404 error page should offer the visitor:

- **It should be obvious that the page is not there.** In other words, tell the visitor that the page they were looking for doesn't exist, and do it in such a way that there is no risk of misunderstanding.
- **Offer alternative routes.** Since the most likely source of hitting a 404 error page in a WordPress setup is a faulty link from elsewhere, you should offer a different route to the content the visitor was looking for. Encourage searching in particular.
- **Open up your site.** The visitor may not care enough to search for the content that sparked the 404 error, but maybe you can snag him or her anyway? Add links to your various categories and offer a very brief intro on what they are all about. Turn your 404 error into a sales pitch for your site.
- **Show the latest content.** It is easy to display a list of links showing the latest updates, so you should do that. Maybe there's something that will appeal to the visitor there?
- **Use humor.** A bit of light-hearted humor can be a way to make the visitor less annoyed by the fact that the content they wanted to see isn't there.
- **Offer a means of error reporting.** Let the visitor get in touch with you to tell you of the missing content; that sends a positive message as well as helping you find any particular faults in your site.

A useful 404 page says a lot about a site, so spend some time making yours a good one.

The WordPress JavaScripts

JavaScript can be a great tool, especially thanks to excellent libraries like jQuery, MooTools, Scriptaculous, and so on. There are a ton of these out there today, making it easy to add visual bling for transitions, as well as more useful stuff as well. Most cool services online rely on JavaScript today,

254

and the WordPress admin interface isn't particularly fun to work with if you turn off JavaScript in your Web browser.

Naturally this is something you can bring to your WordPress sites as well. Whether it is really just some added visual appeal to your theme, with smooth animations or similar, or some actual new functionality added thanks to your brilliant coding doesn't matter. What you need to think about is how you do it, and that is where `wp_enqueue_script()` comes in. With this you can load any of the JavaScript libraries that ship with WordPress, which is quite a few I may add, or you can just attach your own.

The usage is simple. Add a JavaScript to the hook where it is needed, using `wp_enqueue_script()`. So if you want to load a JavaScript as late as possible, since it probably won't be needed before the user does something special anyway, you can use `wp_enqueue_script()` and attach it to the `wp_footer` hook, like this (using jQuery as an example):

```
function load_my_scripts() {
    wp_enqueue_script('jquery');
}
add_action('wp_footer', 'load_my_scripts');
```

The use of `wp_enqueue_script()` also makes it easy to just load the scripts when you need them, with some clever use of conditional tags. If you just want the script on the home page, use `is_home()`, and so on.

There really are a ton of things you can do with JavaScript, and it all depends on the site as well as your own preferences. Some people are more at home in Prototype than in jQuery, and others prefer MooTools or something entirely different. That's why `wp_enqueue_script()` can load anything. You should use it, and you should in particular make sure that you don't slow down your site with JavaScripts if you don't need them, or let them load too early. After all, what's the point of waiting for a JavaScript when there isn't a page to utilize it on?

I urge you to read up on `wp_enqueue_script()` in the Codex, where you'll also find information on the various JavaScript libraries that ship with WordPress, and how you can pass things such as dependencies. Start with the Codex page (`codex.wordpress.org/Function_Reference/wp_enqueue_script`) and then you can move on to the JavaScript library itself.

There are a lot of JavaScripts out there that you can use, not to mention extensions to the popular libraries mentioned. Be sure to read up on them, though, not only to keep your site clean but also to make sure that they work in all the Web browsers you want to support. Barring that, if the extra functionality, flair, or bling does it for your site, it can be a great way to make it more visually appealing.

Speaking of which, you've worked a lot at the front end of WordPress in this book, with themes and how to show the content, as well as using plugins that alter what the visitor sees. There is a back end too, and sometimes you either want to make that more appealing, or perhaps brand it to fit your site. The next section examines that concept and what options there are.

Making WordPress Your Own

Sometimes you'll find yourself in a position where you need to make WordPress carry your brand a bit further than usual. More often than not, it is when you're using plugins or features that let the visitors become registered users, with settings and privileges on the administrative side of things. Or, in plain English: they can access the WordPress admin interface.

This means two things. First, visitors get to log in, and that means that they'll use the login form. The one that doesn't look the least bit like the carefully designed site you're sporting, so naturally you'll want to do something about that.

Second, they get into the WordPress admin interface, and that looks every bit like WordPress and nothing at all like Your Super Brand™. Who would want that?

Unfortunately, WordPress doesn't offer as good theming possibilities for the administrative side of things as it does with your site's front end, but there are some things you can do and if you really want to you can take things pretty far. It all depends on how important it is that the WordPress parts looks as little like WordPress as possible, and how much time you want to spend doing that.

A Custom Login Form

If you need to tweak one thing when it comes to WordPress admin stuff, it is probably the login form. This totally screams WordPress, which in itself is pretty annoying, especially if your site does something totally different from what people usually think of when someone mentions WordPress to them. (See Figure 12-6.)

You can of course just hack the login form by altering the core files in WordPress, but that would mean that you may end up breaking something crucial, and also that you would have to do it all over again with every update, since the update will overwrite your hack.

It is way better to use a plugin then, and if you've paid attention you may have already found a few possible ones in Chapter 11. They are good, so try them out.

However, some of us may want to keep the login form in line with the theme, since it is a design matter after all, and that would mean that you would want the custom stuff with the theme files. Luckily, you can do that by hooking on to the `login_head` action hook, and applying some extra stylesheet goodness. If you think that over for a little while you'll see that it basically means that you can make the login form look just about any way you'd like, so long as you don't need to change the actual layout of the thing. So a black background and your grungy logo is not a problem at all, just do it with some CSS.

First of all, however, you need to create the function to hook onto the `login_head` action hook. You'll recognize this type of code from before, and if not, revisit the earlier sections on action hooks. This particular snippet is from Notes Blog Core, which supports custom logins from the start. There are some minor changes added for this example, though, so if you're comparing code you may want

Figure 12-6: The default Login form

to remember that Notes Blog Core is made to build child themes upon, and these child themes may want some custom login of their own. That's why I'm using the `stylesheet_directory` parameter in the `get_bloginfo()` tag, and not `template_directory`, which is a lot more commonly used.

```
// custom login form
function nbcustom_login() {
    echo '<link rel="stylesheet" href="' . get_bloginfo('stylesheet_directory') . '/custom/login.css"
  type="text/css" media="screen" />';
}
add_action('login_head', 'nbcustom_login');
// ends ---
```

This code is simple enough; the only thing it does is that it adds the contents of the `nbcustom_login()` function to the `login_head` hook. And that is, of course, the `echo` containing a stylesheet located in a folder called `custom` in the theme's directory.

The rest is up to you: just hack away at the new included stylesheet (located in custom/login. css in the previous example). The login page is easy enough to figure out, but a few of the things you may want to change are the background color (using the body tag), the WordPress logo, which resides in the `h1` tag, and the whole login box itself, which is in `div#login`. Happy modifying!

Admin Themes

Theming the WordPress admin is unfortunately a slightly tricky affair. First of all, the only way to do it without hacking or overwriting the core files (which you never want to do) is by using a plugin. What you do, basically, is create a plugin that hooks on to the `admin_head` action, and applies your own stylesheet, much like you did in the login form example previously.

```
function smashing_admin() {
    echo '<link rel="stylesheet" href="' . WP_PLUGIN_URL . '/smashing.css" type="text/css"
  media="screen" />';
}
add_action('admin_head', 'smashing_admin');
```

You know the drill: you're just including the stylesheet smashing-admin.css located directly inside the plugin directory, so probably something like `domain.com/wp-content/plugins/ smashing-admin-plugin/smashing.css` in this case. Then it is all a matter of changing the behavior of the tons of elements within the WordPress admin interface. It is not something for the weak. And, of course, installing and activating the plugin!

You may also want to add something to the admin footer. If so, just hook on to `admin_footer` with whatever you want, in a similar way.

There are some pretty impressive admin themes out there, and some of them were mentioned in Chapter 11, but you should be under no illusions. Making the admin interface look the way you want will most likely be hard work. That being said, sometimes all you need is the little things, like swapping colors and such, and that shouldn't be too much of a problem to do this way.

Polishing a WordPress Site

Learning the various tricks of the trade when it comes to WordPress is important to lift your site from just a mere WordPress theme (no matter how great) to something more complete. It is almost all about polishing, but any good site needs that, so you should experiment with techniques and see what you can do with your site.

In this chapter you played with the design. The next chapter is about adding extra functionality, another way to polish your WordPress site.

13 EXTRA FUNCTIONALITY

You can do a ton of things with WordPress, usually in myriad ways. This chapter is all about showing off some of the functionality you may consider using in a project or on a site of yours, so that you have a decent starting point. Since every site is different, your solution may very well differ a lot from the ideas presented here.

Each element described is also discussed with regard to when it is a good idea to use the technique, and when you should forget about it. Between the plugin expandability and the various features you can put in your theme, there are a lot of options and it is way too easy to clutter a site with things it just doesn't need. You should question every addition, even if it is hard to resist adding some cool features sometimes.

Tabbed Boxes

Tabbed boxes are a great way to save some of that all-important screen real estate. On blogs and somewhat dynamic and living sites, tabbed boxes can be used to show off popular posts, recently commented posts, and other similar things that can be grouped together in a natural way. The key is to make sure that the tabbed content that isn't shown by default doesn't always have to be visible. In fact, that's the key thing with tabbed boxes right there: make sure you don't hide something crucial in a tab.

Technically, tabbed boxes aren't very hard to create or manage. Some of them may not even look like boxes with tabs on them; it is more a type of functionality than anything else.

Smart Usage

Creating the actual tabbed box functionality is easy enough, and there are a ton of scripts available out there if you don't want to do it yourself. The one in the following example is simple enough for most cases, but it would also work well with some bling. After all, if you've decided to use a tabbed box, why not make it look really good and fit your design?

This is the code we'll be working with in this case. It relies on the Prototype JavaScript library, so you need to load that with `wp_enqueue_script()`. See the JavaScript section in Chapter 12 for more on that. In this example, assume that Prototype is loaded. Here is the part that needs to go in the head section in header.php:

```
<script>
// Function to view tab
function viewTab(tabId) {
    // Get all child elements of "contents-container"
    var elements = $('contents-container').childElements();
    // Loop through them all
    for (var i=0, end=elements.length; i<end; i++) {
        // Is clicked tab
        if (tabId == elements[i].id) {
            // - Show element
            elements[i].show();
            // - Make sure css is correct for tab
            $('tab-'+ elements[i].id).addClassName('active-tab');
        }
        // Is not the clicked tab
        else {
            // - Hide
            elements[i].hide();
            // - Make sure css is correct for tab
            $('tab-'+ elements[i].id).removeClassName('active-tab');
        }
    }
}
</script>
```

You may want to put that in its own file, of course. That's entirely up to you.

Moving on, here's the basic markup for the actual tabbed box:

```
<ul id="tabs">
    <li id="tab-content-recent" class="active-tab">
        <a href="javascript:viewTab('content-recent');">Recent</a>
    </li>
    <li id="tab-content-popular">
        <a href="javascript:viewTab('content-popular');">Popular</a>
    </li>
    <li id="tab-content-comments">
        <a href="javascript:viewTab('content-comments');">Comments</a>
    </li>
</ul>
<div id="contents-container">
    <div id="content-recent">
        Content for Recent tab.
    </div>
    <div id="content-popular" style="display: none;">
        Content for Popular tab.
    </div>
    <div id="content-comments" style="display: none;">
        Content for Comments tab.
    </div>
</div>
```

Naturally you'll need to style this to look like the sort of tabbed box you want, which may not be a tabbed box at all, but something entirely different. The key is that the links in the list items are opening a div container with the contents for the tab (or whatever) in question.

You could stop here, by putting the necessary code for Recent and Popular posts, as well as the latest comments, in the corresponding div. No big deal.

However, if you want to make it a little bit easier to manage, you can create a widget area for each tab's containing div, giving you the freedom to easily swap faulty functionality for a new plugin of your choice. If you want to do it that way, you need to widgetize a bit.

First there is the register part that goes in functions.php:

```
if ( function_exists('register_sidebar') )
    register_sidebar(array('name'=>'Recent Posts'));
    register_sidebar(array('name'=>'Popular Posts'));
    register_sidebar(array('name'=>'Recent Comments'));
));
```

Then there are the actual widget areas, which of course go in each containing div, respectively:

```
<ul id="tabs">
    <li id="tab-content-recent" class="active-tab">
        <a href="javascript:viewTab('content-recent');">Recent</a>
    </li>
    <li id="tab-content-popular">
        <a href="javascript:viewTab('content-popular');">Popular</a>
    </li>
    <li id="tab-content-comments">
        <a href="javascript:viewTab('content-comments');">Comments</a>
    </li>
</ul>
<div id="contents-container">
    <div id="content-recent">
        <!— Recent tab widget area —>
        <?php if ( !function_exists('dynamic_sidebar') || !dynamic_sidebar('Recent Posts') ) :
  ?><?php endif; ?>
    </div>
    <div id="content-popular" style="display: none;">
        <!— Popular tab widget area —>
        <?php if ( !function_exists('dynamic_sidebar') || !dynamic_sidebar('Popular Posts') ) :
  ?><?php endif; ?>
    </div>
    <div id="content-comments" style="display: none;">
        <!— Comments tab widget area —>
        <?php if ( !function_exists('dynamic_sidebar') || !dynamic_sidebar('Recent Comments') ) :
  ?><?php endif; ?>
    </div>
</div>
```

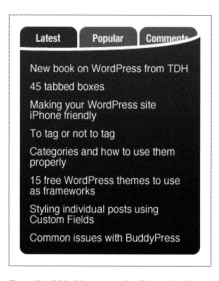

Figure 13-1: Tabbed boxes can help with organization and navigation

Now you can just drop the contents for each tab in the widget area of your choice from within the WordPress admin interface, just like you would with your footer or sidebar widgets.

Figure 13-1 shows how a tabbed box can look with a few minor alterations to the preceding code.

To Tab or Not to Tab

So should you use a tabbed box or not? There are some obvious pros and cons for doing so, and it all boils down to the kind of site and content you're dealing with. Most importantly, you need to make sure that the usage is intuitive and obvious for every possible kind of user. The content you hide away in tabs can't be crucial, since the visitor may not be the clicking kind. Also, content in tabs can be entirely missed when you get an accidental visitor, who scans the site briefly and then decides whether to stay and explore or move on elsewhere. You can't hide away your best stuff in tabs, just like you shouldn't make a menu or search box too obnoxious to actually use.

That being said, for a lot of sites tabbed boxes can make sense. It's all about how much space you want to free up for listings of content, activity, and things like that. Is there, for example, any real reason to show your blogroll all the time? Why not put all links in one tabbed box, having a tab for your social Web profiles, another for friends' Web sites, and so on. That takes a lot less space, and anyone looking to delve deeper into your online presence or the friends and partners of a site is certainly not averse to using a tabbed box. The same user would also most likely appreciate the tabbed box whenever it isn't the focus of attention, since it save space and makes your site a lot easier to deal with.

Overall, you should be careful with tabbed boxes, and the same goes for tabbed menus. It is one extra click, and that can be annoying for the visitor. That being said, it's not so nice to clutter a site with lists and functions that are rarely used either, so it is all a matter of purpose and usability.

Displaying RSS Feeds

RSS feeds are really useful not only for subscribing to updates using a feed reader, but also for displaying content from partners or other projects you may be publishing online. You're probably already acquainted with the RSS feed widget that ships with WordPress; it can display a bunch of updates from just about any working RSS feed.

When you want to work with feeds on your site you're not limited to just that widget, or even any of the available plugins. You can, in fact, tap into the feed parser directly and hence do more custom stuff with the output from the feed. If you want to output the description you can do so, just as you can add HTML code around the various elements to get more control, and so on. If you want to do more advanced stuff with content from an RSS feed you're more or less required to either rely on a plugin, or code it yourself thanks to the built-in functionality. Which, incidentally, often is what the plugin you may be considering relies on in the first place!

One thing worth thinking about, however, is that displaying RSS feeds can slow your site down. If you're fetching the latest updates from several sites (or even just one) you'll find that your site sometimes lags behind. That's because the feed is being queried from your server, to the feed host's server, and then PHP needs to get all the data and parse it to be able to produce the output you want. This is true for hardcoded RSS fetching as well as if you were putting a ton of RSS widgets on your site. If you rely on a lot of feed content you should look into caching solutions to make your site as snappy as possible. In fact, ideally you'd let the server run a cronjob at regular intervals and cache the content for you to output whenever needed. There is some support for caching, but you're on your own when it comes to scheduling the content fetching. Most likely that would mean that you would have to develop your own plugin, or find one that does this already.

So, yeah, feeds are great and really useful, but if you browse the blogosphere (in particular) and pay close attention to what it is that slows down sites, you'll find that feed fetching is one of the culprits, along with other functionality that nabs content (be it badges or ads) from external services. All I'm saying is make sure your site isn't too bogged down by RSS feed content.

The Built-in Parser

There is built-in support for outputting RSS feed content on your site. You can use the feed widget (covered a bit later), but most likely you want more control than that. Luckily this is pretty easy to achieve, thanks to the addition of SimplePie in the core. That's right, there's a new feed parser in WordPress as of 2.8, which means that although your old `wp_rss()` calls may still work, they are outdated and should be changed to something more up-to-date.

Which is to say, you need to use `fetch_feed()` instead, something that may seem a bit daunting when delving into the SimplePie documentation at first. However, it isn't that complicated after all. Here's a simple inclusion of the latest headlines, linked, from my lifestream over at `stream.tdh.me`:

```
<ul>
<li><h2>Lifestream</h2></li>
<?php $feed = fetch_feed('http://stream.tdh.me');
    foreach ($feed->get_items() as $item){
        printf('<li><a href="%s">%s</a></li>', $item->get_permalink(), $item->get_title());
    }
?>
</ul>
```

By including the feed like this, I'm opening it up for SimplePie functions. I'm basically looping the feed here and printing it, fetching the data as I go along. In this case, I'm just pulling the permalink and the title of every post. You can expand on that by adding the description and a date:

```
<ul>
<li><h2>Lifestream</h2></li>
<?php $feed = fetch_feed('http://stream.tdh.me');
    printf($feed->get_title());
    foreach ($feed->get_items() as $item){
```

```
        printf('<li><a href="%s">%s</a></li>', $item->get_permalink(), $item->get_title());
        printf('<p>%s</p>', $item->get_description());
        printf('<p><small>%s</small></p>', $item->get_date('j F Y at g:i a'));
    }
?>
</ul>
```

SimplePie is huge—worthy of a book on its own. What you need to know is available in the SimplePie documentation, which unfortunately isn't entirely compatible with WordPress since it is a stand-alone RSS parser. That being said, you should take a look: `simplepie.org/wiki/reference/`.

We'll return to SimplePie in a little bit. But first, some words about the built-in widget solution.

When to Use the Widget Solution

So when would you want to use the default built-in RSS widget? The answer is simple: never! It may sound a bit harsh, especially since what the widget really does is the same as you did in the preceding section with `fetch_feed()`. That's right, the widget calls SimplePie in the same way.

Problem is, it also slaps on a feed header, linked to the feed URL and everything. That's not really such a good idea, now is it? If you want to display the latest updates from your blog, a news site, Twitter, or whatever, you don't want to link the actual RSS feed at the top of the listing! You may want to link the site itself, but not the feed. I'm hoping this is something that will be changed in WordPress in the future, but it's been around for some time now.

So should you never use a feed widget? That's going a bit far, because others have realized this problem and released plugins that remedy the situation. Refer to Chapter 11 for some cool RSS plugins that may achieve what you're after.

In fact, hacking the RSS parsing code yourself should be avoided unless you need to do really funky stuff. It is better to add a widget area and then add an appropriate feed widget. That means you can easily add stuff around it too, but naturally you have a lot more control if you code the whole thing yourself. As is the case so many times, pick the solution that fits your project.

Multiple Feeds with SimplePie

With the addition of SimplePie you get the power of multiple feeds, and I'm not talking about the capability to display several feed blocks on the same page. No, I mean the capability to take a bunch of feeds and then mash them together and present the content. In SimplePie, this functionality is often referred to as *multifeeds*, which may be a good thing to know when looking for solutions in the SimplePie documentation.

In the next example, we'll put SimplePie to a quick test by taking two feeds and listing them depending on date, but limiting the output to just show 10 items:

```
<ul>
<Li><h2>Interesting Headlines</h2></li>
<?php $feed = fetch_feed( array('http://rss1.smashingmagazine.com/feed/', 'http://feeds.digg.com/
digg/topic/apple/popular.rss'));
    $feed->enable_order_by_date(true);
    foreach ($feed->get_items(0, 10) as $item){
        printf('<li><a href="%s">%s</a></li>', $item->get_permalink(), $item->get_title());
        printf('<p><small>%s</small></p>', $item->get_date('j F Y at g:i a'));
    }
?>
</ul>
```

You're defining the two feeds in an array within `fetch_feed()` rather than just putting the single feed URL in there as you did when you just wanted a single-feed output. You can add several more feeds to this in the same spirit if you want to. After that, an `order_by_date` setting is added, acquired from the SimplePie documentation:

```
$feed->enable_order_by_date(true);
```

This could just as well have been in the single-feed example as well, but if you just output a single feed you can probably rely on the fact that the latest item will come at the top, so it would be a bit redundant.

After that there's the `foreach` loop again, starting at the first item (the `0`) and moving onward to the tenth (the `10`), after which the loop is over and hence you get 10 items.

Again, SimplePie is huge, but this is a start at least. At the time of writing, the help section in the WordPress Codex is pretty scarcely populated given that `fetch_feed()` was added in version 2.8, but I'm sure it will be completed with more examples as time goes on. Meanwhile, turn to the SimplePie documentation for an extensive look to what you can do with this RSS parser.

Sending e-Mail with WordPress

If you want to have WordPress send e-mails for you, you can use the `wp_mail()` function. This can be anything from a verification for some action that you want to confirm went through (or didn't) on your site, to building a full "My blog has updated!" notification list.

The `wp_mail()` function is easy enough to use. This code snippet would, assuming you activate it with a function of some sort, send an e-mail to `smashing@domain.com` with the subject "Smashing Party!" and the content (in text format) "Thanks for the smashing party the other night. TTFN!" (See Figure 13-2.)

```
<?php wp_mail('smashing@domain.com', 'Smashing Party!', 'Thanks for the smashing party the other
  night. TTFN!'); ?>
```

Figure 13-2: A simple e-mail sent from WordPress

You can even attach files and send in HTML format rather than the default text ditto. There's more on this in the Codex: `codex.wordpress.org/Function_Reference/wp_mail`.

As always when sending e-mail from Web pages, there are a few things to observe:

- **Don't spam people.** That's bad form and evil.
- **Beware of e-mailing too much.** That can get you blacklisted.
- **Make sure your code works.** After all, an unintended hiccup can send hundreds of duplicate messages, bringing your server to its knees and getting you into all kinds of trouble.
- **Prevent exploits.** Make sure that some nasty person won't be able to spam through your e-mailing solution. It can be anything from just shooting random e-mails to the left and right, to just being a pain by pumping that submit button a thousand times.
- **Tell everything.** Users like to know what's going on, especially when there are e-mail addresses involved. In other words, be sure to explain how you will use their e-mail address and what they can expect from you. When it comes to e-mail, no surprises is a good thing.

Adding a Login Form

Sometimes it can be prudent to have the WordPress login form (Figure 13-3) a little more handy than just on its own page as it is by default (on /wp-login.php, from your WordPress install's point of view). If your site relies on user features that require logins, then naturally there is no harm in adding a login form to, say, the sidebar or the header. There are a couple of ways to add a login form, but I think the solution outlined in this section is the easiest one to implement. Not counting using a plugin, of course.

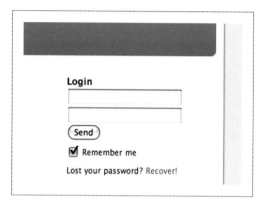

Figure 13-3: A simple Login form

The following example assumes you want to put the login form in the sidebar, which usually is a `ul` in itself, so the form would go in a `li` of its own. However, you may want it in the header instead, or someplace else, in which case you probably should put it in a `div` so you can style it accordingly. This is a bit rough, you see:

```php
<?php if (!(current_user_can('level_0'))){ ?>
<h2>Login</h2>
<form action="<?php echo get_option('home'); ?>/wp-login.php" method="post">
<input type="text" name="log" id="user_login" class="input" value="<?php echo wp_
  specialchars(stripslashes($user_login), 1) ?>" size="20" />
<input type="password" name="pwd" id="user_pass" class="input" size="20" />
<input type="submit" name="submit" value="Send" class="button" />
    <p class="forgetmenot">
        <label for="rememberme"><input name="rememberme" id="rememberme" type="checkbox"
  checked="checked" value="forever" /> Remember me</label>
        <input type="hidden" name="redirect_to" value="<?php echo $_SERVER['REQUEST_URI']; ?>" />
    </p>
</form>
<p>Lost your password? <a href="<?php echo get_option('home'); ?>/wp-login.php?action=lostpassword">
  Recover!</a></p>
<?php } else { ?>
<h2>Admin</h2>
<ul>
    <li><a href="<?php bloginfo('wpurl'); ?>/wp-admin/">Dashboard</a></li>
    <li><a href="<?php bloginfo('wpurl'); ?>/wp-admin/post-new.php">Write a post</a></li>
    <li><a href="<?php echo wp_logout_url(urlencode($_SERVER['REQUEST_URI'])); ?>">Logout</a></li>
</ul>
<?php } ?>
```

What you've got here is an `if` clause checking first to see if you're logged in, or rather, if you're a user of `level_0` or higher, which is the most basic WordPress user level. You may recognize it as the Subscriber role from the admin interface, which means that it can do just about nothing. Read up on Roles in the Codex (`codex.wordpress.org/Roles_and_Capabilities`) and remember that there are 10 user levels; the lowest is level 0 and the highest is 10.

So the first check is to see if you're a logged-in user, basically, and if you're not the site will display the login form. Most of the code is swiped from wp-login.php, but other than the necessary functionality, I think this is the most important snippet:

```
<input type="hidden" name="redirect_to" value="<?php echo $_SERVER['REQUEST_URI']; ?>" />
```

It is the redirection that happens after login, and since I'm assuming you're rolling a site where there is a point to letting users login wherever they want, I think you should be redirecting them to the place where they logged in, as opposed to ending up at the WordPress admin Dashboard. So this takes care of the redirect by reloading the page you're at, but with you logged in.

Moving on, the `else` clause is what is displayed when a user is actually logged in. For the sake of it, I'm outputting a list with a link to the Dashboard in WordPress admin, along with another to the Write Post screen, and finally a logout link. There should probably be checks to make sure you're not showing admin links to pages where the user can do nothing, like I'm doing here. After all, the Subscriber user (level 0, remember) can't write any posts, so they wouldn't be able to use a link to the Write Post screen. A check with `current_user_can()` much like the one done at first would be prudent, or a longer `if-else` logic, perhaps.

Remember, don't put login forms in your designs unless they serve a purpose. After all, why show off a login form and tease those nasty brute forcers to abuse your WordPress install if you don't have to. Also, there is no point in showing off a login form if the visitor can't put it to good use, as that's just poor use of screen real estate. Make the login forms count.

Print That Blog

Sometimes it is prudent to print an article or blog entry on paper for convenience. It may be that the reader isn't comfortable reading on screen (or has a really crummy one), or prints an entry just for the sake of bringing some paper to someplace else. That's why you should make printing easy, if your site is the kind that would benefit from it.

Start with adding a simple "Print This Page" link. This is easily done with a tiny little JavaScript, no extra custom stuff or enqueuing of script libraries needed:

```
<a href="javascript:window.print()" rel="nofollow">Print This Page</a>
```

That's it; the browser will try and print the page. Simple enough, though your site may not be all that print-friendly, especially if you have a big, fancy header and lots of columns. That's why you need to create a print stylesheet. Technically, you don't really have to add another stylesheet, but it may be a good idea to separate print-only things from the regular screen stuff.

First of all, create a stylesheet called print.css and look over your theme for what should or should not be included. Most likely your sidebar and footer will be unnecessary when printing, so remove them:

```
#sidebar, #footer { display:none; }
```

Gone! At least assuming that the sidebar has the ID #sidebar, and the footer has #footer, which they usually do.

Now, make sure the actual content looks decent enough on paper:

```
#content {
    width:100%;
    margin:0;
    padding:0;
    float:none;
    background: #fff;
    color: #222;
    }
a:link, a:visited { color: #000; }
```

Almost black text, white background, full width and no floating or weird margins or padding—that will do it. I also added code to make sure that the links are black (no need for the :active or :hover pseudo-classes, obviously).

You could go on forever on stuff to put in your print stylesheet. You may want to make sure that headings look decent, and perhaps you don't want to have those 637 comments you've got on every post printed either. Just hide the elements you don't want on paper, and style the others. It is as simple as that. You may also want to set all font sizes to points (pt) rather than pixels or em, since that is talk the printer can understand. Also, speaking of printing, consider adding page-break stylings to headings, and possibly also elements like block quotes and lists. It all depends on how you want to present your site in printed form.

Right, the only thing that remains is to include the stylesheet in header.php:

```
<link type="text/css" media="print" rel="stylesheet" href="<?php bloginfo('stylesheet_directory');
    ?>/print.css" />
```

Add the stylesheet below the standard stylesheet inclusion code in the head section of the file. You may notice that I opted to use 'stylesheet_directory' rather than 'template_directory' when passing the stylesheet URL. This is purely semantic, since I imagine you'd want all your stylesheets in the same place, and hence print.css should be in the same place as style.css.

Adding Some More

Expanding a site with necessary functionality is a natural and obvious step in the development of a site. When it comes to WordPress, expanding a site often means that you want to show off or promote content in some way, or add possibilities for interactions, like the login form, for example.

The next chapter is about using images to spice up a site; in other words, another type of element that can expand a site's impact. Remember, though: don't go too crazy with these extras. After all, you don't want clutter.

14

FUN WITH IMAGES

It's said that a picture is worth a thousand words. Or maybe it speaks a thousand words, I'm not sure. The point is that an image can tell a story a lot faster than text can. This isn't to say that images are always preferred over text; I'm pretty sure you can agree that isn't the case. It is no secret, however, that images and text work extremely well together. Other than just spicing things up, an image can also help tell a story and (literally) illustrate a point.

Some sites use more images than others, but most sites are better off whenever they do something thought-through with their galleries and illustrations. This chapter is about displaying images in a WordPress site, beyond the traditional inclusion of illustrative points or inspiring scenery in your posts and pages. It is more about galleries, presentation, and photo-sharing services, not to mention the small matter of actually setting up WordPress image management in a way that makes sense.

Working with Image Galleries

Ever since WordPress 2.5, there has been support for the [gallery] shortcode and the possibilities it brings. What [gallery] does really is output uploaded images in a clickable thumbnail grid. Then you can let your visitors see a larger version of the image, either in your theme's design, or the original file itself. The former is called the attachment page, since that's what images are: attachments to blog posts. This built-in functionality should cover most of the needs you may have if you run a text-based site that sometimes publishes images.

To fine-tune it even further, the first stop after installing WordPress and picking the theme of your choice should be the Media page under Settings in the admin interface. Here you can control the circumstances under which the various images are scaled. Each image you upload is saved in up to four different versions, designed for your needs across the site.

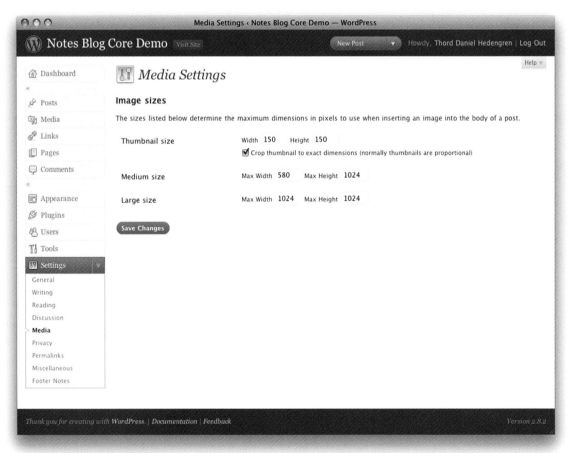

Figure 14-1: The WordPress Media Settings page

Figure 14-1 shows the WordPress Media settings page, which outlines the various sizes your images can be:

- **The thumbnail** is a cropped version of an image meant to symbolize the image in question. You can set it to be cropped to exact sizes, which means that it won't actually show the whole image all the time. It's a small image meant to be clickable. Default size is 150 × 150 pixels, but you can change that to fit your theme.
- **The medium image** is in fact the full image downsized, with width and height proportional to the original image you uploaded. You can set a maximum width and height that dictate how the image should be scaled. This is also the image used in the attachment pages.
- **The large image** is also your full image but downsized proportionally.
- **The original image** is also available, untouched.

There's one caveat: no image version will be created if it is in fact larger than the original image. So if your large image is set to 800 pixels width and height, but the image you're uploading is smaller than that, it won't be created nor will it be available to include or link to in WordPress. There's just no point.

So what about it then? Why bring this up?

Simple. The thumbnail should be in a size that fits your width and the number of columns you think you'll want to use normally in your image galleries created with the [gallery] shortcode. Make it a nice size for your site.

Meanwhile, it is my belief that the medium image should be the exact same as the maximum width your design can manage. In other words, if the max width is 580 pixels, set the max width of the medium image to 580 pixels, to ensure that you can include it in your posts whenever you like. Since the medium image is the one used in attachment pages it is a good idea to make it fit well enough there. Granted, you're in something of a pickle if your attachment pages are constructed in such a way that they can manage a larger image than your traditional blog posts, but if that is the case you'll just have to create custom images for your posts. The important thing is to make the attachment page look good.

Finally, the large image is good for linking a larger variant. One can argue that perhaps the large image should be the one in the attachment page, and it is probably possible to make it so, but by default that's not the case and hence you can't rely on it. The large image is usually only interesting if you're uploading a high-resolution photo and don't want to link the original version because it is 15 megabytes and ridiculously large for Web view, and the large one is substantially smaller and fitted to the screen.

WordPress should promote the image size settings more, I think. They are important whenever you will be working with images, so get them right from the start; otherwise you'll end up with images at the wrong size, and that's not a pretty sight in any design.

Styling the Gallery

Making the galleries included with the `[gallery]` shortcode look good is easy, assuming you've configured your thumbnails according to the number of columns you'll be using. This is something you can choose when you're including the gallery, so you need to be wary of that.

Actually styling the gallery is also pretty simple. The whole thing resides in a `div` with a number of identifying classes to use, one being called *gallery* itself. As is the norm in WordPress, there are unique IDs and classes as well, but you'll probably settle with `div.gallery` for your CSS needs.

Moving on, each item in the gallery is enclosed in a `dl.gallery-item`, which in turns contains `dt.gallery-icon`, which has the linked thumbnail image, and possibly also a `dd.gallery-caption` if a caption is provided for the image in question. You get this for as many images you've chosen to display in a row, then it all breaks down to a new row quite unceremoniously with a `br` tag with `style="clear:both"`, and it begins again.

That means that, for the thumbnail gallery listings, you need to style the following (listed hierarchically):

```
div.gallery {}
    dl.gallery-item {}
        dt.gallery-icon {}
        dd.gallery-caption {}
```

This is the code used by Notes Blog Core, with a subtle font color and size for the captions, and some white space in between because that's always nice to the eye. Naturally your design may be a lot flashier than this, adding background images, borders, and so on.

```
div.gallery { margin-bottom: 14px; }
    dl.gallery-item {}
        dt.gallery-icon {}
            img.attachment-thumbnail { border:0; }
        dd.gallery-caption { margin-top: 8px; font-size: 12px; color: #777; font-style: italic; }
```

Now, that's just one half of it. While you can configure your gallery thumbnails to link to the actual image, you can always choose to link to the attachment page. That's the one showing the image in your theme's design, which probably means that it will revert to either single.php or index.php since most themes lack the attachment.php template file, and very few have ones for video.php, image.php, and so on.

To get your theme to be image-friendly, you really should add a link back to the post containing the actual gallery, and you should add Previous/Next links so the user can browse the gallery from image to image.

Start with the Previous link. The following code fetches the post's parent, which is the actual post the attachment is attached to, and links it. Nothing fancy. You can't use `the_permalink()` of course, since that would indicate the attachment itself, while the_title() naturally is the image title. You probably want to make sure that your attachment template outputs that too:

```
<a href="<?php echo get_permalink($post->post_parent) ?>" title="<?php echo get_the_title
  ($post->post_parent) ?>" rev="attachment">
    <?php echo get_the_title($post->post_parent) ?>
</a>
```

Speaking of outputs, the description you can fill out when uploading or editing an image is in fact output by the_content(), which means that you can add decent attachment support to your single.php or index.php template easily enough. Just use the is_attachment() conditional tag to check for it and output accordingly, and you'll be fine.

Back to business: add those Previous and Next links for navigation within the gallery, in attachment image view. This is done with previous_image_link() and next_image_link(), both of which by default will output the thumbnail, linked, to the other target image. Here you're using div's to float the Previous and Next links to the left and right:

```
<div class="left"><?php next_image_link(); ?></div>
<div class="right"><?php previous_image_link(); ?></div>
```

While the thumbnail output may be cool if tailored to the task, you may want to use text instead. Just pass nothing to the image size parameters (yes, it takes other sizes as well) and it will output the image post title, which is the name you gave it, instead. Or you can add another parameter to pass a custom text link, like this:

```
<div class="left"><?php next_image_link('', 'Next Image'); ?></div>
<div class="right"><?php previous_image_link('', 'Previous Image'); ?></div>
```

That's about what you need to know to work with galleries on a WordPress site. The next natural step, after getting it to work with your theme, is pimping the whole affair using plugins.

Better Browsing with Lightbox

A Lightbox effect is a common name for an overlay that displays an image on top of a site, without opening a popup (see Figure 14-2). You need to close this to access the actual site again, which may sound like a bad idea, but compare it to having to open a new page to view the image in full size and you get the picture. Most decently designed Lightbox solutions have accessible browse buttons as well.

This is pulled off with JavaScript and some design trickery, and there are a ton of possible solutions waiting for you a mere Google search away. Which solution you choose all depends on how much visual bling you want, and what sorts of effects suit you and your site. I do think you should go with one that comes as a WordPress plugin though, because that means that you won't have to add any classes to your images manually to make sure the Lightbox solution recognizes the link as

277

Figure 14-2: Lightbox effect in action

a Lightbox one. The plugins do this manually, and suddenly your image gallery won't have to open those attachment pages at all, and your visitors can browse your photos with ease and flair.

However, there are drawbacks, the most obvious one being what happens if the visitor has turned off JavaScript, or if someone clicks the thumbnail link before the Lightbox script is fully loaded. The result is an opening of the image as a whole, outside of the design and everything, just as if the link pointed to the image itself only. Which it usually does, but then the script puts it right in the effects it adds. It isn't too pretty when that happens, especially if the visitor expects that nice overlay effect and the easy Previous/Next links it probably sports, but then again it is a fully functional solution as well, thanks to the Web browser's back button.

Why wouldn't you use a Lightbox solution? There aren't that many reasons actually, and the plugins available are easy enough to use on just about any theme. The issue with no JavaScript is diminishing predictably enough, but there's another problem here, and that is smaller devices. How good does something like this look on a seven-inch low-resolution screen? Is it really useful then? The same can, in all fairness's sake, be said about attachment pages, but it is a bit easier to style those on a per-user agent basis. You should make sure that the Lightbox script doesn't override any such solutions.

Finally, if you make your money on page views, don't go the Lightbox route unless you think it will bring in more readers. After all, having people load a new page, and hence a new set of ads, whenever they want to view the next image in a gallery can be good business in itself!

Using Outside Scripts and Systems

Finally, a few words about using gallery solutions outside of WordPress. There are several gallery scripts available, some of which are fully-fledged systems in themselves, while others just crunch images to various sizes and output content in physical folders on your server as HTML. They all have their place; I just believe that isn't as a part of WordPress.

Don't get me wrong here, I'm sure there's a reason to use Gallery2 (or any of the other popular image galleries) with WordPress at times, but overall I think you should think very carefully before doing so. The foremost reason for this is flexibility. WordPress can be extended with numerous plugins, and if your images are a part of WordPress they can sometimes benefit. However, if you're running your images in an outside script and just showing them in your theme one way or the other, you won't benefit. And what happens if that outside script suddenly stops working, or starts clashing with your WordPress install? There may be great support and fixes available, but then again there may not. You won't get that with WordPress, and if you do have problems you know what to expect from the community.

The same really goes for plugins that move the gallery functionality from the WordPress core to their own setup. This may mean that they can add new features, better sorting, or whatever, but it also means that whenever the plugin isn't being maintained anymore and it stops working because of defunct WordPress functionality or other conflicts, you'll be on your own in a way that wouldn't have happened otherwise. And besides, instead of the flashy gallery functionality that the plugin you were considering offered, why not look for something that adds that to the core image gallery features instead?

All that being said, sometimes you need more, and then you'll have to move outside of WordPress core features, either by relying on plugins or to external systems and/or services altogether. Just make sure you know what you're doing, and make sure you know what to do if you need to move back, or to something else. Conversion and importing tools can certainly help you to feel more secure in such cases.

Random Image Elements

Adding some random stuff to a site can spice it up and make it feel more alive. In the blogosphere having a random header image is popular, as well as having random posts being promoted and things like that. After all, things that change between visits are always seen as good things, and there is no harm in adding to that illusion with some random images.

The most basic way of randomizing is using PHP and any of the randomizing functions it offers, such as `rand()` and `mt_rand()`. There are also several JavaScript solutions you can utilize. Solutions for both of these techniques are available in vast quantities online so you really shouldn't waste time on hacking your own unless you really need to.

It doesn't stop there, however. Several plugins can help as well, a few of which are discussed in Chapter 11. Randomized content, and especially images, has been done so many times it is almost ridiculously easy to get going. That is, unless you want to display random images from posts you've uploaded. For some reason this is a bit harder.

Random Images from Your Galleries

An even cooler type of random image content would come from your galleries: the images you've uploaded to WordPress. Those are attachments, and you can get to them by doing a little bit of `get_post()` hacking in an additional loop. The idea is to show the thumbnail of any attachment that is an image, and link it to that very image. Since you'll have properly styled your gallery (as you found out about earlier in this chapter) you know that the visitor can continue clicking and enjoying your photos or whatever from there, so it sounds like a good way to catch the readers, right?

This is how you do it, in this case outputting everything in an unlimited list since it seems appropriate:

```
<ul class="random-attachments">
    <?php $new_query = new WP_Query('&showposts=4'); ?>
    <?php while ($new_query->have_posts()) : $new_query->the_post(); ?>
        <?php
    $args = array(
        'post_type' => 'attachment',
        'numberposts' => 1,
        'orderby' => rand,
        'status' => 'publish',
        'post_mime_type' => 'image',
        'parent' => $post->ID
    );
    $attachments = get_posts($args);
    if ($attachments) {
        foreach ($attachments as $attachment) {
    echo '<li>';
    echo wp_get_attachment_link($attachment->ID, 'thumbnail', true, ");
    echo '</li>';
        }
    }
    ?>
<?php endwhile; ?>
</ul>
```

The first two lines are just to get the new WordPress loop started and for limiting the amount of posts to loop out. Then you've got an array belonging to the `$args` function. This is fairly common usage in WordPress, it makes it easier to pass all the parameters and store them in a function. The parameters belong to `get_posts()`, which will control what you'll actually output. We'll get to that in a little bit.

The `$args` array should be pretty self-explanatory, sorting by the attachment post type, showing just one attachment per post (otherwise you'd get several images rather than just one), randomizing the ordering, using only published posts, and limiting things to the `'image'` MIME type. That could just as well have been `'video'`, for example, so it can come in handy. Finally, you attach the parent post's ID as well, for good measure only because it really isn't needed, but can come in handy in other cases so is left in here for info.

So you've got all that information in the array stored in `$args`, now to load `get_posts()` with it. This is done here:

```
$attachments = get_posts($args);
```

Now the whole `get_posts()` with all the parameters from `$args` is stored in `$attachments`, which you'll use in the `foreach` loop. There you'll find the following line, which is what controls how the attachments are output:

```
echo wp_get_attachment_link($attachment->ID, 'thumbnail', true, '');
```

The `wp_get_attachment_link()` template tag outputs the relevant attachment by default. Here you're giving it the ID from the `foreach`, then you tell it that it should display the thumbnail rather than the original size (which is default). The `true` passed after that is whether or not to link the output to the attachment page, and since that is kind of the point, this needs to be passed. Finally, the last parameter is whether or not to display a media icon, which defaults to `false`, so you don't need to pass that.

Putting that little code snippet in the sidebar will get you an unlimited list of randomized thumbnail images linked to their respective attachment page.

More Random Image Options

Not good enough for you? Then you should turn to the wonderful world of photo-sharing sites and their various widgets and embed codes, as well as to the plethora of plugins available. A combination is usually a pretty good recipe for nice image blocks showing off your latest works of art (or just snapped vacation photos), so dig deep into that for more random image goodness. You'll find a bunch of plugins and suggestions in Chapter 11 if you haven't seen that already.

A word of advice, though: beware of clutter, and beware of long load times.

Adding third-party services always adds to the load time, and it doesn't get any better if an image, which may or may not be properly compressed for the Web, is served. I know it's tempting to put in a cool Flash widget from some photo-sharing site, or an Ajax-y plugin that shows off all your best photos in a never-ending slideshow, but you should be careful.

Another thing to remember is whether the image block is actually needed. Just because you've got access to a stream of images doesn't mean you have to use or display it. Will the visitor be interested? If not, forget about it and use that valuable screen real estate to show something else.

Making the Most of Image-sharing Services

For sites running on limited hardware or shared hosting accounts, it may be crucial to save on both space and bandwidth, and what better way than to host the videos on YouTube and the images on Flickr? The same actually applies to larger sites not generating much money, but they tend to be able to afford custom solutions like stored data in the cloud or static files on servers.

Serving the images from any of the photo-sharing sites out there is a sure way to keep both bandwidth and storage down, especially if the site in question is running a lot of photos. A good example would be a videogame site, pumping screenshots not seldom less than around 700 KB in size each, and with larger screens and HD resolutions comes the need to share them in that resolution as well. Say you shoot out two screenshot galleries every day, each containing 10 images. That's 140 images every week, or 560 per month. At around 700 KB each, that adds up for sure; to over 380 MB per month actually. You don't need to be a mathematician to understand that such a site will require a lot of megabytes in bandwidth, as well as storage in the long run.

That's why photo-sharing sites are interesting. Pumping images in to Flickr means that you needn't worry about those things. Now, it may be a bit of a stretch to have the big videogame sites running their screenshot library on Flickr, but what about the ones relying on more traditional photography?

There is money to be saved here, by "doing a YouTube" with images as well. After all, even the best of them are embedding videos these days, so why not images?

Naturally there are drawbacks, most importantly the fact that if your image host goes out of business you'll lose all your images. You can sort that out with backups, of course, but you'd need to put them in again manually. On the other hand, these services are rarely small players, and if you stick to the big ones it isn't likely they'll go away. Again, if you can rely on YouTube you should be able to rely on the likes of Flickr. There is some trust involved, after all.

Another issue is loading time. If your image host is struggling to serve the images, for one reason or another, your site will suffer for it. In the long run I believe that images are more of what I like to call "direct content" than video, and that's why I tend to store and serve them locally whenever I can. If I really need to serve them from someplace else to keep a site up, I'd look into file servers and cloud solutions before relying solely on a third-party service.

However, that doesn't mean that I don't think about going the third-party route, and as a dedicated Flickr user I sometimes use it as an image host. It is convenient and saves both time as well as bandwidth and space. Despite all I've said so far, those are hard facts to argue with.

Posting from Flickr

Flickr (`flickr.com`) is probably the most popular photo-sharing site out there. It lets you upload photos for free, up to a limit, and if you want to upload more photos you can purchase a pro account. It also works very well with blogs, and you can even share your Flickr photos (and those of others) directly to your blog. This is done in your account settings, and WordPress is just one of many types of blogs that Flickr can let you share photos to. To share photos on your blog using Flickr:

1. Sign in to Flickr and go to the Your Account page.
2. Click the Extending Flickr tab, and then click the edit link to the right of Your Blogs (see Figure 14-3).

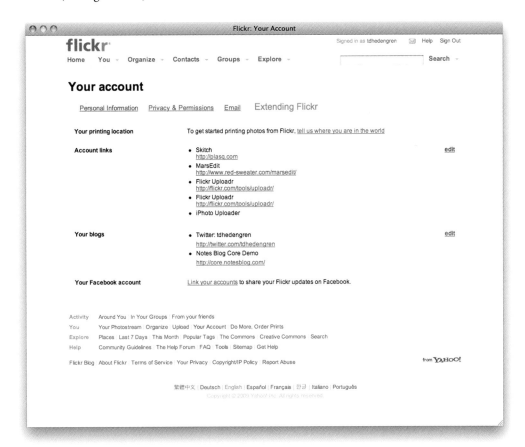

Figure 14-3: The Edit Link is to the right of the blogs listed

Figure 14-4: Add your WordPress blog's details

3. Add your WordPress blog by filling out the details (see Figure 14-4). You need to activate publishing by XML-RPC in your blog's admin interface, under Settings → Writing. The address you'll fill in on Flickr is the URL to xmlrpc.php, which resides in the root of your WordPress install.

4. Go through the guide and be sure to pick (and possibly edit) a default layout for the posts you'll publish from Flickr.

5. That's it!

Now you can send photos from Flickr directly to your blog. Find a photo you want to send, click the Share This link in the top right when viewing it, and then choose your blog under the Blog It tab. You'll get to fill out some more content if you like. Remember, it is not possible to share all photos this way.

Flickr is a commonly used tool not only for posting images, but also for saving traffic. By serving the images from Flickr you won't strain your own server, which can be a good thing. Of course, it works both ways, because if Flickr should go down (or out of business), your images will go down with it, so make sure you've got backups of everything.

The Flickr Slideshow

If you're a dedicated Flickr user you may be interested in embedding a Flickr slideshow. Basically it is a small Flash widget that you can put wherever you want on your site, and even alter the size of. You can get a slideshow of anything grouped on Flickr, be it a full user's photostream or a set of photos. Naturally, the slideshow will only include public photos.

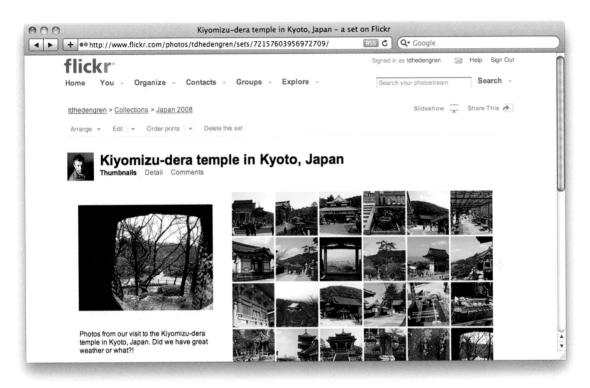

Figure 14-5: The slideshow link is easy to miss, but it is usually there

Adding the slideshow is easy. Just find the set or photostream you want to embed and click the Slideshow link at the top right (see Figure 14-5), next to the Share This link. If the Share This link is present, you can slideshow the content; if it's not, you can't—simple as that.

The slideshow begins. Click Share at the top right (see Figure 14-6), and then click the Customize HTML link below the embed code. This will bring up a new window where you can set the desired width and height, or pick a predefined width and height. Copy the embed code and paste it wherever you want.

So when is using a Flickr slideshow useful? Sites can use it for coverage when they need to lean on Flickr's weight to get the message (and traffic!) across, but otherwise I'd say you're better off creating cool galleries instead. However, the slideshow does indeed fulfill a purpose as an extension to everything else, as in putting a box in the side column showing off your latest exploits and such.

Other than that, the Flickr slideshow is more of a novelty. To really put Flickr to good use, other than to serve static images, you have to dig a bit deeper. There is an API to play with (www.flickr.com/services/api/) and the numerous plugins available can sometimes take things to a different level, depending on what you need from the service.

Figure 14-6: Grab the embed code from the custom page rather than directly from the slideshow; doing so will give you more options
Reproduced with permission of Yahoo! Inc. ©2009 Yahoo! Inc. FLICKR and the FLICKR logo are registered trademarks of Yahoo! Inc.

Beware the Clutter

Images are great to spice up a site, especially when you can utilize services like Flickr and get nifty little widgets that show off your latest photos, or however you may use it. Your visitors will enjoy the living elements you've added, and they all add value to the experience. At least that is the ideal usage; in the real world, a lot of this type of usage means clutter and breaking of the design.

My point is that you need to make sure you put these tools to good use, whether it is a random image element or your latest updates from Flickr. They need to make sense, just like every other element in a good design.

And with that, the next chapter moves on to integrating the social Web, something that also needs to make sense to be valid on any Web site.

15 INTEGRATING THE SOCIAL WEB

Before digging into the various techniques used to display and connect to the social Web, it is important not to forget the most obvious integration tool offered: RSS feeds. In its most simple form, you've got the RSS widget that ships with WordPress, and it easily lets you show off content from an RSS feed. And today, any social Web service, app, community, or whatever has an RSS feed for you to play with, which means that a lot of the integration of these services you may want can be done using RSS. From showing off your latest tweet to mashing up a lifestream, it's all about RSS most of the time.

So when you want to flash your latest finished book saved to www.anobii.com, consider the RSS feed (or their widget) before you start looking for plugins or hacking your own solutions. Chances are the service you want to show off your latest actions/ saved items/whatever from already transmits this data with RSS. You should never make things harder than they are.

Now it's time to get your hands dirty!

Show off Your Twitter

There is certainly no doubt that the rise of Twitter has changed things. These days everyone and their cat tweets, at least among the techie crowd, and it doesn't seem to be slowing down. So while 140 characters is quite a limitation to someone used to punching out 3,000-character blog posts, it can still be quite a tool for online publishers.

If you or your brand are on Twitter, it is likely you'll want to promote the Twitter account on your site. That is easily done with graphics, of course, but you can take it further than that. It works the other way as well: by promoting your content with tweets you can reach an audience that may only know you on Twitter. And that's just scratching the surface; after all there are a ton of cool mashups and services built around Twitter and its API that you may want to mimic or at least get a piece of.

First thing's first, building a cool new Twitter app isn't what this book is about. However, it would most likely be a good idea to take the Twitter promotion one step further than just a small "Follow me on Twitter" graphic, right?

Your Tweets

One of the best and most stylistic ways to show off your Twitter updates is to display the latest tweet. I'm sure there are a ton of plugins that can do that, but the most straightforward way to do it is to use the Twitter API (see the reference at `apiwiki.twitter.com`) and some JavaScript.

This is me, returning the latest tweet from my user account (`twitter.com/tdhedengren` if you're curious), relying on two JavaScripts supplied by Twitter:

```html
<div id="mytweet">
    <div id="twitter_update_list"></div>
    <script type="text/javascript"
      src="http://twitter.com/javascripts/blogger.js"></script>
    <script type="text/javascript"
      src="http://twitter.com/statuses/user_timeline/tdhedengren.json?
      count=1&callback=twitterCallback2"></script>
</div>
```

First of all, the outer `div#mytweet`, is not required, but since you may want some additional control I think it is a pretty good idea to add it. The `div#twitter_update_list`, with nothing in it (at first glance), on the other hand, is necessary. It is inside this one that the blogger.js and the JSON script are returning the status updates requested. Which, in this case, is mine.

In this line you'll find my username, `tdhedengren`, added as if it were an actual file on the twitter.com server:

```
<script type="text/javascript"
   src="http://twitter.com/statuses/user_timeline/tdhedengren.json?
   count=1&callback=twitterCallback2"></script>
```

That's telling Twitter to fetch the updates from my username. Naturally, `count=1` means that just one tweet should be fetched, and you can change that to, say, five if you'd like five tweets. Finally there's the `callback=twitterCallback2`, which is necessary since you're using JSON here and Twitter wants you to.

What you'll get its a bulleted list inside the `div#twitter_update_list`, so style it accordingly.

You can fetch the user RSS feed instead, but that one contains a lot of rubbish, not to mention the username in front of everything, from the tweet title to the actual content. Naturally, you can cut that away with some PHP, but then you're hacking away in such a sense that it may be more prudent to use one of the available plugins.

Figure 15-1: A simple box showing off the latest tweet can get you new followers on Twitter

Full documentation on this method (along with information on other settings and methods that may suit you better) is available in the Twitter API documentation: `apiwiki.twitter.com/Twitter-REST-API-Method%3A-statuses-user_timeline`.

Display a Twitter Search Result

You can use the same method to display a search result as you did in the previous part, but for search of course. The Twitter API offers a lot of information on that, so if that's the route you want to take then by all means dig into it: `apiwiki.twitter.com/Twitter-Search-API-Method%3A-search`.

However, it is good to know that a search on Twitter also comes with an RSS feed, and while displaying just the latest tweet makes sense, just relaying the latest result from a search query does not. You may be better off just doing the search query yourself on `search.twitter.com`, and then grabbing the RSS feed and doing funky stuff with it. Which is to say, output it somewhere using a plugin, the default widget, or some or the built-in methods described in Chapter 13.

Twitter search results can come in handy when watching trends around brands, but also for support. There are trending hashtags, for example, which may work very well as a search query everpresent on a site about the particular topic. A hashtag is a hash symbol (#) and then a word, like this `#smashing` or this `#NotesBlog`, and most of the Twitter apps out there also make them clickable. Some Web services and online products talk a lot about what's going on as well as giving support on Twitter, and then they can use their hashtag to make sure that people interested in the topic can follow it, but also for their own means. After all, it is very easy to search for a hashtag, and the same can, of course, be extended to showing off the results.

Twitter Site Extensions

There are numerous widgets, plugins, services, and applications surrounding Twitter. The fairly open ecosystem around the microblogging service makes it easy to build on, and the ever-increasing buzz around the brand isn't exactly slowing things down. That's why you've got TweetMeme (`tweetmeme.com`) tracking the hottest stories on Twitter, as well as Twitterfeed (`twitterfeed.com`) that lets you post automatic links to your Twitter account using an RSS feed. The list goes on and on, and below is just a tiny little sample of the numerous Twitter services, widgets, and tools that you can put to good use. I'm focusing on things that can help your publishing, so for actual twittering applications you'll have to look elsewhere.

You won't find any Twitter plugins here either: they are all in Chapter 11.

Site Enhancers

These services add functionality to your site by using Twitter, while being a tad more advanced than the buttons and counters listed below.

- **TweetMeme** (`tweetmeme.com`) tracks what's hot on Twitter, and borrows a lot from Digg while doing so. Among other things, there's a button that you can add to your site for even more exposure: `tweetmeme.com/about/retweet_button`.
- **Tweetboard** (`tweetboard.com`) adds a Twitter conversation to your site with threaded replies and everything.
- **Twitterfeed** (`twitterfeed.com`) publishes links from any RSS feed to your Twitter account, so that you won't have to. There are competing services that do this as well, but this is the original one with OpenID login and everything.

Buttons, Widgets, and Counters

There was a time when buttons were everywhere and statistics counters felt like a good idea. Not so much anymore; it's just another third-party server call that has to be made, and it clutters the site as well. That being said, sometimes it makes sense to use anyway.

- **The official Twitter widgets** (`twitter.com/widgets/`) are a good choice for anyone wanting a simple display of their latest tweets or search results. Don't miss the widgets on the Goodies page either: `twitter.com/goodies/widgets`.
- **TwitterCounter** (`twittercounter.com`) is a service that offers a counter that displays how many people are following you on Twitter and more, with an API and everything.
- **TwitterButtons** (`www.twitterbuttons.com`) has a bunch of Twitter buttons for your perusal.

URL Shorteners

The 140-character limit means that long URLs just won't fit into your tweets. Enter the URL shorteners, a necessary evil according to some, and a great tool say others. You can roll your own of course (see Chapter 11 for cool plugins) but if you can't or don't want to, these shorteners are great options. Remember, you may want to pick one and stick to it so that people get used to seeing you use it.

- **TinyURL** (`tinyurl.com`) is the original URL shortener used by Twitter, but it doesn't offer much compared to the competition.
- **Bit.ly** (`bit.ly`) not only shortens your URL but offers statistics as well.
- **To.ly** (`to.ly`) is a short and simple URL shortener with an API.
- **Is.gd** (`is.gd`) is another short and simple URL shortener.
- **Tr.im** (`tr.im`) offers statistics and is built into a few Twitter apps as well.

Of course, sometimes you want to do more than just flaunt your tweets. Maybe you want to show off everything you do online on your site? That's called lifestreaming, and we'll look at that next.

Lifestreaming with WordPress

Lifestreaming is a term commonly used to describe the mashing up of everything you do online. A bit presumptuous, perhaps, to assume that your life is online, but there you go. Usually your lifestream involves links to your blog posts, status updates on Facebook, tweets on Twitter, photos from Flickr, books you read from LibraryThing, videos from YouTube, and so on. Basically, the more the better, with everything mashed together in a chronological list of sorts.

The mashing together of your online life usually relies on RSS, and so, theoretically, you can use WordPress for lifestreaming. Either you do it by creating your theme in such a way that it uses the built-in SimplePie RSS parser to mash up and then output everything, or you use one of the RSS scraping plugins to feed your WordPress database with the content as posts.

Setting up a Lifestream

While you can just pull in all those RSS feeds yourself using SimplePie and the multifeed feature mentioned in Chapter 13, I must say that lifestreaming is one of those situations where I feel plugins are the best solution. Needless to say, it is possible to create a fully functional lifestream using SimplePie functionality, but you would perhaps have a hard time making it load snappily.

In my mind there are three possible setups—discussed in the following sections—for someone who wants to lifestream with WordPress.

The Built-in RSS Way

If you pull in all your content from the various RSS feeds generated by your accounts across the Web, you'll have a hard time managing the feeds. You can mash them up, and perhaps cache the content in either files (which SimplePie supports), or in the database (which isn't officially supported but possible), and then serve it in your theme. This is a stiff project to get working, but it is definitely possible.

A slightly less daunting solution relying on the built-in RSS parser is to have a set of boxes containing different kinds of content, grouped by relevance or just on a whim. It may not be the typical chronological list of updates, but it will serve you just fine in most cases.

Use a Lifestreaming Plugin

There are a couple of lifestreaming plugins available, with the most aggressively heralded one being WP-Lifestream (`wordpress.org/extend/plugins/lifestream/`). It works well enough and lets you set up what sources you want to fetch feeds from, and then you can include the lifestream in your sidebar or on a Page, for example. This is by far the easiest way to get started with lifestreaming using WordPress, but it may not offer you the customizations you crave. Also, there are other issues regarding load times, which I'll get to in a bit.

The WP-Lifestream plugin saves the fetched content to the database. Not all lifestreaming plugins do that, which I think is somewhat necessary. After all, without saving the content (and hence maintaining an archive of your activities online) there really is no point in not just showing the content as it is of this moment, is there? Make sure your lifestreaming plugin of choice has the features you need, and be extra wary on this one.

Feed the WordPress Database

The third and final solution is to feed the WordPress database with content from RSS feeds using scraping plugins. The idea here is to actually create a WordPress post, preferably sorted into a suitable category and perhaps even tagged (although that will probably be hard), and then display it in your theme using the normal methods. This would theoretically mean that you can have a Flickr category containing everything from Flickr, a Twitter category that saves all your tweets, and so on. The fact that everything is stored as normal posts makes it easy to manage, which is a good thing.

The FeedWordPress (`wordpress.org/extend/plugins/feedwordpress/`) plugin is one of several scraping plugins that can fetch RSS feeds and save them in your WordPress install. Using a solution like this may seem a little bit extreme, but it is definitely possible, and with some nifty theming you can get a site with blog and lifestreaming sections and a great database for search and categorization.

About Those Cronjobs

The problem with fetching RSS feeds (and anything that comes from outside the server, really) is that it takes time. PHP needs to ask the target server for the feed, then the server has to send it, and then your server needs to receive it, and PHP has to wrap everything up by doing something with the fetched content. Compare that to querying the database and outputting the data, and you'll see the problem.

Now imagine you have 10 online identities that you want to include in your lifestream. When a visitor comes to see what you're up to online, PHP needs to query them all, receive all the content, and then output it. And that's assuming nothing lags behind, which can cause the script to break (which would be poor programming) or delay until an answer, even if it is a negative one, has been received. Then you'll understand that a lifestream page can take a lot of time to load.

That's why you cache content, and any decent solution will have support for caching. However, the fetching and caching has to be initiated by someone. In its purest form it means that even if the content is cached, one poor visitor every 30 minutes (or whatever limit is set) will have to wait for everything to be downloaded, cached, and then output for it to work. You can do this with SimplePie, and most lifestreaming plugins will have some form of caching solution. Both files (text files basically) and database solutions can be used.

There are better solutions. One is the built-in WP-Cron feature that is something of a pseudo-cronjob called by some plugins. Another, preferable one, is a cronjob. This is basically timed instances run by the server independently, which means that no visitor will have to sit and wait for all those RSS feeds to be loaded. The only thing that will be served is the saved (cached) content, and that's the only thing that is updated as well. How you set up your cronjob depends on your host. Most likely you have a control panel where you can make changes to your site. Look for cronjob settings there. Diehard Linux fans will obviously use the terminal, but that's pretty far from the scope of this book. For the rest of us, the host's built-in control panel solutions will do.

If you plan on running a lot of RSS feeds, which comes with the territory with lifestreaming, you need to look into caching, which should be supported by your solution from the start, and how to run the content fetching scripts without slowing down the site. Again, most decent plugins support this, and so does SimplePie if you want to dive into that. The best solution is a cronjob, so talk to your Web host about that, and make sure whatever plugin or service you want to use supports it.

Social Web Submit Buttons

The social Web is certainly a big consideration when working with editorial content today. While search engines can trickle in visitors for a long period of time, hitting the front page of Digg will boost your statistics dramatically in the short term. If your content is technically oriented in particular, the social Web offers a number of services to submit the story to, but even if you're not you should look around in your niche and see if there is one that suits your site. After all, you all want more visitors, right?

There's a lot to be said about what content works where in the social Web, and every time it boils down to writing good, interesting, and easily accessible content, and submitting it to the right site. Then it's up to the users to vote it up or neglect it completely, which may in fact be up to how many friends you've got that can give the story the head start it needs.

So, yes, it is a popularity contest, and yes, you can easily participate by extending your site towards it.

Using Plugins

The easiest way to make your site ready for the social Web is to use one of the numerous plugins available (see Chapter 11 for suggestions). These typically add links or buttons to the end of each post, where the visitor can vote up the story in question, or submit it to a service if it hasn't been submitted yet.

Adding a plugin to manage these things for you is easy and certainly tempting, but there are some things you should consider before jumping the gun:

- **Which social Web services can the plugin handle?** Make sure the ones for your particular niche are there, and that you don't clutter your site with the ones that never work for you. In other words, don't ask people to submit your site to Digg if you're writing about gardening in Norwegian; that just won't work.
- **Does the plugin look good with your design or can you customize it to?** If not, you should probably look for another one.
- **Does the plugin look the same everywhere?** If it does, chances are the visitors are so used to seeing it that they just don't register it anymore. It's just that block of icons between the post and the comments on every other blog out there, and that's no good since you want your visitors to interact.
- **Is the plugin actually hosted elsewhere?** There are third-party plugins that load everything from an external server. This will slow down your site, so make sure you're okay with that before using such a plugin.

Most plugins, unfortunately, add clutter in the form of buttons or icons that just won't work with every site. Some are limited to a set number of services, while others tempt you by adding too many. Make it classy and don't overdo the number of social bookmarking services; that won't make it more appealing to vote. In fact, maybe just one or two "Please vote for my story" buttons will work better for you than filling the screen with them.

Hacking Your Own Submit Links

You don't need to rely on plugins to add social bookmarking submit buttons. Most sites offer their own buttons that you can embed, but embedding them is something you need to do manually.

Personally, I'm a fan of adding simple submit links to the single post view (see Figure 15-2), prefer-ably in a way that isn't overly obtrusive to the user and doesn't clutter the design. Better to promote the stories that do look like they can go somewhere by themselves, with additional graphics and/or updated stories asking for help. A few sitting links, however, isn't too much in most cases, as long as you keep them relevant.

The following is the code to add sitting links. What you do is submit the permalink of the post in question to the service, so when someone clicks the link they'll go to the submit page:

```
<a href="http://delicious.com/post?url=<?php the_permalink() ?>&title=<?php the_title(); ?>">Save
  on Del.icio.us</a>
<a href="http://digg.com/submit?phase=2&url=<?php the_permalink() ?>">Post to Digg</a>
<a href="http://www.facebook.com/share.php?u=<?php the_permalink() ?>">Share on Facebook</a>
<a href="http://friendfeed.com/?url=<?php the_permalink() ?>&title=<?php the_title() ?>">Share on
  FriendFeed</a>
<a href="http://www.mixx.com/" onclick="window.location='http://www.mixx.com/submit?page_
  url='+window.location; return false;">Post to Mixx</a>
<a href="http://reddit.com/submit?url=<?php the_permalink() ?>&title=<?php the_title(); ?>">Post
  to Reddit</a>
<a href="http://www.stumbleupon.com/submit?url=<?php the_permalink(); ?>&title=<?php the_title();
  ?>">Post to Stumbleupon</a>
<a href="http://twitter.com/home?status=Now reading <?php the_permalink(); ?>">Send to Twitter</a>
```

For the most up-to-date code, along with graphics, logos, icons, and so forth, visit each site individually. The most commonly used ones are listed in the preceding code. It is easy enough to add new ones; most sites have similar share links that can be built around `the_permalink()` and `the_title()`.

And remember to use these on a per-post basis! Otherwise you'll just send your category or front page to Digg, and that will hardly work well. In fact, a nice place to put these links would be between the content and the comments. It makes sense to submit a link to your great content after reading it and then moving onward to the comments. In the next section we do just that and get to pimping the comments.

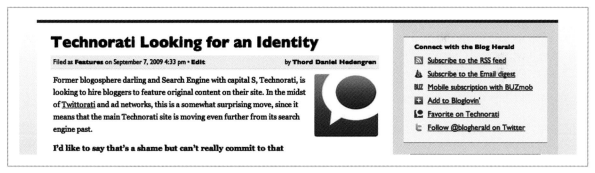

Figure 15-2: The social bookmarking submit links, along with some other stuff from `blogherald.com`

Pimping the Comments

With the addition of threaded comments in the WordPress core, and the excellent CSS styling options that are now available, as well as the ever-present Gravatar (`gravatar.com`) support, one would wonder how it is possible to pimp the comments?

Simple: either by filling them with additional functionality using plugins, or by moving them from WordPress altogether. The former solution can mean anything from user grading of the comments to fetching the buzz from Twitter, while the latter means that you'll rely on a third-party service for managing your comments.

See Chapter 11 for a whole bunch of plugins that make your in-house comments hotter, and a few that help you manage logins and the like. This section will deal with the rest.

Hosted Comment Solutions

Hosted comment solutions mean that you leave the complete comment solution to a third-party service, not rely on the WordPress comment functionality. There are two players in this arena, Disqus (disqus.com) and IntenseDebate (www.intensedebate.com). The former has seniority, but the latter is owned by Automattic, which makes it a tempting choice to anyone loving WordPress. Both of them have their pros and cons function-wise, and both are being actively developed.

To start using either Disqus or IntenseDebate you download a plugin for WordPress and take it from there. It is easy to get started, although localization has proven to be something of an issue for some, as well as customizing of the styling. That being said, getting started with either Disqus or IntenseDebate is a breeze. Incidentally, you can add these services to static sites as well, giving any site a commenting functionality. That's pretty cool, actually.

My main gripe with the concept of hosted comments, however, is the fact that you're basically giving content to someone else to maintain. That means that if your comment service of choice breaks down or goes out of business, you're stuck with no comments at all. Granted, these days there are backup solutions, but it just doesn't feel safe. Comments may be mostly the words of your readers and as such it is not your content, but at the same time it is, since the discussion is a part of your site. With that in mind, would you risk losing that content, even if it is just for the time your hosted comment provider is experiencing downtime or other issues?

Other possible issues include downtime and added clutter because chances are that the comment solution won't fit seamlessly with your smashing design. Also, problems experienced by the commenting system's host will hit your site as well. That's not good.

However, there are some great advantages here too. First of all, spamming is taken care of on a wider scale, and that has its advantages. Both comment systems also offer various login methods, reply by e-mail, RSS feeds, as well as Twitter integration and e-mail notifications. The scope of features you'll get out of the box from Disqus or IntenseDebate is something you'd have to supercharge your WordPress comments with plugins to achieve.

It is often said that sites using these systems get more comments, and that doesn't seem to be just the PR talk of the companies themselves. So with that in mind, if you are to use a service like this, which one should you pick? I have no idea; they are pretty similar. Give them both a go and see which one fits your site better.

Unified Logins

The idea of a unified login system is a great one. Think about it: wouldn't one login for everything be great? Not a ton of passwords to mess around with, and no risk of the "one password for too many sites" security hazard. (Except, of course, for the fact that you can access all those sites with one password anyway.) The idea, however, is that the few providers of these Master Accounts would be so secure that the only risk of users being compromised would be human error, and on your side of things at that. Compared to the risk of some minor site being hacked and your "one password fits all" master password being out there, it sounds pretty good.

That's why OpenID (`www.openid.net`) is interesting, and that's why the giants like Yahoo!, Google and Microsoft are interested in this. For the same reason Facebook Connect (`developers.facebook.com/connect.php`) exists, a unified login using your Facebook account. The Sign in with Twitter (`apiwiki.twitter.com/Sign-in-with-Twitter`) solution is something similar, but using Twitter of course, and the list goes on.

You may wonder why you should even consider using your own sign-in procedure if you can lean on those giants. Most WordPress sites don't have their own sign-in procedures for anyone other than the actual writers and administrators, at least not for commenting. It is usually enough to leave a name and an e-mail address. However, if you want sign-ins, one of the unified solutions is worth considering. I would like to point to OpenID, but the truth is that Facebook Connect is way more user-friendly (right now) and besides Facebook is an OpenID member so it isn't such a big deal after all.

Soon you'll be using your Google and Live.com accounts to sign in across the Web, alongside Facebook and Twitter, all perhaps being connected through the OpenID Foundation. Or not. Either way, the thing is you should consider a unified login for your site if you need login functionality for your users. There are plugins that solve this for you (you'll find them in Chapter 11), but don't let that stop you. Read up on the services themselves and make up your mind regarding any potential user registrations in the future.

About Building Great Sites

As you probably have gathered by now, I find WordPress to be a superb publishing system. It's a lot more than just a platform to power blogs; it is a way to publish just about anything online. Most parts of the system are versatile enough to take you from idea to deployment a lot faster than if you started developing from scratch. Naturally, at times other options are better suited to the task, but despite sometimes stumbling across some of these situations, I often end up using WordPress anyway.

There are, of course, two reasons I usually return to WordPress. The first is that WordPress really is incredibly easy to work with; you're on track really fast and that is always good when you want to launch something. The second reason is that I know WordPress, whereas the alternative may be completely new to me. I think it is important not to forget that, because even though I use WordPress widely, and I hope you will too, sometimes you may prefer other options.

Building great sites is all about having a great idea, and making it work the way you intended it to. For me, WordPress pulls through on this almost every time thanks to a solid foundation, a great theming system, lots of plugins and the option to write my own, as well as an overall friendly community where you can ask questions. All these things, along with the ease of the system, mean that building that great site using WordPress rather than any of the other systems out there is not only a time saver, but also more often than not the best choice in the longer run as well, thanks to the way the system develops.

WordPress has come a long way from just being about blogs. It is a publishing system, and that is the way you should both view it and treat it.

And that will help you build great sites.

Index

Index